P9-EDO-348

By following the tenderly intertwined intellectual and sexual awakenings of three friends, *Buffalo Trace: A Threefold Vibration* eroticizes academia. Their stories embrace the contradictions and rigors and limitations of academia, and yet this trilogy of essays can also be read as an ode to Buffalo, the deeply American town that provided cover and even salvation for these three writers. Who can resist the assertion that "Buffalo was itself a kind of Paris of the rust belt"? Ultimately, this is a love story, among friends, lovers, literature, and even Buffalo.

LUCY JANE BLEDSOE,
AUTHOR OF *A THIN BRIGHT LINE* AND *THE EVOLUTION OF LOVE*

Smart, honest, and beautifully written, these three tales of grad school life in the 1980s could be called Love in the Time of Deconstruction. A hothouse world of brains, bodies, books, and doubt (in Buffalo, no less), it's all a bit mad, but in the exciting, necessary way of life in your twenties. *Buffalo Trace: A Threefold Vibration* is a strange, original, wonderful book.

CHRISTOPHER BRAM,
AUTHOR OF *GODS AND MONSTERS* AND *MAPPING THE TERRITORY*

Left to Right: Walton, Morrison, Cappello, circa 1984

Buffalo Trace
A Threefold Vibration

MARY CAPPELLO
JAMES MORRISON
JEAN WALTON

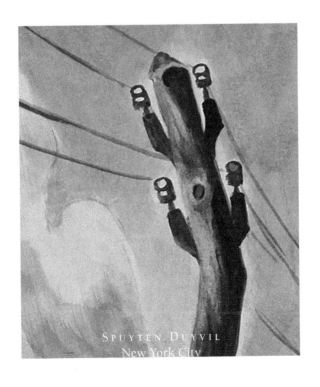

SPUYTEN DUYVIL
New York City

Grateful acknowledgment is made to Robert Boyers and *Salmagundi* where an excerpted version of "My Secret, Private Errand" appeared in the Fall 2013-Winter 2014 issue. Cover painting by Charles Burchfield reproduced with permission of the Charles E. Burchfield Foundation.

Roots & Branches Series

©2018 Mary Cappello, James Morrison, Jean Walton
ISBN 978-1-947980-16-7 pbk.   978-1-947980-18-1 hdc.
cover image: Charles E. Burchfield (1893-1967), "Telegraph Pole" (1935), watercolor, charcoal and graphite on paper, 23 3/8″ x 20 7/8″, Memorial Art Gallery, University of Rochester, Gift of Mrs. Charles H. Babcock

Library of Congress Cataloging-in-Publication Data

Names: Morrison, James, 1960- His masters' voice. | Walton, Jean, 1957-
    Buffalo trace. | Cappello, Mary. My secret, private errand.
Title: Buffalo trace : a threefold vibration / Mary Cappello, James Morrison,
    Jean Walton.
Description: New York City : Spuyten Duyvil, [2018]
Identifiers: LCCN 2017053505| ISBN 9781947980181 (hardcover) | ISBN
    9781947980167 (pbk.)
Subjects: LCSH: State University of New York at Buffalo. English
    Department--History. | State University of New York at Buffalo--Alumni and
    alumnae--Biography. | Buffalo (N.Y.)--Intellectual life. | Morrison,
    James, 1960- | Walton, Jean, 1957- | Cappello, Mary.
Classification: LCC PE69.S73 B84 2018 | DDC 808/.042071174797--dc23
LC record available at https://lccn.loc.gov/2017053505

FOR GWENDOLYN ASHBAUGH

"But the persistence of the twofold vibration suggests that in this old abode all is not yet quite for the best."

Samuel Beckett, *The Lost Ones*

His Masters' Voice

JAMES MORRISON

We shall not cease from exploration
And the end of all our exploring
Will be to arrive where we started
And know the place for the first time.
T. S. Eliot, "Little Gidding"

1.
TAKE A RISK!

So my old friend and erstwhile grad school roommate Bill Bradley used to hector me, usually when he was already a few beers in, half a sheet to the wind, hoisting his can of Milwaukee's Best or Genny Cream Ale to drive the point home.

I thought I had. I'd moved to Buffalo.

I didn't let it get to me. The order of the day those years was not letting things get to you. There was some justice in others' thinking me timid, and it wasn't the first time, not by a stretch. Besides, that was just Bill's way—playful, genial teasing. He did it to everyone and I didn't take it personally. He had lived a life—so he'd given us to understand—that would have broken the rest of us in two: intimations of a rough upbringing even further upstate, in Potsdam, where no life could be free of strife, winters worse than Buffalo's; a bout with cancer in the not-so-distant past; in and out of schools and jobs; hard stints on an oil rig when nothing else came through. He had at least ten years on the rest of us, who were mostly in our early twenties while he was pushing forty. He had earned his right to lecture us.

Take a risk.

A big man, he would hulk over the table, any table, at Anacone's Bar on Bailey Avenue or the Central Park Grill on Main, or our own little dinette, towering over the circular stand on which we took our modest meals, a chiseled chunk of marbleized white formica the size of a medicine-show wagon wheel, set on spindly legs of copper-colored aluminum that Bill could have crushed in a fist as easily as one of his cans of beer. After dispensing one of these antic verdicts of his, he'd dependably soften the blow, leaning in to gently qualify his reproach, flannel-clad elbows on the precarious tabletop, right hand aloft with a simmering cigarette clenched between the fore- and middle fingers. Why take a risk after all? What did it get them, the risk-takers? What did it ever get them? Take a risk, don't take a risk—what did it matter, in light of the futility of human endeavor, what you did? Everyone was deluded anyway, everything vain, everyone blind. "There's a way in which…" That was his characteristic lead-in, contemplative, oracular—"There's a way in which…" There was a way in which…everyone was goaded by frazzled self-interest…There was a way in which Freud, *Freud*…was really onto something—but not what everyone thought it was…There was a way in which—we all knew too many books and not enough pictures…There was a way in which…if nothing mattered then anything might, anything could be done or thought, because the truth was provisional and the world was everything that was the case.

On April 1, 1983, I got a letter from the English department of SUNY—the State University of New York—in Buffalo, offering me admission to the graduate program in the fall, as well as a teaching fellowship in the sum of four thousand and one hundred dollars. It was not lost on me that this life-changing news arrived on the Day of Fools. The timing could hardly have been more propitious. It felt like my last chance. Two of the other places I'd applied had already rejected me, and though three more had yet to report, I knew as soon as I opened that letter exactly where I'd be headed.

I vaulted through the letter some half-dozen times, holding it to my heart between readings and smiling beatifically up at the ceiling, before emerging from my room, breast aflutter, and announcing to my parents that I'd gotten in. Gotten in to what? they mildly inquired. From nearly any vantage point the query was a reasonable one, since I had not told them I was applying to graduate school. Yet its effect was to deflate in a flash my expansive exuberance into shriveled rage. I glared, fuming, into their meek and qualmish faces. In a seething voice I informed them that I would be moving to Buffalo, New York, and there was nothing that they or anyone else could do about it.

All this was business as usual. Around the age of ten I'd decided that they had no right of access to the inner reaches of my life. They could maintain their terrible dominion over my physical being, but my mind would be my own. I would continue to subsist among them—what choice did I have?—but anything of importance to me would be closed off utterly from them. They wouldn't understand anyway, and any effort to explain would only yield puzzled, peevish looks—like the ones my announcement provoked—and inane, fatuous conversations to boot. It wasn't my fault I'd been born into the wrong family. So I resolved that any personal failure would go unremarked and any success divulged, if at all, only in retrospect. I didn't tell them I'd entered a national writing contest until I'd won an "honorable mention" and was about to get my picture in the local paper. I didn't tell them I was going out for the school play until I'd already been cast in the plum role of Doctor Chumley in *Harvey*. Great satisfaction was to be had in such concealments—the moments of revelation even sweeter, when I could vent my outrage at their ignorance of matters they could have had no way of knowing about. Such luxuriant revenge!—to be so vindicated, without ever having been subject to doubt in the first place.

Except that I *felt* doubt, and felt doubted, to the bottom of a soul I was really only marginally certain I did not have.

It was an acceptance, that letter from Buffalo, and a rare one, in spite of Dr. Chumley and the writing contest and the picture in the paper. Those were passing triumphs while this was the invitation to a new life. I'd be graduating from Wayne State the next month, and it had not been at all clear what would happen after that. Now it was. *A new life.* In Buffalo.

To go from Detroit—in the vicinity of which my first twenty-two years had sluggishly unfurled themselves—to Buffalo may fairly be declared a lateral move. The look on my parents' faces when I told them I was going to Buffalo was darkly mirrored in numerous faces over the months, as I busied myself with preparations for departure. Of course I'd had a vague sense of Buffalo as something of a national joke—"To commit suicide in Buffalo," as one of the cutest boys in the road show production of *A Chorus Line* at the Fisher Theater had quipped, "is redundant"—but I learned how widespread it really was in the universal disbelief, however politely repressed, of every friend, relation, co-worker, as I broke the news. Buffalo? Why would anyone move to *Buffalo*? All that snow! And what's that again—S-U-N-Y? *SUNNY*? SUNNY Buffalo? I thought it was cloudy in Buffalo...

This consternation doubtless owed as much to matters of vocation as to those of geography. Why, the question could just as well have been, would anyone go to graduate school? In *English*? An undergraduate degree in that chimerical subject seemed folly enough. To dig oneself even deeper, aside from deferring the inevitable responsibilities of the real world, was likely to render one terminally unemployable. In fact, many of the programs I'd considered, in reply to initial inquiries, had sent me brightly colored brochures filled with ominous forebodings, informing me of the dire state of the job market and advising that I not embark on the high-minded undertaking of a Ph.D. with any starry-eyed notions of actually having a career.

Then as now, arguments on behalf of the real world tended to leave me unmoved. What living among my family had certainly taught me was that it—this so-called "real world"—had many versions, a fractional infinity. Mine was no more theirs than any of theirs was another's, and even mine had many dimensions and was shockingly malleable, even if never, alas, fundamentally so. This conviction translated into a certain indifference to place. Having been outside of Michigan fewer than a dozen times—and then never more than a distance of three hundred miles or so over a period of three or four days—I could not have been called well-traveled. My knowledge of the world came from books and movies, which I knew (thought I!) as well as anyone. But the mind itself being reassuringly finite, everyone else's knowledge derived from similar sources in roughly similar proportions: a tiny slice of direct perception and experience set against a vast, amorphous slab of inference, conjecture, invention, projection, and densely mediated information. That every consciousness was trapped in a single body bounded by time and space seemed like incontrovertible evidence of this surmise, and whatever came of it could scarcely count as a world, much less as real, unless both terms were duly equipped with the safety-net of shudder-quotes. With all of this in mind (and allowing for my withering, unwavering contempt for the sterile suburb of Detroit where I happened to live) it followed that places, all in all, were more alike than they could ever be different from one another. Whether in Cincinnati, Toronto, or Mackinac Island—these being among the coordinate points of my limited reference—one was always treading on terra firma in any of its closely related forms or else, if in some brief dalliance with flight, about to return to it. One was always breathing air drawn, one way or another, from the same sky, however variable its inflections across a given universe, and glimpsing the same celestial bodies, from whatever slightly modified angle. What did it matter, in the end, and assuming a grand scheme of unreckoned things, where one lived?

Besides, my dedication to an ethic of the unworldly (since that is what I fancied it was) was actually shot through with a secret strain of pragmatism. One could just as easily have turned the formulation around on the skeptics: If I *were* merely a quixotic and capricious dreamer, wouldn't I be bound for some more exotic, high-flown locale? Trading one snow-swept industrial province for another wasn't exactly tilting at windmills. I didn't know that Buffalo's English department had enjoyed a reputation as one of the nation's best in the recent past, but I did know that several of my professors at Wayne State—including Charles Baxter, one of the mentors I admired the most—had gone there. They all lived in decent houses and seemed to be making viable livings. I could see the possibilities, envision some positive outcomes, however dimly, and if I *did* fail, as was more than likely, I would not be returning from some abortive excursion to the stars. It was *Buffalo*—three hundred miles away as the crow flew, seven or eight hours by bus.

A few more hindrances remained. A determination to escape being one of the things that bound us together in adolescence, most of my friends had fled for college after high school and never came back. But among other things, there was the guy I'd been having sex with on and off for a while; if he'd told me not to go, if he'd declared that we really *were* "boyfriends," in spite of everything, if he'd promised that we would have a life together—all bets would have been off. Instead he thrust his hands into the deep pockets of his dove-blue Dockers, squared his shoulders sheepishly, shot me his off-center Tom Cruise smile—it was the summer Tom Cruise became famous dancing in his tighty-whities in *Risky Business*—and wished me luck. At the eleventh hour, Wayne State offered me a competing fellowship, and suddenly the idea of staying put, of letting the familiar laws of inertia assert their ready hold, became as powerful as gravity and as alluring as the prospect of dozing in bed on a cold winter morning. From gallingly predictable quarters, the question had been raised of whether I could really survive on that four grand a year. Advised of these misgivings, Buffalo upped the ante to the more princely sum of six thousand four hundred dollars, and the decision was made. I took the risk—and left.

I would "work on"—so I'd written in my applications—"the problem of self-consciousness" in the work of "select modern masters." I had mentioned Beckett, Joyce, and Nabokov, and also indicated an interest in "the cinema."

These assertions were accurate, in their mewly ways. They were more predictive than usual for formulations such as these, in fact: My dissertation, five years later, did indeed turn out to be a study of "the problem of self-consciousness" in late modernist literature and film. So why, when I think of what I wrote, do my ears redden and warm with such tender embarrassment? Why does it all seem so damn naïve? Certainly by the time I got around to writing that dissertation, I knew a lot more about "the cinema," about "modern masters," about "the problem of self-consciousness." I know even more today—or do I? Is that how knowledge works, is it progressive? Could at least some of what I knew when young—in its contours, if not in its contents—have been superior to what I know now? Quantity aside (does knowledge come in quantities?)—might it have been that the best knowledge was the most needed in any given moment, the toddler's tottering first steps, however clumsy, trumping the elder's oft-repeated aphorisms, however wise?

"If I knew then what I know now"…That's the "problem" in a nutshell. You didn't and you couldn't. At least in part, the problem of self-consciousness is a problem of memory.

My undergrad advisers had advised me that if I wanted to sound academic I should say I would "work on" things, and should frame issues in terms of problems, so I did. That was all I meant by "the problem." I'd heard the awkward compound "self-conscious" more times in my life than I cared to recall but had no idea that literature could be self-conscious until I read it in a book (Robert Alter's *Partial Magic: The Novel as a Self-Conscious Genre*). My own limited understanding of Alter's sense was the only one I intended. In ordinary discourse I'd sooner have bitten my tongue than spoken of "the cinema." I wanted above all to be intellectual without being pretentious, if such a thing was possible. Yet my whole application was a farrago of Received Ideas. The "modern masters" loathed Received Ideas. Flaubert kicked off the trend. I knew that. But I had to put down something.

My preference for the "modern" began with no impulse more so-phisticated than an aversion to old books, though to call it aversion is not quite right, since any book was preferable to almost anything else, except maybe some movies. In college at Wayne State I'd discovered there was a thing called "modernism," a cognomen that served as a handy umbrella for most of what I'd been reading, and allowed me to start to think in new ways of how these books related to one another. What did it mean to be "modern"? Hadn't everyone always thought they were modern?

The first line of my dissertation read, "Every age thinks itself mod-ern, but one that *names* itself modern articulates a new kind of self-con-sciousness." I'm paraphrasing here - my copy's been lost for years.

It wasn't that I found old books hard and new ones easy. Among my favorite experiences as a reader had always been, since at eight I'd tried *Moby-Dick*, dim comprehension of books that were clearly beyond me, especially if it was accompanied by a murmur under the surface of something profound that I might one day be able to grasp. I sought the most challenging work; difficulty was the badge of modernist honor, which was why Djuna Barnes made the cut while F. Scott Fitzgerald, for instance, did not. Anything immediately comprehensible was anath-ema. Late James, Eliot, Pound, Joyce, Barnes, Stein, Woolf, Nabokov, Beckett, Proust, Kafka, Musil, Céline, Bely, Doblin—that was my can-on, indiscriminate in its way yet exclusionary as any. I was aware of certain ideological liabilities among members of this pantheon, but I also knew that the pressing work of *epater*-ing the *bourgeoisie* was the first order of business, and a matter quite beyond mere ideology.

Where did the movies fit in? It was clear where "the cinema" might, if that meant European auteurs like Bergman and Antonioni and God-ard and Fassbinder and the rest. But I also, mainly, loved *the movies*. I'd loved them since I learned to talk, because they seemed to offer a site where you did not have to talk, they seemed not to demand speech— and as often as not, that was just how I experienced the imperative of speech: as a demand. It could be said of movies that they demand-ed silence—attention, concentration, observation. I recall nothing of the process by which I came into language but I know that I have, since then, associated language with effort—the work of committing to thought, the labor of accounting for oneself. Having to talk was not often particularly painful, but *not* having to was almost always pleasurable, and many of my most intense experiences involved a rapturous sense of blissful liberation from language. Going to the movies was my favorite pastime because it entailed an enforced period of freedom from speech—my own, or anyone else's. The talking in the movie on the screen didn't count; in my mind it was never really speech to begin with. It was like the lyrics in songs on the radio. It didn't really matter what they said—just as I could never really follow the plots of movies, so I was incapable, most of the time, of deciphering song lyrics. In one song I heard "got some highs, got some lows," as "got some eyes, got some nose"—and went on for years thinking this was a perfectly reasonable thing to sing.

The meaning was not in the content. It was elsewhere.

It's probably not really true to say that movies demanded silence. Like books, they didn't really demand much of anything, on the face of it. They offered, but unless a teacher made you read a book—and nothing turned me against a book faster than any such obligation—they had no way of forcing you to accept whatever they might have to give. You could always just sit there. Whenever it was that I learned that movies played in theaters whether there was anyone there to watch them or not, the discovery clarified something basic about their character. They were not exactly *indifferent* to one's own presence, but like life itself—of which they could be seen as a slightly more manageable microcosm—they were fully able to go on, with or without it. Whenever there was a movie I really loved—and that was all the time, whether it be *Oliver!* with sexy, hooded-eyed, world-weary Jack Wild and sweetly delicate Mark Lester, or *The Out-of-Towners* with Jack Lemmon and Sandy Dennis, or *The Sting* or a little later, *Jaws*—I could scarcely bear the thought that they were ever being shown somewhere without my being there to take them in, and I'd return for repeat viewings as often as possible. Often, the second time, I'd be disappointed, the movie's vividness curiously faded, but then on a third trip I'd love it even more. It was all very mysterious, these ups and downs, the whole wonderful rigmarole of movies. But with any given movie I was usually too engrossed in the experience to worry much about what it all meant. That was the great thing about movies. Their meanings, if any, were elusive, yet vibrant, unfixed, not etched in the dreary solidity of language—and this seemed very much the way that meanings should be.

Modernism had a more obviously vexed relation to meaning. In many of its most inspired moments—*Pigeons on the grass, alas!*—it wrapped nonsense in a warmly whole-hearted embrace. But it was hard to miss the fact that modernist obscurity in most of its forms stood *against* the kinds of culture that the movies, above all, represented. How then to reconcile them? I'd found another book (Alfred Appel Jr.'s study *Nabokov's Dark Cinema*, which I read soon after having made my way through Nabokov's oeuvre) that went some way toward defining their reciprocal relationship, not just in Nabokov but in a range of "modern masters." Yet it did so largely by ignoring the wary association between modernism and mass culture, despite the cultural ground they shared, a mutual suspicion that increasingly interested me and came to seem—by the time I was confident enough to make sweeping claims about Culture—like the defining feature of the twentieth century.

It also had a personal implication. For a long time I read Nabokov's *Lolita* as an allegory of that wariness, that mutual suspicion. In this reading Humbert Humbert was Modernism and Lolita was Mass Culture. He was a creature of High Art, she a voracious consumer of movies and movie magazines, junk food, pop songs, comic books, trashy teen novelettes. Yet the spirit of the book loves Lolita, detests Humbert (despite the dubious identifications with him it lures the reader into). Where, given this paradox, to go from there? I too aspired to High Art, though I too "detested" Humbert, but like Lolita—and Humbert too for that matter—I was stuck in the world of mass culture. What surrounded me daily was the landscape of *Love Boat* and *Tiger Beat*, Hamburger Helper and "Seasons in the Sun," Hai Karate and Shake'n'Bake and Coca-Cola, Highlights magazine and the Wonderful World of Disney. These were among the things, over the years, that had always come to hand. Anything "higher" had to be searched out, with great effort, like a precious needle in a haystack of rubbish. If I was honest, I had to admit that, in my day, I had loved a lot of this rubbish and sometimes still did; the long resolution to wean myself away, gradually, entirely, was still in progress by the time I got to Buffalo. It often seemed that I was wholly alone in my attitudes of ironic detachment from these surroundings, while my parents and my sisters lapped up their TV dinners and microwaved meals and their Brady Bunches, their paperback thrillers and romances and telecast ballgames, their tabloids and their trinkets, with nary an inkling of the degraded quality of the overall milieu. Thus: *I* was Modernism and *they* were Mass Culture. That was certainly, I felt sure, how the situation would work itself out, ultimately. Meanwhile I was also Mass Culture—because I was *in* it if not *of* it and I was one of them and (I might have neglected to mention) I loved them too.

My apartment that first year was on Main Street above Patsy's Hair Salon, with an auto-body shop nudging passive-aggressively against it on one side and a factory a few blocks down on the other—TriCo, a Buffalo institution, maker of fine windshield wipers since the city's boom years. Between TriCo and Patsy's stretched a row of houses that typified a quintessential strain of the city's architecture, somewhere between the severity of Carpenter's Gothic and the symmetry of stick-style construction. All had wide enclosed porches with modest columns supporting iron-fenced balconies on the second floor, above which peaked an A-framed roof with a little round attic window inset near the tip of the triangle in front and dormers on the sides jutting up from the asphalt shingles. The houses were placed close together, and what struck one right away—especially one from Sterling Heights, in the suburbs of Detroit—was the promiscuous blend of residential and business addresses all along the street, law offices and insurance companies mixed right in with domestic domiciles where unruly children tussled on the patchy lawns.

From the start Buffalo seemed like something of a ghost town in two senses. It was a shadow-city, a reflection through a mottled glass of rust-belt burgs like Detroit and Cleveland but also, as the state's second city, a pale, oneiric double of its first. I had never been to New York proper then, but I recognized in every quarter correspondences to that Manhattan-of-the-mind conjured by the culture at large and known to all. Sprawling at the town's center, Buffalo's Delaware Park was the clear analog of the fabled common wedged into the core of the Big Apple (and Buffalo had a Central Park of its own too); the butcher or bus driver was as likely to bark with a Bronx twang as to hem with a more provincial haw. Though poised on the cusp of the country's Midwestern and northeastern regions, Buffalo was a haven for refugees from all five boroughs. My roommate that first year was from Long Island, and most of my professors were either New York City-born-and-bred or had done some hard time there one way or another, and when any one of them mentioned "the city," you could bet it was never Buffalo they had in mind. A subway projected to run up and down Main was under construction—kitty-corner from Patsy's, the Main/Amherst stop, placed at an odd angle to the intersection, was shaping up to resemble a high-end outhouse—and two years later, when the subway finally opened, Buffalo's half-hearted parody of its richer relation would be essentially complete.

In another sense Buffalo was a specter of itself. Along Millionaire's Row on Delaware Avenue or the broad boulevards of Bidwell Parkway, Victorian mansions stood as stately reminders of a glorious past. Yet even the less sumptuous houses along Main, at least to my eye, boasted a grandeur of their own, their triple-decker summits so distinct from the squat, functionalist "ranches" or foreshortened "colonials" of Sterling Heights. If you walked up Main towards the university and made a sharp left turn at Brand Names Wholesale, you would find yourself, suddenly—a block away from the neighborhoods of ordinary people—amid an enclave of veritable castles, multi-winged stone manors that might have housed so many Great Gatsbys; and these, in turn, leveled off in another block or two into street after street of less lavish three-storied abodes which might, in their turn, become just a little grander around the next corner. A few blocks south and just to the right, past a cleaners and an auto dealer in Googie neon-and-glass style with upswept roofs and curvaceous Space-Age pillars, just off Main on Jewett Parkway, you'd happen upon Frank Lloyd Wright's Darwin Martin House, with its clean lines and its sleek slopes—a new definition of symmetry. All of this seemed of a piece with the same ethos that interspersed factories, shops, bars, and restaurants with family homes, indifferent to the laws of zoning that had reduced the rest of the nation in a matter of decades to a barren but neatly stratified grid of subdivisions. What was still visible in Buffalo was not just the residue of a former boom town, but the vestiges of an urban ideal, where people of the working classes might be able to live in nice houses within view of their richer neighbors, and where boundaries among the zones often seemed auspiciously vague.

The betrayal of any such ideal was the real story of postwar America, and by the turn of the next century even its vestiges would mostly be but a dim memory. As it happened, in 1983, my apartment on Main Street straddled a class divide that was also, as in most American cities, largely racialized. On the West Side—where, after that first year, I would spend the rest of my time in Buffalo—lower- to upper-middle-class neighborhoods alternated peaceably, with a fair degree of overlap, the stores and delis of Hertel Avenue in North Buffalo tending to be only a little less upscale than all but the trendiest boutiques or most exotic bistros along the Elmwood Strip downtown. Though these neighborhoods were rarely segregated entirely by race, the clusters that tended to be called "ethnic" were occupied mostly by lower-middle-class Italians. On the other side of Main lurked the porn palaces and strip clubs of Bailey Avenue or Genesee Street, which cut at severe angles through the East Side and partitioned the few remaining Polish and German enclaves to the north from the African American neighborhoods to the south. From my front window, above Patsy's, I looked down on Main, where mingling yuppies lounged on the patio of the Stuffed Mushroom, the new hot spot just across the street; from my bedroom, in the rear of the house, I glimpsed a completely different world out on Fillmore Avenue, where formerly famed Blues clubs had declined into dark dives, and black kids in vacant, rubble-strewn lots played stickball—a blast from the past—or coasted coolly on skateboards, the wave of the future.

It was the perfect city, just close enough to what was familiar, and just far enough from it, genuinely urban, yet posing few of the threats of a real metropolis. For one thing, it seemed, I really *could* live there on that six thousand and four hundred bucks a year. Could I have survived in Manhattan on the paltry stipend Columbia would have paid me, had they not, as it happened, spared me the pains of finding out by rejecting me? But that was just the thing. Buffalo accepted me. What could I do but love it? And what better place for a cautious young person, eager to believe he was taking a risk?

My real home was Samuel Clemens Hall, quarters of the English department, the imposing vertical monolith that bounded at one end a cluster of squatter buildings, one enclave among many on the university's North Campus, all of the same drab industrial-red brick, each linked by enclosed elevated walkways to limit contact with the punishing winter climate. By contrast with the Main Street campus within the city limits, dating to the nineteenth century, with architecture in a more classically academic style, the North Campus had an impersonal corporate look. Erected in the '70s, it was designed in response to uprisings of the '60s, when the university roiled with protests against the war in Vietnam, earning UB (as the locals called it) the moniker "the Berkeley of the East." To forestall any further such disruptions, the new campus was planned along the lines of a business school, on the assumption that such a model would produce a general effect of stupefaction at odds with bothersome dissent. It was also made sprawling and de-centralized, isolated complexes placed randomly across the campus, like the "Ellicott Complex," rising up at a distance on the near horizon from Clemens like the Emerald City above the Land of Oz. The elevated tunnels linked the buildings of each enclave, but not any one enclave to the next; each was placed at such a well-calculated distance that each was effectively inaccessible to the others, especially when winter turned the ample grounds into non-negotiable expanses of tundra for months at a time. The intent to deter any critical mass of assembly could hardly have been clearer.

Some members of the department still grumbled about the move north from Main Street, even though it had occurred nearly a decade before. For me the suburban setting provided a surprisingly agreeable element of familiarity; in its cellblock style, the campus resembled the high school I'd attended, grotesquely outstretched in keeping with an expanding universe. As much as I'd professed to hate it at the time, I welcomed this uncanny return—it was as if I was re-enacting over and over my longtime fantasy of escape from suburbia, obstructed for so many years but now accomplished daily, whenever I boarded the Lockport bus that would bear me back to the city and a life that might finally be called my own.

It had been about twenty years since the Big Bang, as they called it, just after the then-private University of Buffalo became a branch of the recently established State University, when Al Cook, as Chair, had been given carte blanche—by Nelson Rockefeller himself, it was said—to assemble the best English department he could. Within a year or two he had lured a dazzling array of literary stars to Buffalo. In the first waves alone came John Barth, Donald Barthelme, Robert Creeley, Leslie Fiedler, Charles Olson, and many others. Cook's inspired idea was to hire people who were writers before they were scholars, at a time when the now-entrenched alliance between writers and the academy was only beginning to emerge. Cook sought the most original thinkers he could find, without regard for covering literary fields or periods, and without particular regard for schools or orthodoxies, such that relative traditionalists like the poet Carl Dennis, a recruit of the second wave, found themselves side by side with dyed-in-the-wool postmodernists like Creeley.

The result was one weird department—one might even have called it queer, in another time and place, if not for the dearth of queers, not even, it seemed, the closet cases that had populated literature departments in such robust numbers in days of yore. A large constituency consisted of men who were unmarried—or divorced, or perennially between girlfriends—in their forties and fifties, whose main ties of affection appeared to be their friendships with one another, but most of these more than fulfilled their clichéd roles as rakish English professors in their debonair flirtations with female graduate students at department parties. Leslie Fiedler had made his name by writing about flights from marriage and adult responsibility in classic American literature and the pervasive homoerotic ethos that resulted. It was striking to find these Bachelors of a Certain Age in a department where Fiedler was a figurehead, but the straightness of the arrangements seemed impeccable in the end.

By the eighties, among the celebrities, only Fiedler and Creeley remained of the original lineup, and we grad students joked that Buffalo was the place where Everyone *Had* Been, and Left. René Girard had formulated his theories of triangulated desire in Buffalo, as well as his ideas about violence, scapegoating and the sacred, before moving west to Stanford. Michel Foucault had paid an extended visit soon after the publication of *Discipline and Punish*, though I wouldn't learn until many years later that he'd frequented some of the same gay bars in Allentown that I ventured into from time to time. Olson decamped to the University of Connecticut after holding office hours in a hotel room across the street from the old campus for a semester or two, and meeting students there in his pajamas. Barth moved to Johns Hopkins, Barthelme to Houston by way of New York. Almost all the so-called "New York Intellectuals" passed through at some time or other, some like Dwight Macdonald tarrying for extended periods, while the most cantankerous of them all, Lionel Abel, held out until our day, treating many of us in our first year, just before he retired to Manhattan, to racist bromides in his sparsely-attended seminars. Asked how best to deal with America's race problem, he would snarl, "Give 'em Texas!"

Anyone who'd spent half a day there would not have been likely to doubt ever again the momentousness of the practice of criticism. Lives depended on it, though whose was less clear. The shelf life of an idea was about a week, yet no appearance of intellectual trendiness ever settled in or had to be denied. Times being what they were, almost everyone sounded a little deconstructionist. To most, it did not come as news that it was possible to claim that language constructed reality rather than the other way around. Even the few real die-hard deconstructionists, though, on the lam from Yale or Johns Hopkins, tried to think beyond that approach. The questions remained basic—what was language, what was literature?—the past tense more than apt, because there was always the possibility that any thought-formation was at its end or already defunct. Foundations were routinely put to rest with the wave of a hand. What most defined the climate, in a way, was all that was taken for granted. Ideas were not introduced but explicated. If an idea seemed entirely new it was only because you had not come across it before. All the groundwork was already laid, and it was no more interesting than the ground. It was only to be walked upon. What mattered was what you could build on it.

Any idea deemed too stable, too grounded in the un-thought empirical, was suspect.

History and politics were basic, which was to say assumed, which was to say absent. Direct recourse to either, crucial as they were, could lend itself too readily to establishmentarian programs. There were rumors that Cook had intended to staff the place with conservatives at Rockefeller's behest, but if so—though his recruitment did favor anti-Communists—the plot failed. The department's progressive credentials were more than solid, certified in town-and-gown conflicts like the community outrage that greeted nude sunbathing and casual pot-smoking at the Fiedlers'. Many faculty had radical pasts and most were card-carrying liberals. Carlene Polite was among the first black women to be tenured at an American university, and there were more tenured women at Buffalo than in most Ivy League English departments then—about five, out of sixty.

Eclecticism was regarded as a virtue, but too great a tolerance for critical pluralism could be seen as a liability. Most of the faculty had some version of what Norman Holland, a pioneer of reader-response theory who had founded the Center for the Study of Psychoanalysis and the Arts at Buffalo, would have called an "identity theme." Marcus Klein brought an anti-Communist edge to the study of proletarian literature. John Dings countered with a commitment to Marxism, reading through the lens of class, Raymond Williams-style, before it was broadly fashionable to do so. Art Efron's credo was *Pay attention to the body*—though, by the time this mantra became a widespread theory-slogan in the '90s, it was not at all what Art had had in mind, awash as it was in an updated variant of D. H. Lawrence's sex-in-the-head. Marty Pops was a reconstructed Jungian who was considering then the relationship between what he called the Appollonian and the Dionysian impulses in culture, the penitential and the celebrational. Irving Massey was thinking about literature as a form of philosophy decades before the rise of Theory redefined the field of Comp Lit along just those lines, and he was doing so without any loss of sensitivity to literature as art. A few built their reputations on an aversion to Theory, like Alan Spiegel, the film specialist, who would stand next to an old 16 mm. Bell-and-Howell projector at the back of the classroom and shout over its whirring motor and creaky reels, riffing brilliantly on whatever pictures poured out onto the screen—from *Adam's Rib* to *Woman in the Window*, *Double Indemnity* to *Strangers on a Train*.

The recommended course load for graduate students was two seminars per term, but I always took three. After years of laboring to pay tuition as an undergraduate, the idea of free education was one of the great boons. In the first semester, I took Romanticism, Critical Theory, and a course on Literature and War. It became clear right away how these courses would be different from the ones I'd taken at Wayne State, though it took longer to figure out how those differences reflected in turn the oddities of Buffalo's English department. Even when they followed the syllabus, the focus of a particular session was never solely on the announced text. Usually the books became occasions for the professors' larger reflections on whatever they happened to be thinking about—nor was this exactly the right way to put it, since happenstance played a small role. They were thinkers, without even trying, and that meant they were always, for the most part, following a line of thought, not unrelated to the thoughts of others, but somehow quite specific to themselves, a rigorous trajectory in which dense clusters of ideas led logically to other clusters, with certain basic assumptions in play about what you had to have read if you wanted even to begin thinking about a particular idea with any degree of seriousness. This meant that the same books could be thought about in a potentially limitless variety of ways. Even if books themselves were not ideas, they were central to whatever it was that made ideas possible. I suspected almost everyone there knew exactly what that was but that I wasn't allowed to ask because you had to figure it out for yourself—the same reason the Good Witch of the North held off telling Dorothy that all she'd have needed to do to get back to Kansas was to click together the heels of the ruby slippers.

In Irving Massey's seminar on Romanticism, it was assumed that we would already have read Byron, Coleridge, Keats, Shelley, Wordsworth. They were referred to mostly in passing, though often with a sense of great moment. Though Irving remained committed to an ethics of value, he never supposed it was obvious how such value was to be adjudicated, nor that it should be clear. In 1983, the literary canon as it then stood was starting to come under fire for, among other things, its rank exclusionism, but in Buffalo it had never had much of a foothold to begin with. Canons were just as likely to be filled with dross as with gold, and they were not for readers anyway. They were for people who did *not* read. A real reader would never need to be told to look beyond a canon—that was the conventional wisdom at Buffalo, and it went without saying. Among the main texts of Irving's seminar were Dorothy Wordsworth's journals, John Galt's *Annals of the Parish*, and John Clare's poetry and prose—hardly the stuff of doctrinal orthodoxy, then or ever. Anyone on the lookout for the best and the highest would have come away with dashed hopes, no doubt—and while that wasn't exactly the point, it was no accident that these and other selections called for a rethinking of what the best might include. Irving knew as well as anyone that these writers were marginalized—and how and why they were—but that wasn't why he taught them. He taught them because he thought they were great.

Art Efron's course in Critical Theory was, if anything, even stranger. I'd become vaguely aware at Wayne State of a thing called Theory, but I'd only been required to read a couple of early staples like Michel Foucault's "What is an Author?" that had started to seem like old chestnuts by the time I arrived at Buffalo. Art's seminar paid lip service to the already-entrenched pantheon—Derrida, de Man, Barthes, Foucault—and concentrated instead on such unlikely figures as Wilhelm Reich, John Dewey and Stephen Pepper. Reich I knew only from Dusan Makavejev's movie about him, a wild fantasia that had left me feeling queasy. Dewey I knew chiefly as a culprit behind the supposedly progressive system of education of which I had been a victim. Pepper I'd encountered by coincidence—how great a coincidence I only came to appreciate on learning how little currency Pepper's work had ever gained—in one of the dire courses I'd taken in the Education Department at Wayne State, with a professor who bore an uncanny resemblance to Art (same darting glance, same glancing smile, same chinstrap beard). That course had been one of the factors that made me give up the hope of ever getting credentialed as a high school teacher, and perhaps for that reason—and because I could not shake an unpleasant association with my childhood reading of the "Five Little Peppers" books—I never could move beyond an initial impression of Pepper's work as schematic and dull-witted, however Art lobbied for him.

In Literature and War, Rodolphe Gasché sat with his head tilted down, peering at a single sheet of paper on the table in front of him, which was entirely covered (as far as one could see from across the room) with microscopic inscriptions, so dense that they left no margins anywhere on the page. He seemed to be reading from this sheet as he spoke, but his lectures lasted ninety minutes, and he never once turned a page. The mystery of how all those sentences could be contained in a single folio was never solved. Without fail, the lectures were shapely and intricate. At the end of every paragraph, Gasché would glance up at the class and blink. During the lecture, he kept his legs intertwined, coiled under the table as he arched his back and leaned forward over his piece of paper, elbows propped on either side of it. When he was done, he unknotted the legs and leaned back, signaling that discussion of what he had said was now authorized to commence. The general idea, as far as I could make out, was that the literature of war could not help but be self-reflexive because literature at its essence *was* war, and war literature.

By the end of the '80s, the triumvirate of race-class-gender had risen to power in English departments—a strange kind of power, that was— and come to hold sway even at Buffalo by the end of the century. In retrospect, I did come to regret a lack of explicit attention to such concerns during my time in the program. By the time I left, colleagues were starting to speak of graduate study as a training ground. *Where were you trained?* they'd ask at conferences. Who—me? I'd think. *Trained?* I'd been left to fend largely for myself in a vaguely welcoming atmosphere of tumultuous intellect, and that had been fine with me. I'd been forced to figure out—or simply to presume—that everyone was really always talking about selves and others, centers and margins, subjects and objects, even before they got around to talking about *which* selves, *which* others. You could not do everything at once, though at Buffalo it sometimes seemed you had to.

My life was dividing, though I wanted it to converge. My home life, my reading life, my social life… (My "sex life" was another matter altogether.) My teaching life: English Composition 101 met on Mondays, Wednesdays, and Fridays from eleven o'clock to ten of noon. By pacing back and forth to bide the time amid between-class swarms along the hall one flight above where my class was scheduled to meet, and allowing thirty-five seconds for an unhurried descent of the stairs to the floor below, I timed my arrival to eleven on the dot, thus avoiding any pre-class complications. On the first day about twenty students were propped in their chairs like dummies in the passenger seats of crash-test cars. Despite the glazed-over eyes, the students still managed to convey an air of dour expectation. The room was flooded with it. Even after the calculated leisure of my approach, my breathing seemed compromised, strained. I stepped gingerly around the desk, breaching that mildly comforting boundary between myself and the space of the room at large, to pass out the syllabus. On returning to the zone of relative safety behind the desk, following a cursory and humiliating shuffle through some irrelevant papers, I discovered I'd handed out my own copy, which meant I had to venture once again back out into the bristling territory fore-desk, to collect the extras. A somnolent student supplied them in slow-motion, with a repressed yawn and an arm outstretched unnaturally, straining to reach far, far in front of her, to stave off even the slight possibility of unwanted contact.

The halting trek through the syllabus provided another safety-net of sorts, as the page it was printed on served as a kind of screen. As I held it up and read from it, it trembled a bit—in tandem with my traitorous hands—but I could hide myself behind it, to a point. Peeking around the edges, I saw them all, all twenty, looking down, away from me, at their own copies. My heart, which had been bouncing around my rib cage, with a brief excursion into my throat—where it inflated suddenly to push against the sides of my neck—returned to an approximation of its proper location, but when they looked back up at me, all at once, it broke in two, lickety-split, the parts shooting down the lengths of each arm to the fulcrum where, one half squished into either wrist, it throbbed. We reached the end of the syllabus. Were there questions? There was one: "Do we have to type our papers?" That matter settled as gently as possible, the class was dismissed. With the wobbly, harried gait, hesitant yet aggressive, of subway riders churning through a turnstile, the students filed out the door. I sat alone at the front desk. That dreamlike journey down the hall to the first class of my life as a "teacher" had to have been at least an eon ago, but the irrefutable clock said that seventeen minutes had passed. How could I ever return?

How could I return? What could possibly fill the full *fifty* minutes of the next session, to say nothing of the fourteen weeks after that, three times a week, nearly an hour each and every time? If I told them everything I knew in the world I could fill, maybe, half a session. I watched the smirking clock tick away a full minute, second by endless second. There was a rent in time. Maybe in this new and unwelcome dispensation all I knew couldn't even fill up a minute's worth.

That afternoon, also for the first time, met SuperTeach, a handy portmanteau of "Supervised Teaching." This was a seminar on the ins and outs of instruction that the department offered to keep us first-years from feeling that we'd been thrown into the classroom like so many Christians to the lions. That was exactly what *was* happening, of course, and the department's efforts to show otherwise were half-hearted at best. One indication of this was that the class was perennially staffed by faculty who, by and large, were not active participants in the life of the program, and did not otherwise tend to offer graduate courses. The thankless assignment of SuperTeach had to have been a kind of punishment to those deemed unproductive, but I knew nothing of academic politics and such thoughts never occurred to me then.

Certainly Vic Doyno, who was running SuperTeach that semester, had little air about him of one who was being chastised. He was genial to a fault, a remarkably avuncular man, cheerfully moon-faced, with a large round head and loose limbs that gave him something of the look of the Scarecrow of Oz in a plumper incarnation. The looseness of the limbs extended, somehow, to the neck—the round head, as if precariously placed, bobbing constantly, even when he was standing still; and when he moved his motion was a slack, twitchy jig, legs swaying and arms floundering. He would have seemed like an entirely buoyant presence if not for his voice, which was shot through with a quality of earnestness and urgency, a low-pitched murmur unpredictably punctuated by unsettling, breathy giggles that swallowed the last few words of every other sentence he spoke.

What counsel he provided was puzzling in its dichotomy. Sometimes he encouraged us to treat our "kids," as he called them, with kid-gloves, like tender little lambs who were all too easily bruised. Other times he urged upon us a tough-as-nails approach, as if they were

23

nothing but an unruly mob of juvenile delinquents, forever hatching terrible plots, ready to pull off a mile-wide con if you gave them half an inch. On the one hand, we weren't supposed to overwhelm them with too much commentary on their compositions, since cascades of red ink in the margins had a tendency to traumatize the poor dears and turn them off learning for life. On the other hand, we were advised to adopt an unusual watchfulness, the utmost vigilance, to brook no mischief, to suspect every excuse of concealing some nefarious pretext, and to guard constantly against the wily ulterior motives that surely lurked under the most innocent-seeming activities. Vic never tired of sketching the students' demographics, perhaps to account for this essentially divided nature of their characters. They were predominantly on the low end of the middle-class, he explained, innocuously ethnic in some vague senses and typically the first generation in their families to go to college—a lot like me.

That sense of identity was just what bothered me. For one thing, they were eighteen and I was all of twenty-two. The only thing that differentiated us, aside from the gulf that separated each human from every other, was a few years. As a student I'd always resisted considering my teachers as parental surrogates, though I knew it was common to think that way. I didn't welcome the tutelage of my own parents, let alone that of substitutes. Now I wondered if it really wasn't a necessary part of the arrangement, to instill the respect any heuristic transaction, for all I knew, might require. But respect was a thing to be earned—that was axiomatic—and I had thought of most of my teachers before college, even those I was fond of, as bureaucrats of a sort, who shared the same basic indifference to the Life of the Mind that flourished among my peers.

What could I teach them? What did I know about teaching? What did I know about anything? I could not remember, myself, ever having been "taught"; in my sense of things, everything I'd ever learned I had taught myself, or learned from books—which came to the same thing. Even in college, I'd never expected pedagogical revelations in the classroom, even in the presence of teachers I *knew* were great. I always thought that I was supposed to be gathering material to be culled later, on my own, and that that's what a great teacher was—one who could show you how to do that. And if I was so untaught, and maybe unteachable, how could I transmit a sensation I'd never experienced? And what was I doing in graduate school in the first place?

Friday morning I arrived once more most carefully upon my hour—eleven on the dot, no muss no fuss—and decided on the spur of the moment to abandon my lesson plan on paragraph form and to wing it. How many thought writing was hard? Most hands went up. They went up languidly, but they went up. That in itself was remarkable. They would, it turned out, respond to my prompting. Even if the reaction resembled the dead-alive reflex of so many comatose frogs attached to a galvanic battery, it was still something. How many, then, thought *talking* was hard? No hands. Just blank looks. But wasn't writing really just talking, encoded in scripted signs? What was the difference? Blank looks shading over into weary mystification. Human presence—that's what! In speech you have the illusion of *being there*—you can use your hands, you can use your voice. You can ask your listeners questions and answer them. But writing—most writing is characterized by *absence*—the absence, at least, of the speaker. That is one of its defining qualities, and what made Plato so unhappy about it. Did they know that? It was all right there, in the *Ion* (a Platonic dialogue, like the *Republic*, I added helpfully)—that writing was always to be distrusted, because the writer was not present, and you could never be sure, therefore, whether he was lying or telling the truth, because you could not witness for yourself the deceiver's blush or the truth-teller's confidence.

And then—it was ten to twelve. I had just gotten started. The same hour that had limped by only two days before as if it would never end had just sped past in half a heartbeat. I'd only scratched the surface of the problem. And that was exactly what writing was, I told them—a *problem*. Writing a paragraph was like solving an equation. And next time, I proclaimed, I would give them the solution.

After they shuffled out, I lingered behind alone again, marveling that the same empty room could contain both the despair I'd felt the last time and the exhilaration that now buoyed me. The feeling was short-lived. A minute later it occurred to me that I had a single weekend to figure out what I was going to tell them—what this advertised "solution" was going to be.

I spent the weekend reading Derrida. From that quarter, the boiled-down source at third-or-fourth hand of my absent/present gambit, no solution was forthcoming. Meanwhile, I was haunted by the possibility that the students had heard my impromptu lecture as gibberish, rather than as the inspired disquisition I'd imagined. I pictured myself standing before them, a blubbering, clownish figure, babbling on about blushing liars while sporting, myself, florid cheeks of shocking-pink, the damn ruddiness that flooded my damn Irishman's face any time the going got rough. That constant flush was another thing I'd have to resign myself to, if I ever really *was* going to be a teacher.

By Monday morning I had decided I was going to let them talk. They'd heard just about enough out of me for the time being, and I planned to test a hypothesis I'd spent the weekend nursing—that they would not recall my promise of the week before to let them in on the secrets of the universe. I wouldn't say a word about this pledge, and wagered—in a hopeful little bet with myself—that they wouldn't either, even if they were permitted to take the floor. I asked them to tell me what they wanted to learn. Blank looks, then, one by one, some tentative hands. One wanted to write in a less "flowery" way. One wanted to be less wordy. One wanted to be more concise. One wanted to get right to the point and be done with it. The word "flowery" recurred. I wondered if they themselves were discerning the pattern. The most original contention—from a young man named Hal with steel-blue eyes, acne-spangled cheeks, and straw-colored hair, tightly cropped in little yellowish curls—said he wanted to "inject humor," reminding me of Mary McCarthy's student who apologized for a story he submitted to her in draft, saying it wasn't very good but he was planning to go back through and put in the symbols.

They all seemed to be saying that they did not want to write at all. That didn't surprise me.

The hour went by—not fast, not slow. Just regular minutes, ticking themselves away. I assigned their first composition, a short diagnostic essay. Were there any questions? There were two: How long did it have to be? And, did it need to be typed?

In the weeks that followed we worked our way through tedious lessons on process analysis, inductive versus deductive reasoning, and logical fallacies. A gap in communication somewhere along the line led the class to the calamitous misunderstanding that the logical fallacies really *were* logical, and that I was encouraging their use. In the surprisingly lengthy span during which they labored under this erroneous impression, they perked up for the first time all semester, as if they thought they were finally getting their money's worth, but when I realized their mistake at last, and clarified that the logical fallacies were actually *fallacies*, to be avoided, they reverted promptly to their usual despondency. In SuperTeach, with disproportionate alacrity, Vic Doyno recommended various techniques to promote class participation, like bringing in a ping-pong ball or a little mitten, and tossing them around the room, starting with the first student elected to speak, who would catch the object in question, say his or her piece, then in turn toss ball or glove, as the case may have been, to the next student, and so on. The simple raising of hands, it seemed, smacked of an authoritarian atmosphere in this age of the de-centered classroom. Vic was so taken with the ball and the glove that he instituted their use in SuperTeach itself, to show us what fun they could be. I wished there were some way to let my students know what I was sparing them—how much worse the class could have been if I'd adopted such madcap antics, sure they would agree that a whiff of authoritarianism was preferable in a college classroom to the hijinks of the nursery.

Hal became a problem. He was one of those guys whose intelligence manifested in aggression, as manly straight-from-the-shoulder-talk or smart-alecky joking or frank argumentation. He'd sit in the middle of the room with his arms crossed and his biceps bulging, pointedly *not* taking notes. Instead he stared at me (they *all* stared at me), a look of wry pity constant in the steel-blue eyes. He seemed to feel sorry for me, stranded up there at the front of the class, getting into constant pedagogical jams. But he didn't make it any easier. When we read Orwell on politics and the English language, he said he'd heard Orwell was a Communist. That was easy enough to deal with, since it was plainly wrong. But when we read Gore Vidal's bold and breezy plan to legalize all drugs in the U.S.—an idea the class greeted with unanimous outrage—Hal said he'd heard that Vidal was a homosexual. Did that discredit his proposal? I asked (voice cracking a bit). What about the logical fallacies—remember them? Was this a "hasty generalization"? An "*ad hominem* argument"—or maybe "*ad* homo-*nem*," I added, a little joke that elicited a few noncommittal titters, including one from Hal. I felt a little burst of satisfaction when I saw him grin, but I knew it would turn to lasting shame by the time everyone else had forgotten all about it.

In SuperTeach, amid the whizzing projectiles, I thought about how to broach the issue of problem students. But what exactly was the problem? It was hard to pinpoint. The ping-pong ball soared at my head and slipped through my fingers when I tried to grab it, and as I groped for it under a chair I grunted a general question about how to handle hostility in the classroom. Vic uttered a few bumptious truisms and asked to see me after class, when he grilled me in a raspy, conspiratorial whisper about the nature of the difficulty. After I filled him in he nodded knowingly and told me to keep a sharp eye on the boy's pupils. And the lips, *watch the lips*—sometimes they'd get a white powdery substance in the corners of the mouth, a telltale sign. What tale it might have told remained a mystery to me.

The real problem was that Hal was obnoxious and unappealing and somehow, despite the acne, awfully sexy at the same time. Through September and much of October he wore short sleeves and, arms crossed as usual, flexed his biceps from time to time, right or left at random. As a site of affect under erasure—as Derrida might have put it—the classroom supplied so little visual stimuli from the teacher's panoptical vantage (don't forget Foucault!) that I found myself, amid the arrested motion and depleted expressions, scanning the unpromising field of vision in hopes of glimpsing the periodic muscle-twitch. But I was still relieved when the cold weather brought on the season of long sleeves.

So it went, week by week, in the usual onset of the ordinary. If anyone *had* ever thought to ask what that promised "solution" was, what could I have said? *I* was the one who was learning—among other things, that teaching was part stand-up-act, part pep-talk, part showdown with the Enormous Other, part five-finger-exercise. Most of what you "taught" dropped directly into the ocean of oblivion like Ahab's tear near the end of *Moby-Dick*. That nobody ever did ask proved that collective amnesia might be the hardiest tack, the handiest tool. Assume everything was new each and every time and, who knows, maybe something might stick. Even when you thought you knew what you were saying you could never know what they were hearing. My lessons were really terribly simple and that was foremost among them. But I was learning you could never hope to put any of these lessons over directly. If I'd ever tried to tell them straight out all I wanted them to learn, they'd have hauled me off to the booby-hatch, pronto. Other "lessons"? Just for instance—*take heed.* Observe the unreachable. Note the slow movement and the quickening end, the stretch of time, and time itself, the clarion call, your tacky dreams, the dazzling airs, the Big Subjects, the dim rewards and light fulfillments, the desperate hungers, the stern commands and fiery particles, the many immensities, the brazen touch, the grandest prize, the changes and the whelming eyes, the beaky bomb, the stains of youth, a long illness and avalanche, the disasters you could never have and all the ones you could. Keep your mind in hell and do not despair. Know the look of the oppressor. Know your way back home.

My "social life"—little by little I was meeting everyone. Everyone came from somewhere else. Mary from Darby PA just outside of Philly, plain old Darby, never to be confused with hoity-toity *Upper* Darby; Sheila from steel country in the same gray state but closer to Pittsburgh; Karyn and Dave from the nation's clamorous capitol, Karyn by way of Reston, VA and Dave, with his non-stop one-liners, by way of the Catskills; Gwen from an old Denver family with deep roots in Colorado and some obscure connection to the Unsinkable Molly Brown; Doran from Santa Cruz, still beach-ready in shorts and flip-flops well after the first Buffalo frost; Liz from Chippewa Falls, a real-life Annie Hall down to the tweed vests and the la-di-dahs. Even the New York contingent— Bill from Potsdam and Neil from Syracuse and Maria from East Aurora, right on the city's outskirts—lent their portion to the cosmopolitan company. All converged willingly and willy-nilly on this city of such small consequence, this odd urban lump of spiritualized rubble, with something of the same sanguine anticipation. To go to grad school was always a kind of a bid, a wager that things might actually work out. Maybe that's why the image of Buffalo in my memory, in all its shabby beauty, its laughable dilapidation and splendor, is always burnished with hope.

My roommate was from Hicksville, an unpromising name for a town considering the exotic Long Island address. It was just up the road from Cold Spring Harbor, Billy Joel country, and Dan would listen to Billy Joel when he got homesick, and to Jerry Garcia and the Grateful Dead— whom he'd followed for many summers as a die-hard Deadhead—when he got nostalgic for his rebel past. He was in the law school at Buffalo, to which he had matriculated by way of Oberlin College, where he'd studied philosophy as a classmate of Richard Gere's younger brother. My expressions of enthusiasm for this connection were intended to convey something of my proclivities, but it took Dan an unnaturally long time to catch on. There was something of an inverse ratio between my categorical insistence that I was already "out"—as well as my dog-matic refusal to perform endless rituals of disclosure for the straight world—and the subtlety of the indications. Dan was lithe and slender with olive skin and a trim beard, the upkeep of which, always somehow out of sight even in the close quarters we shared, required that he be at least a little vain, despite his self-deprecating wit. I was always on the lookout then for an exact blend of conceitedness and shyness, a delicate alchemy that was among my most reliable turn-ons. Dan was quiet and retiring with an odd streak of exhibitionism. Around the house he wore tight-fitting denim overalls with no shirt underneath, even in winter, and with the left strap always undone, hanging down in front, revealing a smooth naked shoulder, half a neatly symmetrical thatch of sparse, dark chest hair, and a chiseled, plum-colored nipple. His diligence and reserve made him a perfectly fine roommate—like me, he spent most of his time working in his room—but there was always something a little vexing about him too, because I thought I should, by then, have been well beyond having crushes on people.

But I had crushes on almost everyone and began to pride myself on this promiscuousness. After my first trip back home to Michigan for the holiday break, it was clear that whatever had been going on there with That Guy would not be going on any longer. In spite of my—not pleas, I was *certainly* above that—entreaties, there was not even destined to be one last time for old time's sake. The rejection was perfectly timed,

I decided. I'd spent my first sixteen years discovering my spiritual self and the next five discovering my sexual self—wondering all the while how my sensibility (a word I'd picked up from Susan Sontag), if I should ever really happen to come into one, would accommodate either. Both, as far as that went, were fully wrought and utterly known. Now it was time for something else, something even deeper and yet to be explored that would blend all three—sensibility, spirit, sexuality, preferably in that order—and integrate my life, which only seemed one with itself so long as it was unsundered by want. That January I returned to my adopted snow-bound city determined to desire less.

2.
"The problem of self-consciousness":

*D*on't be so self-conscious! People were always issuing their injunctions—*Take a risk!*—and this—*Don't be so self-conscious!*—was a favorite of my mother's during all of my childhood. It seemed at odds with her accompanying plaint: *Take more pride in your appearance!* The latter appeal was spurred by my general indifference to attire and hairstyles. Nothing placed me in any more direct contact with the void at the core of Being than the task of shopping for new school clothes, and my aversion to barbers was such that, from the moment I gained even a modicum of personal autonomy, I'd sport an unkempt thatch of finger-combed hair for weeks or months on end, until this wild pilosity threatened to blot out my very sight, like liverworts overgrowing a headstone, and there was absolutely no choice but to cut the infestation back.

Yet the two demands could not be reconciled. Didn't my refusal to take "pride"—a deadly sin, after all, by her own reckonings—in this thing called my "appearance" mean, precisely, that I was *not* "self-conscious"? Didn't self-consciousness imply a certain vanity? Clearly, in spite of my commitment to inner experience, I did not want to be "self-conscious" in whatever shameful, debilitating sense *she* meant. There was only so much that could be known by a mind, though a mind itself could have little inkling of this limit or even of its own content, strictly speaking. In this sense a mind could not even really know itself, let alone another mind. It seemed there were at least two variations. There was the kind of self-consciousness that crippled and the kind that assuaged. The first lured you into yourself as a refuge, breeding insularity and solipsism, engendering an obliviousness one could wear like a cloak. The second did not tempt but threaten. It followed long dark nights of the soul that might be followed by a crisp, wintry but inspiriting morning of surcease only if you happened to survive the nights, and that meant coming to terms with nothingness, and with the impossibility of knowing another, even though the need to comprehend otherness was the only end that justified such turning inward as anything *but* vanity and pride.

You do things, and you watch yourself doing them. You think things and observe yourself thinking them. You say things and hear yourself saying them. You cannot do both at once. (Can you?) There is an interval between the doing, the thinking, the saying, and the hearing, watching, seeing. That gap explains in part why watching is not the same as seeing.

Self-consciousness was imputed to me most insistently in moments of social silence. (*Don't be so self-conscious! Put yourself forward! Make a social effort!*) It wasn't rare for the elated silence of my cherished solitudes to turn into an involuntary speechlessness in public. At times the words just wouldn't come. It was not that there was nothing to say. Usually there was too much, too many words, and it was as if I could hear and almost *see* them, legions of words, speakable, unspeakable, in some inner mysterious place, along various strange corridors, murmuring themselves to themselves, but they were all behind a kind of door and the door was firmly shut. Which hallway—if it ever opened—which passage to pursue? They were not legion, the passages, but they were many, each swarming with possibility, all that might be said, and therefore could not be. Even when, especially if, what was called for was a simple nicety, this linguistic impotence could overtake me. Forcing the words felt like trying to push a boulder through a mouse hole, and when they emerged they came then with the spasm of a stutter.

Unless words come naturally, they had better not come at all. Words can be forced from us, by need, or by love; sometimes, fortunately, the two can even coincide. But to take a stance from which one inflicts words on others...is presumptuous, even violent. It presupposes self-satisfaction and a certain coarseness. It infringes on the fragility of our texture.

A startling paragraph—this is the opening of "Escape from Fiction," an essay that was the first piece of writing by Irving Massey that I encountered, in a college seminar a year or two before going to Buffalo. I no longer doubt the presuppositions—that our "textures" are "fragile," of course, but also that language is implicitly violent and mired in self-justification. Rather, I view them now as axiomatic. (Is this, finally, what I have learned from him?) My first reaction, though, was shocked resistance. How, for starters, could such earth-shaking claims be stated with such tranquility? Why didn't the language seem as hortatory as the content suggested it should, what kept it from being dunning or hectoring? The tone suggested something ripened, something long thought. You would have to believe such things for a very long time to be able to write them so calmly.

Even on that first reading of the passage, I recalled aphasic episodes of my childhood. They had become less frequent, but there were still—are still—occasions when, embarking on a sentence, I'd pull back into sudden silence, like a dazed acrobat about to step from the platform who suddenly realizes the tightrope's been ripped away. Was there, behind all this, some awareness of the "coarseness" of human speech, some withdrawal from the self-satisfaction that speech required in a way that writing, perhaps, did *not*? To speak, you need not assume you have anything to say, but you *must* assume that others want to hear. You have to take responsibility for what you say but not necessarily for what you write. (Could that really be the case?) Sometimes words came streaming like afternoon sun pouring over a westward sill. You only had to say them.

In large part the appeal of modernism was that it trumpeted a collective answer to my mother's injunctions. Its credo was "BE self-conscious!" For the modernists, as I saw it, self-consciousness was more of a solution than it was a problem—though it was a problem too, of course, self-consciousness being what it was and modernism being what *it* was. But mainly it was an answer to the *real* problem —that of the *lack* of self-consciousness fostered by the new conditions of historical being that went by the name of modernity, the new worlds of industrialization and its aftermath, of the machine-age and the Culture Industry, whether in the form of mind-numbing, spirit-killing work (and I'd done my share of that, nearly ten years' worth) or just the bare fact of the human condition—that any given consciousness is oblivious of infinitely more than it can ever be aware of.

Be self-conscious.

That directive remained its sole positive motto, as far as I could tell. Insofar as the Church of Modernism provided rules for living, all the others were prohibitions, suggesting the penitential character that was another of the features that drew me—a lapsed Catholic, like many of its adherents. Irony and skepticism remained the orders of the day. In essence, modernism was cautionary, even its comedy—of which there was plenty, once you managed to find it, or else I'd have had none of it—erring on the side of the cautious and constrained. Don't be naïve, chided modernism. Don't be gullible, don't be foolish. Don't make yourself out so important, don't imagine you're the center of the universe. Despite the fetish for taboo that stood somewhere near the center of the movement, and even though much of its abundant contempt was reserved for any whiff of the didactic, modernism offered these unforgiving lessons of its own, and it could, in its way, once it got going, sound an awful lot like one's parents—who, however, would never have given the time of day to a dogma so impudent, so indifferent to ordinary success, so lacking in horse sense.

Modernism boasted more than its share of "masters," but perhaps more than in any prior movement in cultural history, they tended to be derided, loathed, outcast, not least because of their propensity to inflict upon their audiences assaults of various kinds. When you first come upon a book like *Ulysses* you could be forgiven for making the mistake of imagining that it aspires to some kind of ordinary greatness, just because of its epic bulk. Begin to read and no such error can persist for long. First it just seems dull—like *Dubliners* but even less eventful. Then it takes a turn, and paragraphs start to trail off into a kind of lovely gibberish, the "story" meanders in a few errant directions, nothing seems to be getting the right emphasis. Halfway through you know it's great, but not because the story grabs you and your heart starts to race. Your heart does *not* start to race—not until maybe the last hundred pages, and then forever after, whenever you think of it. But even then you can see, sort of, why so many thought it was just bad. It was *not* "great"—not in any Shakespeare-or-Rembrandt kind of way. It was not even trying. And that was part of the greatness.

It was the ambiguity of the modernist project that clinched the deal—its refusal not just to provide ready-made morals to its favored stories but, as often as not, its refusal even to tell stories in the first place. Modernism cherished its secrets and operated on the assumption that you wouldn't understand anyway. But for its paternalist overtones and its vaunted sophistication—a self-styled sophistication at that—it might have been an angsty teen, even in, especially in, its notorious difficulty. Like Kafka's lawgiver, it closed the door to the complacent, the smug, the self-satisfied, to those who thought they already knew what was what; but, covertly democratic, it opened the door to the suspicious and the doubtful, the raisers of questions, anyone with the wherewithal to abandon all hope as a requirement for entry, half-knowing all the while, it seemed, that hope might be reclaimable, only ultimately, only after its repudiation, if that surrender was deemed just.

After nearly a month in Michigan I was glad to be back. I had been just as glad to be away. Each place was an escape from the other, the trips between them rituals of passage. When the Detroit skyline receded in the dusty glare through the rear window of the lumbering Trailways bus, the strings of my heart tautened with sad nostalgia, but by the time we'd reached Toledo, miles of indifferent highway streaming past, I'd turned my thoughts to the new semester, and hours later, when Buffalo swung into view through the broad front window, my heart would leap, shucking off strings or any thought of strings, as if it could scale in a bound the heights of the Marine Midland Tower that loomed in the gathering twilight over the downtown waterfront. But the trips back repeated the cycle in reverse—the melancholy leaving of Buffalo, the excited return to Detroit—so the whole process was probably ascribable to nothing more than the predictable rounds of arrival and departure.

Many were as glad to see me as I was them. A rare mutuality! I'd worn a coarse, scraggly beard in the fall and had shaved it over the break, and since I always feared that I would not be recognized from one meeting to the next, even unchanged, I worried all the more that nobody would know who I was. Everyone did, some without even noting the difference, which was fine with me. It suggested I was right in supposing a core of selfhood that could be gleaned independently of outer manifestation, a hypothesis that had lurked somewhere behind the beard-growing experiment in the first place.

Those who did notice were all the more heartening, because that implied certain refined acts of acknowledgment. Dan folded his arms, pursed his lips, tilted his head appraisingly, then giggled. Mary threw her arms around me in the hallway of Clemens, a beautiful spontaneous greeting, and said she would not miss the beard because beards were too easy to hide behind. Bill told me it was a definite step forward, nixing the beard, but I should not get ahead of myself because one did not come into the face one deserved until forty.

Uneasy as it was bound to make me—all this having of thoughts, such reflection by others on what was after all my very self, raw and unprotected—there seemed to be, there, the material of something forgeable, assuming the necessary alignments, into future intimacies.

I became ever more aware, ever more fond, of academic time, its self-contained spans and penchants for renewal. The academic year began as the calendar year waned, touching the autumnal light with a freshness and a prospect. Measured in terms, academic time quickened ordinary time into two seasons of a little more than three months each, infused and bordered by periods of enforced repose, the pace hasteless, even though there was always more to do than could ever be accomplished in such spells. Our seminars met once a week, the classes we taught no more than three, so the weeks flew by but the days were long and slow. By the time winter set in the fall term was winding down. Whether just before or only a little after one had grown sick of it all, it came to an end, paused at agreeable length, then started over, the second term all the more cheering for its exact correlation with the world's rebirth, its emergence into spring.

My class that winter met only twice a week, Tuesdays and Thursdays, for seventy-five minutes instead of three times a week for fifty. It seemed a measure of how seasoned I had become as a teacher that I did not view this hour-and-a-quarter as a great and unfillable chasm. It helped that the course was Freshman Literature rather than Expository Writing. I assigned short stories I loved and I knew I would always have something to say.

In fact, I talked far too much. The words poured forth. I astonished myself with an unprecedented loquaciousness. I thought it was because I was given, in the classroom, a permission, an unimpeachable permission, to speak. In a way, that was what I was being paid for. Even if it would prove to have limits of its own, as yet untested, it was a permission I had felt nowhere else before. I did not really know where it came from. I would go into class with a dozen points jotted in my notes and cover only one or two before the time was up. I never doubted that the students were fascinated by the spectacle of my jabbering. They had to realize they were witnessing a virtual mute learn to speak before their eyes. On some days I felt like Helen Keller at her water pump; I was sure it had to be contagious, this exhilarated sense of my discovering, not all there was to be said, for I thought I'd always known that, but of all that I had to say and, quite suddenly, could.

I also knew I'd need to reign them in, all these bursting words. It would not do to leap from lumpish taciturnity to unbridled logorrhea with no stops in between. If I could ever blend these seemingly involuntary monologues with the considered dialogue I knew true teaching had to be, then I might really start to get the hang of it.

January, February: the gray city covered in snow, invigorating cold lodged in the air, a permanent visitor. It was buried, the city—buried under banks and crusts and layers of snow, the roads carved out of snow narrow crystal trenches with great mounds rising on either side, buried cars visible here and there through crevices in the frozen dirty white, like squat beasts entombed in glacial fossils. Peaks and valleys swirled across the yards, hills of snow piled against the houses. Everywhere else snow meant movement and change, falling, gusting, turning to sludge, to slush, melting, flowing away. In Buffalo it stayed, encasing everything for months, becoming the very ground, and holding everything else under, rendering the whole city a subterranean land, its stunned, bundled population trodding back and forth upon the cold surface that covered it, like hapless explorers in search of a lost continent. Snow: any other place where it was so constant, so present, so much a part of the landscape, they'd have had many, many words for it. In Buffalo—where it settled in with the same tenacity it demanded from its people—there was only one.

I was a professional reader now, or at least I thought I might be, and was reading more voraciously than ever. When I'd punched the clocks at my old jobs in high school and college I'd always thought about the reading time I was losing, but even then I could usually manage two or three hours on a bad day. Now, especially with my two-day teaching schedule, it wasn't uncommon to devote five or six. Aside from the material for my class or seminars, the equivalent of three or four books a week, I insisted on carving out time for reading of my own, the equivalent of another two or three. I tore through John Cheever, Muriel Spark, James Baldwin, Mary McCarthy, Jean Genet, James Purdy. Something fortuitous—I felt I was *finding* things then, stumbling upon them in delight. Old books. Sylvia Townsend Warner's *The Corner that Held Them*. George Grossmith's *Diary of a Nobody*. Italo Svevo's *Confessions of Zeno*. Alexei Remizov's *History of the Tinkling Cymbal and Sounding Brass*. New books. Edmund White's *A Boy's Own Story*. Rachel Ingalls's *Mrs. Caliban*. Renata Adler's *Pitch Dark*. Denis Johnson's *Angels*. Marilynne Robinson's *Housekeeping*. I liked talking about the books everyone else was reading in the seminars, but I liked even more having these books to myself.

I was readying myself for something I might never be—that was what graduate school was, preparation for a future that might never arrive—but what? A teacher? A writer? The "honorable mention" in that writing competition back in elementary school had provided an encouragement that could have been less palpable had I paused to consider more fully what it meant to be so honorably mentioned. The honor itself was all very well, but the mention might have raised an eyebrow more self-conscious than my own. A mere mention was hardly an unmitigated proclamation. But nobody else had been mentioned at all, apparently, let alone honorably, and the teacher and my classmates—the latter a bit grudgingly, it must be said—made such a big deal of the whole thing when the Daily Tribune came to photograph me in my natural habitat for their article on the award that I fancied myself poised on the threshold of fame. Yet I couldn't shake the feeling that my entry had not, all in all, been very inspired. The contest had required aspirants to make up the words for a picture book called "What Whiskers Did," itself lacking in spark, by my lights. A cute mutt, Whiskers, ran away from home on the first page, gamboled in the snow with an assortment of creatures, taking refuge with a family of rabbits after

being chased by a wolf, and in the end returned to the welcoming arms
of his mop-headed owner, a pale stand-in for the already bloodless Jane
of Dick-and-Jane fame, with a touch of Little Orphan Annie in the mix.
That was it—not very heady stuff for one who was a third of the way
through Bram Stoker's *Dracula* at the time.

My idea was to have Whiskers himself tell the story and make him
into an insufferable grouch, belying the appearance of cuteness and
giving a little snap to the proceedings. There was some logic to this
conceit: Why would Whiskers have run off in the first place, if not out
of a certain dissatisfaction? His frolics with his woodland counterparts
looked convivial enough, as illustrated, but it wasn't hard to put over
the idea of Whiskers secretly nursing hidden animosities the whole
time. In episode after episode, in my version, Whiskers arrived on the
scene, scoped out the territory with a dour air, vented his unbridled
scorn for each species he encountered in succession, and took his imperious leave, typically with a venomous parting shot. "I never could
stand RABBITS!" Whiskers sneered in my rendering, leaving the warren
of maligned hares in his disdainful wake, while the conclusive homecoming, far from the warm-hearted reunion pictured, found Whiskers
plotting his next escape just as soon as he'd had his fill of chow.

A stately-looking letter accompanied the little wrinkled ribbon that
came from the sponsoring publisher—Henry Z. Walck, such a fine
name for a publisher, so aptly in keeping with the other names of pub-
lishers I happened to know of: Grosset, Dunlap, Scribner, Jovanovich.
(And what *could* that tantalizing Z stand for?) Then unacquainted with
the conventions of the form letter, I assumed Mr. Walck had taken
a special interest in me and my career, and I resolved not to let him
down. Over a weekend I wrote a three-page narrative in verse for his
consideration—"The Jacqueline Jacques," about six daredevil cousins
in France, all with the same name and the same sense of adventure
and derring-do, who collectively undertook a series of feats ranging
from mountain-climbing expeditions to aeronautical escapades. (Ame-
lia Earhart was somewhere at the back of my mind as I wrote—though
I vowed that the Jacqueline Jacques would all come to a happy end—as
was the character played by Natalie Wood in *The Great Race*, my favorite movie in third grade, with perhaps a dash of *Thoroughly Modern*

Millie.) The story unfolded mostly in Seussian couplets that detailed the characters' exploits, taking full advantage of the rhyming possibilities of their names: "They scaled giant peaks as if only rocks,/Such were the skills of the Jacqueline Jacques." Or again: "They played every piece by Beethoven and Bach/ On six grand pianos, those Jacqueline Jacques!"

With the handwritten manuscript I enclosed a note to Mr. Walck, suggesting that he might be able to find a suitable artist to draw the pictures prior to publication—not, I secretly hoped but tactfully refrained from saying, the illustrator of "What Whiskers Did," whose simple black-and-white sketches lacked the requisite color and flair to bring the tale of the Jacqueline Jacques to vivid life.

The thing sent, there followed that time of waiting known to any scribe, when every hour dawdles and all the pressing matters of life seem a bit beside the point, and the coming of the mail turns into a daily ritual in which torturous rounds of flittering hope and plunging disappointment repeat themselves over and over, until the breath-stopping moment when the arrival of the anticipated reply ends the cycle in a final precipitous rush of exhilaration or despair. The outcome in this instance perhaps goes without saying. Though the rejection was kind as it could be, "The Jacqueline Jacques" never did see the light of day. Fifteen years later, in 1984, I read by chance with a terrible pang Henry Z. Walck's obituary in the *Buffalo News.*

I still thought I might be a writer. I'd kept at it all those years, after a fashion, with the usual detours. My next major work, in fifth grade, was a sixty-page novelization of *Sunset Boulevard*—a movie that had supplanted the likes of *Thoroughly Modern Millie* among my favorites as my tastes took a darker turn. It began with what remains my own favorite opening line in my oeuvre: "There's been a murder tonight." The same year I wrote a long pastiche of Poe and Agatha Christie in which a very proper Englishman recounts a sojourn in an old dark house where inhabitants are bumped off one by one, culminating in the revelation—not unforeseeable, all things considered—that the narrator himself, in a diabolically altered state of mind, is the killer. A series of similar Gothic tales followed. The most fully realized was "The Crosstown Bus," the story of an ordinary businessman—Mr. Jenson by name—who slowly realizes that his morning ride to work has taken an unfamiliar route. When he tries to raise a fuss, the driver does nothing but stare ahead with blank white eyes, while his fellow passengers go on staring out the windows, turning from time to time to give him inhuman, vacant looks, revealing their eyes too to be without pupils. In the first draft, Mr. Jenson dramatically leapt from the bus into the road and threw a big rock through the window, striking the driver and causing the bus with all its unearthly commuters to plunge over a convenient cliff. On further reflection this seemed a bit much. A grimmer but more satisfying revision found a benumbed Mr. Jenson slumping back into his seat, defeated, resigned to the hopelessness of his situation, waiting with a sense of doom to see where the bus would take him. This alternative ending showed the direct influence of Shirley Jackson, a new favorite, with shades of Dickinson's "Because I Could Not Stop for Death" and the unresolved conclusion, maddening but strangely haunting, of Hitchcock's *The Birds*.

A writer is a reader driven to emulation, said Henry James, and this was certainly true in the case of my juvenilia. Reading *Lolita* at the age of fourteen changed everything. The book embodied a kind of literary greatness beyond any I had ever fathomed. I might have read greater books before—I'd dabbled in Shakespeare and given Tolstoy a not-very-fair shot—but I had not been capable of responding to them with anything like the intensity with which I read *Lolita*. I had found just the right book at just the right time, it seemed—though in truth, in spite of the shivers of joy the book sent through me page by page, I really understood little of it on that first encounter. Only after the initial aesthetic bliss had worn off did the downside of this milestone dawn on me: I had to admit that everything I'd written, and much of what I'd read, was child's play. So distinctive was this work, so utterly itself, so unlike anything else, I knew I could never hope to imitate it. Even so, the rest of high school was occupied with predictably failed efforts to mount a quasi-Nabokovian piece, driven by sexual obsession and mordant lyricism. Typical of these attempts was *On Hermaphrodite!*, a picaresque novel about a bi-sexed character, living as a man, traveling by bus across America from New York to Big Sur, hoping to reunite there with a man he loves, but who has rejected him on discovering his dual sexuality. I had chosen Big Sur only because I thought I could cull descriptions of it from *The Sandpiper* with Liz Taylor, which had been shot there—a motive that indicates, perhaps, something of the fated nature of the whole enterprise. Not only did the desired style elude me hopelessly, it quickly became apparent that I didn't know enough about love, sex, America, or even buses to pull it off. I wrote about thirty pages and then gave up. Over a period of years, not one of these endeavors came even close to fruition.

By the time I got to college I began to consider the possibility that my talents were critical, not creative. My first year, I wrote a series of movie reviews for the school paper, bemoaning the success of unmerited American hits like *Bloodbrothers* with Richard Gere (not really, in fact, a "hit")—I knew I was being disloyal in this to Richard Gere, whose shirtless pose on the cover of *After Dark* would remain with me forever, but such betrayal, it was clear, came with the calling to serious criticism—and lamenting the obscurity of masterpieces like the Italian *Bread and Chocolate* with Nino Manfredi (not really, in fact, a "masterpiece"). These pieces were as flagrantly derivative as my efforts at fiction had been, trying to mix the donnish, lapidary common sense of Stanley Kauffmann with the headlong energy of Pauline Kael, the bitchy wit of John Simon, and the commanding elegance of Vernon Young. At Wayne State, peers were taking courses in creative writing, but the principal writer-in-residence had a reputation for cruelty and I wasn't sure I could survive that. On the faculty were two professors who would go on to become renowned American writers, Charles Baxter and Edward Hirsch; Charlie was the Buffalo graduate who had encouraged me to go there. But though I'd read some poems and a story or two he had published—most memorably "Xavier Speaking" in an issue of *Antioch Review* I happened to come across in the third-floor reading room of the Detroit Public Library—I knew him then mainly as a scholar and critic of modernism, and as a wonderful teacher. Eddie taught folklore, a field I snobbishly disdained, and I was surprised on running into him once at the McDonald's on the corner of Woodward and Warren when he told me that he went there to write poetry in a plastic booth looking out on the busy street. A few years later, when I read his first book, *For the Sleepwalkers*, I found it hard to imagine poems of such accomplishment being composed there, amid all that hubbub.

My own energies went almost exclusively into the papers I wrote for English and film courses, which proved to be a more than satisfying outlet. You didn't have to worry so much about what your subject would be because it was, in a sense, given in advance, already determined by the limits of the course. And if you started to worry that you didn't know enough, you could just pretend that all that needed knowing was contained within the borders of the texts under consideration. Besides, sentences were sentences. It didn't matter so much what they were "about," as long as you were composing them.

What I discovered at Buffalo almost immediately was that critical and creative work did not have to be opposites. Nearly everyone at Buffalo considered himself or herself a writer, and few doubted that writing criticism was a profoundly creative act, or that authentically creative work inevitably reflected critical sensibilities. Nobody ever talked about "research" or "scholarship"; they talked about writing, and they were more likely to publish in the quarterlies that had supported critical writing for decades, *Kenyon Review* or *Partisan Review* or *Salmagundi*, than in the specialized academic journals that proliferated as the study of English became ever more professionalized throughout the '80s. Questions of intellect remained paramount but questions of literary style ran a close second. An imaginative new interpretation would always trump an archival discovery, however significant—not that anyone engaged in that kind of empirical research would have had a chance then of being hired at Buffalo in the first place. Leslie Fiedler was unusual among his colleagues in that he wrote in nearly every genre—not just criticism, but autobiography and cultural history and fiction—but he was emblematic in fashioning himself a public intellectual addressing that general readership whose demise seemed inevitable even then and whose disappearance Leslie, ever on guard against being late to any party, was among the first to remark.

It was from Fiedler that I learned some of the lessons of humility that would allow me to persevere as a writer for a while longer, surprising as it may be to anyone who knew him to find the word "humility" in any proximity to his name. One of his merriest and most oft-repeated slogans, describing himself, was "Often wrong but never in doubt!" His egotism was really something of a pose and had its self-effacing side—

both features deriving from his paradoxical experience as a prodigy, a young upstart, and a late bloomer at the same time. His best known essay, "Come Back to the Raft Ag'in, Huck Honey," appeared in *Partisan Review* in 1948, when he was thirty, and he'd already been established for a while by then as a provocative Young Turk. Yet despite his association in those years with the New York Intellectuals, he lived in Montana, stuck in the boonies for decades, all through the forties and fifties (though as it happens he'd loved it there, and always spoke of returning). He did some major work in those years, but he was forty-three when he published *Love and Death in the American Novel*, both his masterpiece and his "first" book, his previous publications having been collections of essays. He was nearly fifty in 1964 when he moved to Buffalo, where he would reside for another forty years. He used to say he'd lived a whole lifetime before ever setting foot in the city with which he would become so inextricably associated, living proof that there was a second act in at least one American life.

As a critic, Fiedler's seeming irreverence toward his subjects stemmed from the same impulses that made him think about literature in much larger terms than were common at the time—to the extent possible, in terms of the whole culture that gave rise to it. Literature was part of life, life took place in the world, and even the greatest writer, therefore, wasn't really that different from the guy across the street. What might have seemed like a populist mannerism was really the simple result of reading more than almost anyone else. If you only read the great stuff, there should be no surprise that it all seems great. But if you read it *all*—all of Shakespeare, all of Melville, all of American literature itself—then you could not miss the ups and downs, and these, for Leslie, were always definitive. Most literature simply wasn't "great," and if you were going to try to place it in its widest contexts, questions of greatness fell inevitably away. That didn't mean you stopped knowing what greatness was. It meant that your sense of what it could be grew larger.

Fiedler was surprised when I showed up in his office one day wanting to talk to him about his fiction. Hadn't I heard how bad it was? he asked with a chuckle. I expressed my admiration of his short stories and novels and compared his work to that of two other writers who seemed similar in content and technique, and in their satirical stand-points, Cynthia Ozick and George P. Elliott. Elliott's story collection *Among the Dangs* struck me in subject and tone as being especially close to Fiedler's own collection, *Nude Croquet*. Surprised that I'd read such a little known writer—just the reaction I'd hoped for, of course—Leslie told me he happened to know that Elliott, who had died a couple of years before, had gone on writing every day of his life, even after nobody would publish his work any longer. That, said Leslie, was what made him a real writer. I learned later that one reason for Elliott's inability to publish late in his life was that he had written a virulent assault on the "literary establishment" called "Who is We?" that alienated him from many powerful figures in the industry. Published in *The Nation* in 1959, the essay railed against the domination of American literary culture by a small group of East Coast urbanites—mainly, the New York Intellectuals, Leslie Fiedler foremost among them. On discovering this connection years afterward, I was moved that Leslie had refrained from embarrassing me by telling me that I was unknowingly comparing him to a nemesis; in fact, he spoke of Elliott kindly and generously.

It seemed clear that he thought of his own work in fiction as "minor," even though he had devoted an entire decade of his life, all through the sixties, to writing it. But he accepted this status with equanimity, maybe because his criticism was undeniably "major." Elliott's essay had been criticized for implicit anti-Semitism, among other things; was Leslie's fiction considered "minor" because it was so steeped in his "minority" identity as a Jewish man? Certainly that identity was part of what led him to look so deeply into what had traditionally been marginalized in criticism and in the study of literature. In fact, though, Fiedler's work ultimately demanded that we move beyond limiting distinctions like "major" and "minor." That was what made it so open to writing and culture of all kinds—the idea that anything might matter, if you thought about it. Whether any given work or body of work was major or minor, you still had to learn how to understand it.

In its second semester SuperTeach turned to the question of how to teach literature, having dispatched writing in the previous term, and the genial Vic Doyno was replaced by the decidedly less affable George

Levine. As we were all getting to know who was who in The Profession, we came to a fuller awareness of the standing of particular faculty members in our own department. Levine shared a name with another George Levine in the same field, Victorian Lit, who was widely published and highly regarded. We had to distinguish between that Levine and our Levine in order to discern that our Levine had published next to nothing, and we learned that he made no secret of his lack of interest in graduate students, if not his outright disdain for them. He disapproved of their careerism and thought they were prone to adopt high-flown theories as a cover for their ignorance of what he called "the basics." None of my peers had seemed excessively career-minded to me, nor especially dogmatic, though the semester would put the latter premise to the test.

Levine wore tailored business suits with matching shirts and ties, like the well-heeled administrator he would eventually become. This alone distinguished him on the faculty; among the rest, most usually looked like they had just come from a sit-in, a hayride, or softball practice. The first time I saw Leslie Fiedler in the hallway he was dressed in rags, and I held the door of my office open for him as he passed, not recognizing him from the photos on his book jackets and thinking he was the janitor come to take out the trash. Levine's uptight stylishness was complemented by a scent of acrid cologne and Maalox, his face fixed in a dyspeptic snarl that took on a crocodilian cast when he tried to smile. He would stand at the podium in the front of the class and hold forth. He stood extremely upright, so erect in his posture that the very act of standing came to seem a kind of brag, as if he took a special pride in his status as a vertebrate.

In the second session Levine passed out copies of Browning's "My Last Duchess" and proceeded to lead us through the poem, line by line. It was, he informed us, a dramatic monologue that illustrated the principle of structural irony—an intelligence that could have come as news to nobody, inconceivable as it was that there should have been an English graduate student anywhere in the world unfamiliar with the work or its significance. He asked us pointed questions. How did we learn what we knew about the speaker? How did the poem make us aware that the Duke was not trustworthy? Exactly when did we come to realize the full extent of his perfidy, his moral bankruptcy? Around the room, looks were exchanged. Some of us ventured puzzled, hesitant replies to the pointed questions. Weren't we supposed to be learning how to teach literature—not, ourselves, having to endure being taught it?

A less hesitant voice rose with a question of its own: "What exactly do you mean by `moral'?"

The inquisitor was Mark Fleissig, with his big Harold Lloyd glasses and face so gaunt and hard it looked like it was carved from a long, thin block of wood, like a nutcracker's. He'd shown a gift for wordplay when I had privately suggested that Levine seemed insufferable and he replied, "I suffer him." His claims to rigor resided mainly in keeping a serious look and asking interlocutors what they had meant by each word of the sentences they spoke. This practice did confer upon conversation an appearance of exactitude, and in light of it, his question to Levine came as no surprise, but it seemed a bit early in the term to challenge so openly the authority even of one so obviously unconscionable.

Levine snapped that he meant what anyone would mean by the word *moral*.

That was only if you assumed that language was referential, Mark rejoined in his maddeningly even tone. If you did not, then there were as many meanings as there were people in the room.

Levine looked stunned. If he could have become any more erect, he surely would have.

An intervention from an unexpected quarter saved us for the moment. Fatima Lim, a gifted poet from the Philippines who was so shy she rarely spoke, raised her hand and answered Levine's questions in her high, sweet, trembling, musical voice, and Levine seemed mollified, the crisis temporarily averted.

By the fourth meeting, though, it was clear beyond any doubt that Levine had every intention of continuing to treat us like undergraduates. The exchanges of looks grew more alarmed as the outrage of what we were being subjected to became undeniable. We spent that session scanning Shakespearean sonnets. After class was over and Levine had finally taken his leave, we lingered and discussed what was to be done, in low voices shot through with the agitation befitting a nascent revolution. Three factions emerged, one led by Fleissig, fomenting open rebellion in the next session. Another cabal opted for circumspect inaction, while the third counseled in favor of constructive dialogue. I could see the wisdom of each. Off in a corner, Fatima whispered hopelessly, half to herself, that such things were unheard of in the Philippines. Only later did I learn that she was involved back home in the beginnings of the uprising that unexpectedly led a woman, Corazon Aquino, to power there.

Levine strode into class the next time in an uncharacteristically cheerful mood, with no inkling of what lay in store for him. Since the factions remained splintered, we didn't know ourselves what was going to happen. Levine asked for a volunteer to read the poem of the day, Robert Frost's "Stopping by Woods on a Snowy Evening." No one came forward, though I flirted inwardly with the idea of raising my hand and singing the poem to the tune of "Hernando's Hideaway." In the absence of a willing dupe, a visibly vexed Levine embarked on an uninspired rendition of his own. A long silence followed. One might have thought the speaker was pausing to let the profundity of his recitation sink in, if not for the accompanying scowl, a look of pure hatred, hardly in keeping with the humanistic spirit of the piece. In the blink of an eye, his good mood had become a thing of the unrecoverable past. Levine let this silence stand long enough for it to gather all his hatred of us into its steely, sulfurous hands, and weave around the room, just above our heads, a long, baneful ribbon of loathing. Even Mark Fleissig squirmed a little.

Now, snarled Levine, startling us out of the gnarled silence he had wrought. How does it *scan*?

One timid appeaser supplied an answer. The poem was composed in iambic tetrameter. This seemed sufficient to satisfy Levine, as he launched into a conventional analysis of the poem along formal lines, until an apparently reenergized Fleissig interrupted him with the cool observation that all language was performance and that scansion was the merest of inventions. This sally prompted two of Fleissig's followers to pipe up in their turn. One, who wore black corduroy pants and black corduroy shirts, both covered with grayish lint, and whose whole body quaked with an involuntary twitch every few minutes, observed that the poem appeared to critique the logics of property but was actually in collusion with them. Levine was sputtering in reply that "critique" was a noun, not a verb, when another added, with an exquisite Fleissig-esque tranquility, that scansion, like morality, was the province of a dominant class.

These forays briefly achieved the desired effect. Levine was pitched back into a silence not his own—one imposed, not chosen. But Mark's lackey was the last to speak calmly in that room for quite some time.

The prelude to conflict lingers in mind more vividly, perhaps, than the actual hostilities, once the ignorant armies start to clash, even by broad daylight. The room dissolved into a chaos free of the adventitious detail that memory requires. It must be enough to say that a general hubbub ensued—all hell, in the act of breaking loose. Cries of recrimination. Shouts of indignation. It was difficult to hold one's own in such a skirmish from a seated position; Levine, the only one licensed to stand, towered above the fray, rasping, The *basics*—you need to know the *basics*, you don't know the *basics*! If anything of the kind had occurred in the halcyon days of Vic Doyno the mittens and ping-pong balls would have flown like missiles. Only one image of the fracas do I clearly recall: Fatima Lim—the only one of us with a real political victory to her credit—put her head face down on the top of her desk, her limp arms dangling over the sides, and waited for it all to end.

Which it did, though how, the turmoil of memory obscures. It is scarcely possible to imagine how such mayhem could have reached any end, short of mutual annihilation. I only know that academic time breaks into pieces for a reason, so that virtually nothing can run its course in a single sitting, always leaving open the possibility that saner heads might still, later, prevail. It also compels return to the scene of perpetually unfinished business, however noxious. That was the only reason we found ourselves back in that room the next week, after seven days of intervening life, hunched again at our desks, giving off a quiet little church-mouse hum as we waited to see what the fallout would be. It was just possible that Levine would go on as if nothing had happened and maybe that would have been for the best—that he'd just break out another poem and start in scanning it, pedantic as you please. Or perhaps the very same breakdown of order that had occurred the last time would have to run its fulsome course once more, mere anarchy unloosed again.

Levine came in seething, as if not a second had elapsed since the prior conflagration. I realized in an instant that this mattered to him much more than to us. The rawness and intensity of his scorn were shocking. He leaned on the podium and thrust his face forward. *You people*, he croaked, *make me sick to my stomach*. He intoned the words slowly, squeezing every ounce of bile from each one. He went on and on, a quiet, scorching tirade, upbraiding us for crimes of the spirit of every variety—rudeness, arrogance, ignorance. In the end, he said he was going to leave the room for half an hour, and he wanted only those willing to learn from him to remain when he returned. All others would be excused without penalty for the rest of the term.

I was starting to think that we had to keep learning the same things, over and over, and that they recur to us, much of the time, as if we had never really known them to begin with. What it all had seemed to come down to, the whole failure: Levine had not trusted us, and we could not trust him. But what did trust really have to do with it? What knowledge worth having required a basis in trust? A thing was true or it was not. The main consequence of the whole sorry episode was that Mark Fleissig's junta was consolidated once and for all, and the bunch of them became ever more imperious and doctrinaire as the semesters wore on. We called them the Markists. A semester or two later Mark himself was subject to official discipline for having told his entire class of freshmen that they were all whores. This incident only served to enhance his credibility with his disciples.

Bill would run into Levine on the Hertel Avenue bus from time to time. He'd even shared a seat with him, and chatted, and discovered that George was really a very nice guy.

I did not doubt it for an instant.

Mostly what SuperTeach had taught me was what *not* to do. The question of what *should* happen in a classroom remained open. Probably I would have to figure it out for myself, and I would do well to keep in mind that it meant more to me than it did to the students. I was still reeling off monologues much of the time, though I was pretty sure that would not work as a strategy for the long haul, if there was, in fact, to be a long haul. But the novelty of hearing my own voice hadn't worn off. Often these lectures went off in directions of their own, riffs of unexpected thought about whatever texts happened to be at hand. My notes were usually sketchy and thin, but the streams of words I heard pouring out of me sounded, at least to my own ear, surprisingly ample and cohesive. I was doing what the teachers I most admired did, just talking about the stuff, raising questions and saying how and why the questions seemed to arise. It came as something of a relief that I could do this at all. It had not been evident by any means that I would ever be capable of the public performance required to be a teacher in the first place. In a way it still wasn't.

And all the while I knew that nobody ever learned anything just from being told it.

What I wanted to think I was really doing was *showing* them something. But what? The general line of the English department was that we were teaching the students "how to think." Even if it had been more humbly formulated, this slogan would have been hard to endorse. Everyone thought. What would a brain be doing if not thinking? Were we supposed to be teaching them to think better, to think like us, to translate thought into some variant of language, to think beyond their own capacities, to think themselves beyond wherever they happened to be? This last, certainly, was what I always saw myself trying to do, and if my monologues had a saving grace—if there was anything that kept them from being simple self-regarding preening—it was to whatever extent they managed to model that effort. The thoughts were not really mine, I told myself. Ideas belonged to no one. That was what made them beautiful. My sense of the genesis of those monologues was that, essentially, they had none—they came out of thin air, channeled from the general intellectual ether. I was not just saying the thoughts that I thought; I was saying the ones I hoped to think. *It's not enough to know what you think*, I'd hector my captive audience. *Try to know as much as possible about what can be thought.*

The monologue form has obvious limits toward such dialogic ends. It always tends toward bombast.

Literature, I told my classes, is a conversation in which only one party gets to speak. The other, the reader, gets to speak later, as part of another conversation. And that goes on and on.

But wasn't literature also always in conversation with itself?

We were working our way through the *Norton Anthology of Short Fiction*. One great story after another. If nothing else the course was giving them Kafka, Chekhov, Tolstoy, Flannery O'Connor. When the masterpiece of the day left them stubbornly unimpressed or nonplused, I couldn't hold it against them. It had taken me, too, a while to come around to, say, "Metamorphosis." It was the second time I'd read it. It had suddenly occurred to me that Gregor Samsa's plight was comparable to a young gay person's. Most people with a minority characteristic shared it with their families. Being gay, though, was different. It separated you from your family. The story seemed to express an infinite understanding of exactly this. I did not see how I could have missed it the first time. The story also conveyed that what the family saw as disgusting—Gregor's condition as a cockroach—was really only a matter of perspective. The story's expression of love for Gregor, though there was no spokesperson within the story for that feeling, was one of its most remarkable features.

Once I'd read it that way, the story broke my heart.

Was Kafka gay? Are you saying that Gregor Samsa is gay?

No. I was not saying that.

I did not want them to think that one had to have a "personal" relation to every text, or any text, but then you could not do everything at once. Take "The Dead," Joyce's "The Dead." It had left me cold on a first reading, moved on a second, and devastated on a third. *How was such a thing possible?* What, that is, would possess anyone to keep reading a story he didn't like the first time?—the question under the question, but I chose to hear it differently. The first time through it just seemed like a story about a boring party. The second it seemed like a story about a marriage. But the third time I knew it was really about Gretta—the wife, Gretta. She seems like a marginal character, yes—in fact, you lose sight of her all the time. It's like the story *wants* you to. The narrator calls her "Mrs. Conroy" or "his wife" all through, until the last scene. And all through the story she's being reminded of this dead lover, this Michael Furey of hers. And the first time through we have no way of knowing that. How could we know? And it's like the whole thing was written just for that, for that last scene and that discovery. And that's part of the whole point and it's why the story starts off with "free indirect discourse" (remember we talked about that?) but then it gets more and more restricted to Gabriel's perspective, because that's what the story's *about*, it's all about *perspective* and how hard it is to see anything from another person's perspective, impossible really, but how that doesn't mean you shouldn't try, how it's the most important thing, really; but then when you read it again you *do* know, you do know she's thinking about Michael Furey and then *that's* really the point, it's like the emotional core of the whole story but it's not *at* the center, it's pushed to the side, and that's the really interesting thing the story's *doing*—it's displacing and deferring what is actually most crucial, and it's showing us the way important things get marginalized, all the time. So now look, look—near the end, turn to that page, when they're talking and Gretta says, "You are such a generous person, Gabriel." So you see how, when you read the story *this* way—as a story about *Gretta*, about Gretta's *voice*, about the *repression* of Gretta's voice—do you see what happens to that line, how it's totally different, and when I read it that third time it just totally hit me, I got all choked up just like I'm doing now, because *we* know, we know he's *not* generous, but at the same time, she's not wrong, you know, I mean, what does it even mean to say someone's generous, but see, what *she* thinks in telling him about Michael Furey is that she's sharing something with him, she is being intimate with him, she thinks she is deepening their intimacy, but he can't think of it that way at all, he's incapable, totally incapable, all he can do is just keep thinking about getting her in bed and harping on his own stupid frat-boy jealousy and it's just so so sad, and it all comes down to that line, see? He can't hear what she is saying. But *we* can. And that's how it works. It deepens. It deepens. Believe me. Please. Trust me.

3.
WAS I IN SEARCH OF MASTERS?

I was ten or so when I saw *The Heiress* on TV. It was adapted from Henry James's novel *Washington Square*. I hadn't read a word of James then but I knew his name from the credits of a previous broadcast of *The Innocents*, based on his ghost story *The Turn of the Screw*. I'd been thunderstruck by that movie so I had high hopes for *The Heiress*, but it unfolded slowly, quietly, not a ghost in sight, and as they had during *The Innocents*, as they often did when we watched TV, my family all fell asleep around me. In that case, their slumber had somehow seemed to contribute to the power of my reaction to the film. I knelt before the TV, my elbows propped on our big green ottoman, leaning in toward the screen, alight with its vivid images—images seen, now, only by me!—undulating in silver and silky gray, so brilliant I could feel them piercing my eyes. Every so often I'd glance around to make sure the rest were all still out cold; if my mother woke she'd make me move back from the TV for my vision's sake. And they were (my heart leapt!) they *were* asleep. They lay with limbs splayed, askew, my mother curled on the couch, my father reclined in his chair, my sister lolled on the floor, their heads listing, mouths a bit ajar, lips pulsing with helpless little sighs, dead to the world, as if they'd been stricken all at once with a deep spell that put them under, leaving me alone, awake, alone-awake, awash in electric wakefulness that charged what I was seeing with a still greater intensity—the unforgettable image of the sad, spectral governess, among shuddering reeds in a field across a lake amid a glancing storm; or the demonic valet with his aquiline nose, his scowling visage floating hideously behind a misted glass—or the stricken face at the end of the little boy whose soul he wanted to steal.

There seemed to be little hope of recapturing any of that effulgence with *The Heiress*. Never mind ghosts; there weren't any kids in it either. The main character, Catherine, was a skittish old maid even though she was played by the lyrically named Olivia de Havilland, so lively and spunky in *Four's a Crowd* and *The Strawberry Blonde*. Everyone murmured tastefully and the costumes rustled with gentility and there wasn't much to look at except for a striking young man with dark, melting eyes. Catherine's father was an awful old buffoon. He didn't murmur, he yowled. He treated her slightingly every time he appeared, and she, to my great annoyance, seemed not even to notice. The striking young man wasn't present enough and I wasn't supposed to like seeing him so much anyway and it appeared he was not to be trusted anyhow. Far from reveling in my solitary consciousness as I watched the leaden spectacle roll on, I felt myself being pulled down into the general somnolence, though shocked awake every few minutes by a sudden blast of tinny music.

Then in the last few scenes I sat up at attention: Catherine was turning the tables. She was confronting those who had wronged her, getting a bit of her own back (as Eliza from *My Fair Lady* might have put it), humbling her persnickety aunt, spurning the deceitful young man, handsome as he was, all with a new self-composure, a cool calculation that was exhilarating to witness. The only disappointment was that her father had not lived to get *his* comeuppance. He seemed to have died off somewhere along the line.

"Can you be so cruel?" gasped the humiliated aunt, in the face of these reprisals.

"Yes, I can be very cruel," Catherine replied with an exquisite calm. "I have been taught by masters."

A startling revelation—there was a story beneath the story, in which the inert Catherine, to all appearances submissive and oblivious of the injuries visited upon her by those who thoughtlessly deemed her inferior, had been fully aware of them all along. Did this mean she had never really been inferior, that her final usurping of power only realized the powers of understanding that had been hers from the start? That understanding really was all that mattered?

That galvanizing line—*I have been taught by masters*—seems quintessentially Jamesian, in its way, but it does not occur in James. Like *The Heiress*, *Washington Square* ends with a final meeting between Catherine and the deceitful young man, but in the book she does not spurn him, exactly. She remains the same sweet, timid, patient, tiresome Catherine she had been throughout the tale. She tells the young man that she has long since forgiven him for his dissemblance, but that they can never be friends. Then, as he departs in a huff, she goes on with her embroidery. The final image is not of a stern and righteous retaliation against a lifetime of petty cruelty, but of a sad, still quiescence, an ultimate paralysis: "Catherine, meanwhile, picking up her morsel of fancy work, had seated herself with it again—for life, as it were." The end of *Washington Square* is true to James's bleak sense of human nature, his conviction that people remain very much themselves, too much themselves, in the face of any challenge. His conclusion denies us the invigorating satisfaction of Catherine's final empowerment.

In such denial resides the crux of James's mastery—and if ever a writer was a Master, it was James. The last installment of Leon Edel's definitive biography proclaims him one in its very title—*The Master*—though even in this final volume, Edel paints a portrait of a fearful and insecure man beset by unconscious impulses and anxieties. The same can be said of many of James's own characters, who either thrive in states of unknowing, like Strether in *The Ambassadors*; submit to the terrors brought on by their own dire imaginings, like the governess in *The Turn of the Screw*; or languish in oblivion or outright denial, like John Marcher in *The Beast in the Jungle*—whose lifetime's anticipation of a special destiny blinds him to a deep love that hovers right before his eyes—or the narrator of *The Sacred Fount*, crazed yet hyper-rational.

The voice of James's fiction uncannily simulates a logic of oblivion and denial—even his omniscient narrators are unreliable, comically heedless, more often than not, of the implications of the stories they're telling with an intricacy that offers pleasures of its own, but denies the ordinary pleasures of fiction, including straightforward action and empathy or direct insight. To love James you must assent to excruciation, you must come to take pleasure in it, because that is the work's dominant mode. It brooks little else. In one sense this subordinates readers' common desires to the strange, unyielding demands of the texts. Yet "the Master," too, takes intense and complicated pleasure, however obscurely expressed, in the same torturous tidings that he himself has wrought, and brings us into communication with him, little by little, through the demanding medium of this shared acceptance.

I have been taught by masters—the line seems Jamesian not just in the irony of the fact that these "masters" would never have deigned to teach her if they'd known she was capable of learning as she did. It expresses something of the same contempt for "masters" that "the Master" himself does. Especially in its late phase, as his work edges more and more away from realism and toward a nascent modernism, his work becomes increasingly preoccupied by the question of what it means to be a "Master"—and it means nothing good. A series of late tales pivots on the figure of an author explicitly posited as a "Master," most obviously in "The Lesson of the Master." In most cases the story is told by a disciple of the Master in question, and the point is to expose the teller's errors of spirit and soul, brought about by a woefully misplaced reverence. In stories like "The Figure in the Carpet" or "The Author of *Beltraffio*," the Master is vaguely mortified by the idolatry of his followers, who remain steadfast in their search for the ultimate hidden meaning, "the figure in the carpet," of the Masters' work. In these tales the Master is finally marginalized or absented entirely, ironically displaced by the devotees' feverish and increasingly absurd quests for fulfillment.

But many of James's Masters are far less benign, even when they too are absent—like the Master who owns the house in *The Turn of the Screw*, whom the governess obsesses about even though he never appears in the story.

To aspire to mastery might mean to desire a measure of control or understanding, to achieve a balance of will and want, that self-sufficiency that could enable one to move among others as a putative equal.

But it might mean subordinating scruple, hoarding power and abusing it, dominating those who lack it, or repudiate it, or eschew it.

The latter scenarios form the substance of James's dramas, perplexed and knotty power-plays, wherein even small stakes (think *The Golden Bowl*) yield grave and disproportionate consequences. Though James's moral schemes are as gnarled and mazy as his plots, his clearest ethical objections arise against the holders of power. Wary of surrendering his own authority, yet always trying to tease it into something queer enough that it might not seem like power, he can love among his characters only those who *lack* power—the children perhaps above all, Miles and Flora and Maisie and others, including the child-like Catherine. His work stands against the will to domination and attests to its grim persistence. We have all been taught by masters.

The second year we moved to the West Side—Mary and Bill and I. An intimation of compatibilities and a reserve of accumulated affections had induced us to find a place together. Dan wanted to be out closer to school anyway, and since my crush showed no sign of waning, I thought some distance could be just the thing. We moved into a big Victorian house on Norwood, halfway between Bryant and Summer, a midpoint that marked a dividing line between the middle-class homes at the Bryant end of the street and the more lavish ones that lined the rest of the block, growing more palatial the closer you got to Summer. The houses were set close to the street and slightly above it, giving the rooflines an even more imposing air.

Ours was something of a hybrid, grand and elegant but with hints of an impending decline. Green with yellow and red highlights about the gingerbread trim, it had a canopied wraparound porch fenced with ornamented spires and eight carved pillars that held up the balcony above. It was winged and bayed, with a steep, multi-faceted roof and a pentagonal cupola, complete with weathervane, jutting up at the top in the front northeast corner. I dubbed it the House of the Six Gables.

And it *wasn't* ours, of course. We entered by the back way, a route that confronted us daily with the stark contrast between the lush garden we had to walk through to get there and the untended back door and dusty hallway onto the dark stairs that led up to our quarters. We had the whole third floor, part ballroom and part attic, with a crooked hallway leading back to the large bathroom and three bedrooms. There was one big open room with little alcoves and cubbyholes here and there around the perimeter, a five-sided nook at the far end corresponding to the outer cupola. At the center a large shaft rose from floor to ceiling, a conduit for the chimney of a fireplace below, with four wooden benches built in around the base. A single high wooden shelf ran the length of two walls, a foot or two below the high ceiling. These touches gave the place a rustic air.

The owner was Carol Simmel, a psychotherapist who met patients in the downstairs parlor. She had a chilly manner and a habit of gazing beyond one in conversation. She'd studied with Erich Fromm but her own practice seemed to have a faddish, est-y quality. She spoke often about "getting in touch" with this or that. She treated only women, as far as we could tell, and had women-only gatherings every Friday night. Despite the presence of two or three dour teens skulking about the premises, no husband was in the picture. In fact, Carol lived with Molly, a much friendlier woman with a toothy smile and a mop of gray hair. The living arrangements down there were as much of a mystery as ours would have been, if we had not been able to say we were graduate students. That always explained a lot.

Mary had a gift for creating environments, a poet's spirit and a curator's hands. The only decoration at my place on Main had been an artificial plant that I placed in a corner as a joke, and the only thing I brought to the new household was a long couch upholstered in cheap tightly-knit blue polyester. Mary's inspired yard-sale finds furnished the rest of the place with a surprising warmth, matching perfectly with the blue couch and the one real piece, an elegant cherry-wood side table Carol had given us, one of her cast-offs. Real, living plants prospered in every corner, the walls lined with colorful posters. A used, beat-up brown Barcalounger looked unpromising at first glance, but Mary was sure it would blend in perfectly once set into its proper place at Norwood, and she was right. It was the finishing touch. Mary cooked real meals, and many evenings a week an aroma of garlic and oregano would hover over the apartment until being dispelled later the same night by the smell of Bill's canned corned beef hash with onions.

The atmosphere seemed free and rich, full of energy, a place where one could really live, a place like home.

Under Mary's influence Norwood became a hub of the grad-student community. New students came to stay while they were looking for places of their own. One of them, Jake, as soon as he arrived, took up the slack left by Dan's departure, crush-wise. In the few days he stayed with us, he would loll about the place wearing nothing but a skimpy pair of white shorts, and I was enamored of the way his brownish-blond chest hairs curled around his little pink nipples. He was All-American Boy with a bit of a dark edge, a type I went for at the time. The second night I invited him to share my bed; he said the blue couch would be fine. I told him it was a standing offer, and he thanked me. Sometimes the All-American Boy side took over, and he was too polite to know when he was being hit on.

Hardly a day went by without a visitor—Gwen clambering up the fire escape and coming in through the kitchen window calling "Yoo-hoo! Yoo-hoo!" Or someone coming home from school with Mary for a dish of pasta with homemade gravy. (I was learning slowly you were not supposed to call it "sauce.") Hardly a week went by without a party, spirited gatherings around the blue couch and the brown Barcalounger, hardly a month without a banquet. We were supposed to be having "round robin" potlucks in the neighborhood but most of the time it ended up as dinner at our house. Shrimp scampi was the biggest hit, though Mary and I'd had to spend most of the day on the unappetizing task of de-veining the shellfish. Once, at one of these feasts, Bill insisted on serving up his corned beef hash, and Mary and I worried that it might be an embarrassment, but the guests loved it. "I think it's a *charming* meal!" Gwen exclaimed.

Our routines were familial yet happy, even the ones entailing drudgery. Every few weeks, when the counters grew slick and the dust-bunnies rampant, we'd haul out the brooms and mops and pails and mount what we called a "cleaning frenzy," Joan Armatrading wailing joyously on the tape player while we swept and scrubbed in time. Thursday nights Dan would come over and we would gather around my little portable RCA solid-state black-and-white TV with the broken antenna and watch *L. A. Law.* Sundays we went to the launderette on Bryant, where the attendant, a greasy-haired man in gray horn-rimmed glasses who was missing every other tooth, would climb into the big aluminum trash bin and jump up and down, condensing the already-discarded garbage and making room for more. Sitting out in front one afternoon waiting for clothes to dry, we saw a boy walk by holding a long stick with a dead bird hanging by the neck from a string attached to the end of it.

Sunday nights Mary and I would lounge in one of our beds, hers or mine, and listen to Dr. Ruth give sex advice on the radio, guffawing at her blithe discussions of the mechanics, her meticulous instructions to callers about the best techniques for masturbation. We were each realizing new facets of our queerness mutually; we ventured to a "gay/

lesbian social" at UB, one of the first ever, where I hit on a shy kid who practically dashed away. It was probably for the best; it was not good form to be fraternizing with the undergraduates anyway. "You like the little guys," Mary observed slyly as we left, impersonating Hansel and Gretel freshly escaped from the witch, with put-on Dr. Ruth-ish accents, all the way home.

Due to the shift in space or the sufflation of time, I saw Buffalo differently from there. Walking east on Bryant to catch the Lockport bus on Main, I would traverse neighborhoods from the West Side's decrepitant elegance, past the stately Manhattan-style apartment buildings that hemmed the breadth of Delaware Avenue, to the once-fine houses along Linwood broken into roomers' dwellings, all scarred edifice, chipped paint, and sagging shingle.

I was one of those who saw the city by foot or by bus. We who knew it that way were different from the seldom-seen residents of the townhouses along Richmond down by the Music Hall, or the mansions up and down Oakwood. It was not a city of pedestrians, all in all. The few you met might have mean, cracked lips, hard chins, hard eyes. They were to be forgiven. In spring and summer they'd look to the skies, stunned by the rare clarity, in fall and winter turn their gazes down, empty them out, incurious, in no hurry to learn what new tricks the ground beneath their feet, cloaked in leaves or snow, had up its sleeve. The going was always rough.

A hard city to live in, I would sometimes think, watching from the warmth of my table through the big side window of the Elmwood Lounge. The bald tire of an old man's late-model Mercury spun in a rut of ice out on Utica, an old woman in an astrakhan coat and gray babushka pushed her hobbled-wheeled grocery cart through a driving snow against a cruel wind.

It was not as hard for me because I did not really live there. I was a mere tenant, passing through. Yet I would have to join them. I too would have to go out and face the weather, to get home.

On Norwood the wiring was iffy. Any jolt could seize the power, the house plunging into darkness, and we'd have to call down to get Carol to throw the circuit-breaker. It created a peculiar rhythm, a sense, always, of something a little precarious. You could be robbed of light, any minute. Mary's hair-dryer cut the power every second week or so, in a cycle that was completely unpredictable. There was no telling when it would happen—the dryer's screech going still in a flash, the split-second jounce, the electrical whoosh, like an in-suck of breath, announcing the blackout—then the whoop of Mary's dismay: "Aw *shee*-it." Bill had taught us that word was properly spoken in two syllables.

We were poor and we were not poor. That was the life of a graduate student. Living on Main, I'd taken meals at a card table in the kitchen with folding chairs. When my family had visited for Easter I heard my little sister, twelve, whispering to my mother: *This looks like a place where poor people live...* I had come up in the world, moving to Norwood, but I still walked to the grocery store and lugged my bags back home. On these missions especially I rubbed elbows with the salt of the city's earth. But no, I was not really one of them. My condition was temporary. Theoretically I was preparing to be *not* poor. You could never tell how things would work out though. Every condition was temporary.

Theoretically. In the department we were taught never to fear an idea. Not even the dangerous ones.

A movie every Friday, at least. A matinee at the Amherst or North Park or University Plaza by bus. *Garbo Talks. Body Double. Made in Heaven. Witness. After Hours.* Or an evening screening at the Albright-Knox, all the way up Elmwood, by foot. *L' Argent. Chimes at Midnight. Tokyo Story. The Reckless Moment. Jeanne Dielmann.* "Film shows us what we want to see and what we do not want to see and what we don't know we want to see, over and over, until we can't tell the difference." *Take notes,* I urged myself. *A more systematic approach would serve you better.* A thought was still real before it was written but completely lost when it was not.

And what was *he* on about—this Lacan? The Symbolic, the Imaginary, the Real. Well, yes—the Real. Of course; what else? Let us say that Freud knew consciousness was split but understood that people needed to believe their selves were whole. Let us conclude that this mirage of coherence was the only illusion he was willing to let stand.

Let us surmise that Lacan thought the illusion was much too powerful and that people needed to learn, by force if necessary, how to accept the divided nature of the self. How to love it, if such a thing was possible. Was this, somehow, the key to the difference between modernism and—a new thing, it seemed—"post-modernism"? Every understanding required a leap of some kind.

I acquired a rowing machine and worked out for an hour every other day. "You're getting a V-shape!" Mary cooed. Downstairs, Molly moved out, after what seemed like a bit of a scene. As she packed her things into a little van parked at the curb, distraught, we heard Carol below serenely playing "The Moonlight Sonata" on the piano. A few months later another woman moved in.

In the department, the newbies seemed rather hopeless, on the whole, taking over the seminars, saying their ideas, their urgent sentences. Had *we* been like that? One of them felt the need to relate everything mentioned to Husserl. Another insisted on calling Satan's second-in-command in *Paradise Lost* "Beezel-bub." A third wore one green and one red tennis shoe and thought the time was ripe for a revival of Situationism. The Markists never ceased to make their galling presences known. They liked to argue over who was disagreeing with whom.

Still and all, it was easy to lose sight of the oddity of the whole enterprise.

Bill had never really been crazy about the place on Norwood to begin with. He'd wanted somewhere with an upstairs and a downstairs, and though the ascent to our apartment required scaling two flights, the place itself was a single story. The claw-footed bathtub had no shower and could barely contain bear-like Bill. He had the room farthest from the main space, but as sociable as he could be, he never really got used to the salon-like quality of the environment, the comings and goings. The queerer things got, the more uneasy he seemed. One night at a party at Gwen's place around the corner on Richmond, Mary met a woman named Jeannie Walton. She was a year or two ahead of us in the program, with all of the advancement in sophistication that implied. Jean was involved with a man, but she sat next to Mary on the sofa in the dim light and erotically stroked a cat in her lap the whole night as a light rain fell outside the open window. After that, the more Mary talked about being smitten with this Jean, the more Bill seemed to withdraw. He spent more time watching TV back in his room, emerging every half hour or so to lumber down the hall and grab another can of Milwaukee's Best out of the fridge. One night he told Mary she was making a mistake, that this Jeannie Walton was "unprepossessing." At the end of the year he moved out and went back home to Potsdam. Dan moved in. I had mixed feelings about that, mostly good ones, in the long run. I was used to my crush by then, and so was he.

Then Ronald Reagan taxed me. I have been trying to evoke here some of the varieties of happiness that were mine during my years as a graduate student in Buffalo, New York. An irreducible fact should never be forgotten. Reagan was the president. During the entire five years I lived in Buffalo, Ronald Reagan was the President of the United States. There were severe limits to any happiness to be enjoyed under that reign. I implore the reader never to lose sight of that most basic of circumstances.

There came a point, because there was not enough to occupy his time—no High Crimes and Misdemeanors to cover up, no particular plagues to speak of—when Reagan turned his brisk attentions to graduate students, graduate students who were on the dole, in effect, because their scholarships were free of duty. That made them a drain upon the federal fund, already otherwise mysteriously depleted. The problem needed to be addressed, with all deliberate speed. It was a matter of sufficient urgency that mere months elapsed between the day the idea popped into Reagan's head and the day the tax was levied.

That tax may have been the least of Reagan's crimes, but it had an immediate effect on me. It meant I could no longer afford to live on my stipend and had to take out student loans. I borrowed lavishly. My income doubled overnight. The debt would be a burden all through my thirties but for the moment I was rich, and I bought a car.

A sporty 1977 Oldsmobile Starfire, silver with beet-red interior, it gave me yet another way of seeing the city I already knew so well. I drove down to LaSalle Park, past D'youville College and the Peace Bridge and Ted's Hots, and watched the tug boats mosey up the Niagara

River past the Horseshoe Reef toward Grand Island, as the mosquitoes came out and the late-spring evening shadows lengthened into night. I drove out Main past Williamsville into the country, where the water tower of Clarence rose above the woods and meadows. I ventured over to the East Side, past the patchy parks along Best Street to the Walden Galleria, to remind myself how segregated the city really remained, despite the relative integration of the West Side.

But mostly I had sex again. Though my celibacy had been Buffalo-specific, three years was a long time for that. Back in Detroit, my old pal Paul was available almost any time I could borrow a family car to drive all the way out to Fenton. The sex was fierce and friendly. One-night stands with pick-ups from the Man Trap or the Male Box or the Gold Coast were more frequent than their reliance on the same contingency, the loan of a family car, had seemed to promise. The contingency had an inhibiting potential; sometimes in a stranger's bed, at a crucial moment, I'd have a mental flash of my Mom's LeBaron or my Dad's New Yorker, parked just outside.

I was not the only one in history to link cars with sex but the connection ran deeper, it sometimes seemed, than a healthy sexuality could readily accommodate. The back seat of a car had been the breathless site of a primal scene in high school. My oil-burning '72 Ford Torino had managed to get me out to the Blind Pig in Ann Arbor for an occasional quickie, and to get me back by two or three in the morning, engine light flashing. During my undergrad years, my cream-colored '81 Dodge Omni was a fixture along Seven Mile, where a few of Detroit's gay bars stood in a bright, thrumming row. That was the car I'd had to sell to move to Buffalo. In a way I'd been glad to be free of it. Maybe it meant my promiscuous past was behind me.

Reagan was president. It was 1983. I thought it might be wise to cool it a little. Three years later, thousands of gay men had died, lungs imploded, organs shriveled, skins sprouting tumorous purple blooms, bones turning foam. The Supreme Court handed down a decision that affirmed the criminality of homosexual acts. Gay sex, said the Court, was "an infamous crime against nature," one "not fit to be named." *Fuck them*, I thought. They'd even taxed my fucking stipend. I got a loan, bought a car, went driving, and picked up a guy named Joel at the Villa Capri on Main, where Foucault hung out in his day.

A "healthy sexuality"—that *was* what I wanted to have. But was sexuality really to be designated by the indefinite article? Was it a thing to be "had," like a body—like fingers, like toes? (Anonymous phone sex: *What kind of body do you have?*) Why "healthy"—because the Masters had declared queers sick for all those years? And why "promiscuous"—because it was the word the Masters used? It was hard to compare a piece of experience so intimate, but the dozen or so tricks I'd turned in a decent year did not approach a world record, as far as I could tell, and I was not ashamed. I surprised myself with how little shame I ever felt about that.

I was determined not to consider those encounters inadequate substitutes for some real thing. What exactly would it—that "real thing"—have been anyway? The transient quality of the assignations was *not* a problem; sex was intimate by definition; it did not have to be, *should* not have been, the most important of intimacies. Sometimes after sex we'd become friends. I was always glad of that. I thought sex was supposed to be an extension of friendship. Joel and I ended up working together at the Western New York AIDS Project, trying to get the governor to adopt humane policies and to get the president, for starters, to utter the name of the disease. I was not averse to repeats but thought it just as well that they were rare. The point was to experience a particular, passing intimacy that produced intense affections of its own, and to act according to that understanding.

If I was ashamed at all, it was of a thing difficult to articulate to myself. I would not have known how to think of it if not for sex ads in tabloids: *Top, Bottom, Versatile.* If you were going to do this at all, then it should be done right, I told myself, and the first in the series was, in my own theory of things, the *least* queer. I wanted to be anything but that, anything but the first. There seemed to be no way around it. Desire was desire. I wasn't into S-M but I could understand the versions that tried to neutralize the play of domination and submission. My own experiments along those lines never quite did the trick. Did the unavoidability of it come from a secret wish to dominate—secret even from me? In S-M the dominant one was the Master; was I so alert to Masters, so contemptuous of their power, because somewhere in the depths I really *was* one, or wanted to be?

So many of my Buffalo family were coupling too. Many had arrived that way, each known in relation to the other. To be past the rituals, beyond the game of seduction, the discipline of courtship. I'd been a curator of couples since the second grade, when I had pressed Glenn, whom I'd loved, to go kiss Suzy on the playground, if that was what he really wanted. They liked me for giving them the gift of themselves as an item. I urged Mary into the women's room at Nietzsche's Bar to find out once and for all what was what with that Jeannie, only really half-knowing they would be the ones to answer each other's most ardent letters, and tend the same gardens.

I may have wanted to have secrets from my family in Michigan but not from my families in Buffalo, so I kept the encounters there to a minimum and stayed on the lookout for whatever might be possible with the materials furnished by the things of everyday life. The pickings remained slim. Unless I were to couple, how would I ever integrate "my" "sexuality" into that life? But it wasn't just the absence of opportunity around the department; I really *didn't* want "to couple." Being queer was supposed to be about the creation of new kinds of intimacies.

By the time Mary and Jean had committed to each other some months later, they resisted referring to their "relationship." The word seemed too trite. They called it their "basket." All the words had always seemed that way to me (the usual problem of public language—could *that* have been what Irving meant?). "Dating" was for kids, and I hadn't done it even when I'd been one. "Sex life" was beyond the pale. Whenever anyone tried to "woo" me, I could not help but respond with fond amusement, and the word seemed every bit preposterous enough to name such a silly pursuit. Our lives were so important. They were all we had. Why would we want to trivialize them? I despaired of ever having "a" "healthy" "sexuality" with no language fit to describe it except the language of high school. Many were surprised that I—sometimes so playful, on the surface—could be so painfully earnest underneath. But they were missing the point. *Serious does not mean solemn*, I would speechify, hoping they would not realize I was quoting Susan Sontag.

One spring I flew to Denver to see my high school friend Joey, who lived there with his lover Thom. They had an apartment on the eighth floor of a high-rise near Cheesman Park, and a wonderful group of friends, gay, lesbian and straight. We went to clubs and danced to De-Barge. We drove into the mountains, where a hot cowboy in a convenience store followed us out to the parking lot and told us we'd better watch who we looked at and how we looked at them. We squealed with laughter all the way up Pike's Peak. I got a taste of what a real gay life would be, but I was not disappointed to return to that very different queer life of my own, in Buffalo.

4.
EVERY CONVERSATION WAS ALWAYS IN PROGRESS.

You could not enter any dialogue worth having at its beginning. It was already underway, no matter how you sliced it. You only needed to find the way that you could join it. Irving Massey shared few of my enthusiasms. Nobody has ever brought me into the conversations I wanted to have more fully than he.

Irving's writing had a conversational tone at times that differentiated it from the other "academic" writing I was reading then. One essay began with a description of a stroll in Delaware Park, another with an account of Irving's musical dreams, followed soon by a recollection of an afternoon of berry-picking. In a later book (*Identity and Community*, 1994), Irving remembered the Montreal neighborhood where he grew up and recalled the anti-Semitism he encountered during his boyhood in Canada. One was never surprised to come upon passing references to personal conversations, including chats with students, from which Irving blithely conscripted observations to propel the line of his own thought.

These interludes were introduced casually, and integrated into the sequence, not exactly seamlessly, but offhandedly. In its frequent appearances, the personal pronoun was decidedly nonchalant, though little else in the writing was. A typical piece would begin with a direct statement of its plan: "I began this essay with a simple paradigm in mind…" A few lines later the pattern might become irreparably complicated: "[T]he whole model I was trying to use was unexpectedly threatened…and I shall have to cope with the far-reaching, not to say universal issues [this] raises before I can consider going on."

Were we to assume that the writer had already "coped" with these issues and that the essay we were reading was the outcome of those travails? The use of tenses suggested otherwise—the conflation of future ("I shall have to…") and present ("…before I can consider…"). And the modesty ("…I was trying to use…"). What was striking, always, was how Irving's work conveyed a sense of thought as process. To convey that sense was among the principal aims of his writing, taking priority over any effort to develop a conventional thesis or pursue a straight line of argument. I came to know that Irving was a devoted reader of William James; the distinctive rhythms of his own writing reflected a commitment to a Jamesian notion of the "stream" of consciousness.

Not just in its conversational aspects but in its more exegetical or philosophical moods, the writing was always direct, line by line, never obscure in the then-current de Man-or-Derrida sense, exemplified more by their followers than by de Man or Derrida themselves. In fact, considering its density or the abstractness of the ideas with which it contends, Irving's writing was a model of clarity. Yet reviews of his first two books—*The Uncreating Word* (1970) and *The Gaping Pig* (1976)—sometimes placed them in the deconstructionist tradition of opacity. This misreading derived mainly from the novelty of deconstruction in the seventies, and the critics' desires not to be its dupe—as well as the fact that Irving's work, though very different, undeniably shares some of the strangeness of deconstructive writing.

Every paragraph of Irving's work is packed with ideas, and if you wanted to seize on them and convert them into some Burkean equipment for living, you could. "As for our redeemed selves, it is not literature that will reveal them to us. That is for life to do, at its best." Or again, "In order for us to trust each other, we must be able to abandon the strenuous search for truth and let our language make a detour through God." As maxims, these are more than viable; that Irving granted himself permission to render such flourishes was among the things that set his work apart from ordinary practice.

But to take these aphorisms as axiomatic, as simple truth-claims, would have been a category mistake of the first order. Leading up to the latter example, for instance, is this qualifying excursus: "In dialogue… the figural founds the literal in a special way: by guaranteeing the provisionality of truth, revealing that it is just an eddy in the stream of thought, and so ensuring the continued possibility of dialogue itself." Still less is it the point, however, to persuade readers of the "provisionality of truth"—to persuade readers of anything, for that matter. Resistant to stating "points" in the usual sense, Irving's work seeks to capture something of the elusiveness of thoughts, without confining even that aspiration to the fixity of some ultimately determining pattern.

On the first day of the Romanticism seminar, Irving came in carrying a celery-green, medium-sized suitcase full of books. He opened the suitcase on the table and looked down at the books doubtfully. "I would say that this is a definite sign of over-preparation, wouldn't you?" he asked the class at large. A disarming self-effacement, a certain conspiratorial companionability, was characteristic of him in person; it appeared in another way in his writing. If he was aware at all that graduate students were unlikely to be conversant with such matters—it had never occurred to me that professors ever had to "prepare" anything, even once I'd begun teaching courses of my own—he proceeded exactly as if we would all be in effortless accord.

Yet I came to understand that he regarded conflict and strife as baselines of human experience. Fighting, he wrote in *Identity and Community*, "may be what life is mainly about." His congenial demeanor was perhaps a kind of defense mechanism, a presumptive counter-action to this perceived state of affairs, but there was never any hint of mortification or abasement about it.

A burst of collective laughter came from the hall, interrupting the lecture, and Irving paused to observe, "They must be reading *A Confederacy of Dunces*."

It didn't seem unusual for a professor—especially one of Irving's generation, especially in graduate school—to cite widely and to proceed as if everyone would get the references, whether to Fichte, Alfred de Vigny, or John Kennedy Toole. For my part, I'd never heard of the first two, but I had loved *A Confederacy of Dunces* and was delighted to learn that a man of such learning had found it hilarious too. (I'd always worried that being an intellectual might mean you had to give up on having any fun.) Usually the assumption that listeners would recognize recondite allusions struck me as pompous and pedantic; if I ever ascended to a position to make such allusions myself, I planned to avoid this pitfall somehow. In Irving's case it seemed like a gesture of respect, to avoid condescending to even the least schooled of his auditors by over-explaining.

I think he understood himself as being engaged in many conversations at once, each of them quite far along, all going on simultaneously, on parallel tracks. He was, in his thinking and his writing, inviting others to join those conversations, in whatever ways might be available to them. "There are many different ways to grasp ideas," he would say.

In Irving's classes I revisited my old experiences of pleasurable incomprehension. It was surely odd to *enjoy* a lack of understanding, even to welcome it. It was so anomalous, I thought, that there was really no way to find out whether anyone else ever felt the same way. You couldn't exactly ask. Privately, some of my peers admitted to being confounded by a particularly difficult text now and then, usually a work of Theory, but in class the custom was always to profess some form of mastery. The only thing that enabled me to forge ahead was my ability to take a certain pleasure in confusion and bafflement, the same resource that got me through the more offish works of modernism. I had taken to reading Theory as if it were a species of poetry, its truths, if any, figurative rather than literal. Thus was I able to say a thing or two in company, when called upon to do so, about books as daunting as *Of Grammatology, Discipline and Punish, Écrits.* I often found in dialogue that I understood more than I thought or that others—perhaps even better—understood as little.

To reach some ultimate condition of understanding was not what thought was about in any case. That was what Irving taught, perhaps, above all, that there was always a *perhaps*, and that knowledge was inexpressibly dynamic—"historical, flowing, and flown," in the words of Elizabeth Bishop, whose lyric tale "In the Village," set in Irving's beloved Nova Scotia, he especially admired.

It wasn't that I failed to "understand" Irving's lectures, exactly, only that there was, as in his writing, an elusiveness about them, however lucid they remained moment by moment. You could ever only *almost* grasp his meanings; I heard his words in an ecstatic state of *almost*-knowing. Irving gently discouraged efforts to extract the essence of his thought, or try to pin it down. People were constantly re-wording what he had just said and then asking if that was what he'd meant. He would smile sadly and quietly demur. No matter how painstakingly the asker revised the gloss, Irving would never grant these paraphrases equivalency to his initial formulations. Eventually his questioners would give up, or Irving would bestow a patient but humorous shrug, less to indicate the futility of the quest than to acknowledge the nature, perhaps regrettable, of dialogue itself.

These exchanges were usually more fruitful than ordinary conversations anyway, and only the most restive or earth-bound found Irving to be a frustrating presence. His refusals were too gentle for that. In person he had an otherworldly quality, a deep tranquility, though he spoke often of anxiety and trauma. As he lectured, he would turn a lozenge in his mouth and rhythmically stroke his long gray beard, gestures that produced a combined effect as soothing as that of his low, even voice. He was fortunate in these characteristics; without the sense of reassurance they provided, many might have found his teaching too much to bear. The world was riven by violence. Almost everything he said or wrote turned on that simple fact.

I urged a series of books upon Irving; I wanted to try to give him something like what he was giving me, a pitiful aspiration, I knew even then. I lent him once a copy of Paul Auster's *The Invention of Solitude*, a memoir about the death of Auster's father that Charlie Baxter, in a letter from Michigan, had recommended to me. The book ruminated philosophically with lyric overtones on the theme of fatherhood, and it contained a long digression on *Pinocchio*. I'd risked appearing juvenile by mentioning to Irving that *Pinocchio* was one of my favorite books, and I was terribly relieved when he told me it was a favorite of his too. Auster's take on it included unexpected juxtapositions and odd turns that reminded me a little of Irving's exhilarating logical leaps. He returned the book the next week and when I asked if he had liked it he answered regretfully, "Not very much, I'm afraid...There was something, something about the author's style..." I can see now that Auster's style, even in that early book, was too willed, too performative, for Irving's taste. As he wrote in *Find You the Virtue* (1987), the artist has to be "secure enough to *surrender* what he has produced, to give it up entirely, to become his own auditor." Surely that lack of "surrender" was what he had found wanting in Auster's book, and in most books. As he surely knew, in giving him these books I was beseeching him: *Do I understand you? Is this anything like it, is this close? Am I anywhere* near *to understanding you?* Although the question was never abjured, it could really have no answer. "Three knocks at the door of truth," Irving wrote. "Good thing it never quite opens."

He was puzzled by my love of movies. I knew enough not to defend it or to persuade him to see the greatness of certain beloved films. Only injustice or cruelty required defense, and persuasion was among the most regrettable acts of the will. Irving admired Cardinal Newman's *Grammar of Assent* as much as he did because it concerned how human accords might be reached without coercion or coaxing. For his part, the French farce *La Cage aux Folles* was among his favorites, and for a while he mentioned it in company almost any time the subject turned toward movies. He took a special delight in the opening scene, where what looks like a tryst between gay lovers, an older and a younger man, turns out really to be an expression of affection between a father and son. I did not exactly think this indifference to the cinema constituted a blind spot; although Irving speculates in *The Gaping Pig* that literature is essentially *about* "blind spots," I could never really allow myself to think that he had any himself. I thought he should be fascinated by movies because of his interest in the nature of "the image," but in our talks it emerged that he did not think movies *had* or *were* "images" in any real sense. Maybe, I thought, I didn't even know what he meant by the word.

To give up will—what else would it have to mean? Those who master the world are creatures of the will, so it would have to mean giving up any hope of taking a place among them—as I already gladly had. To submit to fate? To renounce desire? Irving seemed to have done neither. To me, he seemed gloriously self-sufficient, though I knew he was tied deeply to relations of all kinds, familial and otherwise. At least twice married, he was a beloved father, adored by former students, a respected professor with countless collegial connections, deep friendships of long standing. Getting to know him meant constantly being surprised by how much in the world he really was, constantly being drawn up short by the ever widening circle of these affections, marveling at the extent and the significance of these bonds. My own friendship with him, I thought, attested to the ease of his affections, his remarkable capacity to accept others as they were.

The last line of *The Uncreating Word*: "If such a reconciliation could take place"—a reversion, that is, to "a humbler language" that could "renew its compact with reality"—then "we might no longer have to feel that our only refuge from pride or falsehood lies in silence." Could one who wrote words like these with such conviction really, for all that, still have a life? If so—and it was clearly so—did the words mean something other than what I took them to mean?

The idea of "coping" recurred in his work. "I shall have to cope…" he wrote in the passage previously quoted. In *The Gaping Pig*, he observes that the caterpillar in *Alice in Wonderland* "seems to accept his metamorphic fate with as much aplomb as Alice lacks in coping with hers." Always, everywhere, this problem of "coping," contending, struggling, seeking refuge.

The question was how to reconcile this pervasive sense of strife with the underlying tranquility. The strife I understood. As far as I could see, it was everywhere. The tranquility I longed for.

As I read Irving more widely and tried to listen to him more deeply, I thought it was important to keep in mind that the peculiar serenity expressed in his work and his person had to have been, for all its seeming ease, hard-won. It was not purchased through a denial of suffering. At the same time, the exact nature of the suffering he acknowledged was still not entirely clear. Was it the oppression of exploited workers? The trauma of helpless hysterics? The repression of peons in the throes of a dualistic morality? Hardly. Perhaps again, though, each of these. Marx figured not at all in Irving's work, though I knew that Marx had dominated his earliest studies forty years before. Freud and Nietzsche appeared regularly, but in passing, more as background figures in a larger pattern than as truth-giving oracles to be supplicated.

In time I began to see Irving's work as being fundamentally about domination and the suffering it engendered. *The Uncreating Word* considers how language becomes an instrument of control over a reality it also constructs, and in that book Irving subtly cultivates and fosters a language of intransitivity in place of the transitive one that inevitably turns us into master-ful Subjects, always striving to make the world into our Object. *The Gaping Pig*, about literature and metamorphosis, takes up the domination of forms, especially the forms of public language that impinge upon the private languages of individual experience; in its odd way, the book celebrates the metamorphs who rebel against the restrictive forms imposed on them. Later books are more explicit about this theme—one about, among other things, colonial ideology (*Identity and Community*), another about anti-Semitism (*Philo-Semitism in German Literature*, 2001).

I knew that his work took this turn in part because he grew weary of being suspected of "universalizing," but these books bear little resemblance to the countless others on similar subjects that the second wave of Theory washed up. For one thing, Irving's post-colonial subject is Canadian, like himself, while he approaches pre-Nazi anti-Semitism through its opposite, as the title of that book suggests. For another, he feels called upon to prove neither the existence nor the ravages of either imperialism or racism. He takes their entrenchment as his starting point.

Even so, his work retains mystic overtones, with affinities to the work of Martin Buber and Walter Benjamin, to whom Irving dedicated an essay ("Escape from Fiction") but who had to be shorn of his own mystic impulses to be fully embraced by the Age of Theory. The concern with origins, with where thought or language comes from, had to engage at some level the very metaphysics that hasty readings of Derrida had rendered unfashionable. "In a deeper sense than the Derridean," Irving wrote, "all we are ever doing is reading or writing."

That "detour through God" he spoke of, certainly, gave me pause; there were even times when I resented the ethic of effortlessness ("Unless words come naturally they had better not come at all...") that Irving espoused. *He* wasn't the one toiling helplessly over unintelligible books, after all, or scraping along on six hundred bucks a month, or cobbling together quarters to wash his clothes at the launderette on the corner, not even to mention the real suffering that flourished in every quarter and roiled the very earth. Of course Irving never really "espoused" anything, and I knew that he meant something else, he always meant something else. For him, there was something "irreducible"—that was the word—in any thought or feeling, in any experience, and that was what needed to be discovered, remembered, and cherished. It was why he always remained so intent on the problem of metaphor—because metaphors are the only almost-direct expression of this mysterious "irreducible." In a way, Irving's ideal of the effortless (except that it was not an "ideal") was a way of thinking about the problem of self-consciousness, though he would never put it that way. One needs to be "secure enough to surrender…" But where is that security to be found? *Be self-conscious*, he seems to be saying—then don't be.

As I met more and more writers I learned to stop expecting that qualities of their work would be reflected in their human forms. John Ashbery was funny and warm, when I'd expected that he would be caustic and tart; his reading at Buffalo was like a Bob Newhart routine—I'd never noticed that his poems were comical until I heard him read them. Based on his fiction, with its streams of unstoppable talk, I had expected William Gaddis to be sarcastic and garrulous. Instead, at the reception in his honor when he visited Buffalo, he hunched in the squared corner of a long white sofa all night and gazed around the room through watery eyes with an expression of sadness and fear, answering any query with as few words as possible spoken in a scratchy whisper, and gathering his gangly grasshopper limbs every half hour to retreat to the bathroom.

Rarely, though, does one meet a writer closer in person to the spirit of his work than Carl Dennis, who taught the first of the three seminars in creative writing I took at Buffalo. Notable for the likeness of each of its verses to every other, Carl's poetry was quiet, calm, gentle and—in passing moments when its evenness might be briefly ruffled so that it could be carefully re-composed—occasionally jocular, and so was Carl. The "I" of those poems essentially *was* Carl, chronicling the placid days of an attentive yet retiring, law-abiding Buffalo resident. With their level, moderate lines, clipped just sharply enough to avert an oppressive exactitude, they were decidedly the work of a man who, as Carl did, ate two eggs for breakfast every morning until a doctor warned of cholesterol trouble, when he switched to oatmeal.

Carl used to ask people new to Buffalo for afternoon tea in his garden, an invitation that might have struck a certain type, me, for instance, as precious and fey, as Carl himself might have, if it were not issued—and he were not gifted—with great directness of a kind, even candor. In the event, the request to attend was disarming enough that it hardly seemed like a throwback to an earlier era at all. On arriving I felt I was stepping inside one of his books; from the biggest to the most minute details—the aura of Ashland Avenue, the street where he lived;

the spacious porch; the big blue house; the paintings on the walls inside—his poetry was writ large in his environment. What little about his work had seemed even mildly fanciful proved to be nothing more or less than fact, finely wrought description of his everyday surroundings. Maybe it was enough to evoke one's own experience, however circumscribed. Carl knew the scope of his work was localized; in fact, this was a commitment of his—the book he'd just published at the time was called *The Near World*. Maybe it really was enough, and what was to be admired was the steady perseverance in the task of telling what little could ever be told of what was at hand.

No more than Carl's work did, his seminar seldom defied expectation. It met on Tuesday afternoons, and Carl wore the same clothes every week, blue twill slacks and a wool sweater in a slightly different shade of blue. All that changed was the color of the shirt that peeked out above the sweater's crew-necked collar—sometimes light blue to match the rest of the outfit, sometimes auburn to match Carl's fastidiously trimmed russet beard—and the shoes, which got sturdier as fall descended into winter. Though too benign to impose an aesthetic, Carl clearly wanted us all to write poetry that was modest and modulated, controlled and unperturbed—exactly the opposite of what would-be poets in their twenties were likely to be inclined toward. Yet we were all Carl's friends as well as one another's, so we tried to oblige, probably to the detriment of the work. Only one participant, a non-matriculated student, refused entirely to get with the program. He was a wild-eyed fellow with tangled locks and heavy breath—you could hear him practically the whole three hours of the workshop, wheezing off in a corner like a winded wolf—who wrote of sex, politics, viscera, and took to placing himself sulkily askew to the congenial circle in which the rest of us sat, to lodge his overall objections to the genteel atmosphere—not, despite its irksomeness, an altogether unworthy protest.

The work submitted to the workshop was the predictable complement of good, bad and indifferent poetry. In accord with Carl's goal to maintain an even keel, he treated every piece with the same equanimity, holding the manuscript pages up to the light as if they were odd exhibits inviting greater or lesser degrees of mild curiosity or mild distaste—a bit like the cavalier Parisian in Buñuel and Dali's *Un Chien*

Andalou who happens upon a severed hand in the street and gives it a gingerly poke with his walking stick. He never delivered verdicts, but carefully described the poem in question, in his slow, reedy, slightly nasal, trance-like monotone, his eyes half closing, as if the mellowness of it all were apt to put even him to sleep. As weeks of this went by it seemed the wolfish heavy-breather might snap—he started furiously scratching at the pelt of his own arms—but he only came close once. When he submitted a Brechtian ode to Nelson Mandela, one meek, un-informed soul ventured to ask who Nelson Mandela was, prompting a snarl of contempt and a spasm of disbelief from the author that such ignorance was before him. The spectacle was dramatic—the craggy whiskered jaw convulsing under the sloping vulpine brow—and it silenced and shamed the inquisitive peer, but Carl registered neither the outrage nor the humiliation fermenting in their separate quarters. He explained who Nelson Mandela was and moved serenely on.

My own contributions to the workshop ran the gamut from bad to worse. I'd only dabbled in poetry, but I had the sense that I thought mainly in bursts and starts and streaks and details, like a poet, not in arcs and lines and diagrams, like a fiction writer. Now I started to wonder if I was not some unworkable hybrid, a terrible Jekyll-and-Hyde crossbreed, inclining toward the prosy and the linear when I was supposed to be being poetic, and going all lyrical and flighty when I was supposed to be writing prose. After a fashion, the genre liberated me to write love poems, but I wasn't in love with anyone, and crushes did not appear to lend themselves to serious verse. I addressed the safely ungendered "you" of poetic convention, working from memory and committed to avoiding the lachrymose, melancholic and dejected intonations of so much gay love poetry. But this freedom didn't seem real and the workshop duly found these pieces abstract and bloodless. Meanwhile, Carl noted privately, more in sorrow than in anger, that my senses of line and meter were just too set, too regular, to enable any effects but artificial ones. Under ordinary circumstances I'd have mounted a spirited defense of artifice—the real problem, after all, was a knee-jerk aesthetic transparency—but it seemed more circumspect, in keeping with the spirit of the seminar, to accept the sad fact that I'd never be a poet.

I hadn't really thought I was; that was why I'd started with poetry—it seemed less likely to spur the identity crisis that always lurked just around the corner. I did continue to nurse some thought of writing stories, and the first of my two seminars in fiction posed even more of a risk to my conception of myself than I could have foreseen. It was taught by Ray Federman, a Beckett scholar who also wrote postmodern fiction of a sort that moved its admirers to energetic debates regarding the proper name for it: Was it *sur*-fiction, or *meta*-fiction, or better yet some alternative coinage yet to be devised? The experiments ranged from tried-and-true measures like omitting punctuation to more complicated stunts of deranged typography. As a child in Europe, Ray had eluded capture by the Nazis by hiding in a cupboard, and this terrible primal scene haunted such of his books as *Double or Nothing* and *The Voice in the Closet*. Yet his work lacked the gravity (I had the temerity to think) to communicate the full horror of this experience; it was often blithe and playful, like Ray himself, who carried as little outward sense of a traumatic past as anyone I'd ever met. Dynamic, theatrical, gregarious, and witty, he held the class in thrall with his grand gestures and his melodious accent, the voice of a more gravel-throated Charles Boyer. He began every session by reciting great opening lines as models for how to begin, like the one from *One Hundred Years of Solitude* in which the Colonel facing a firing squad recalls "that distant afternoon when his father took him to discover ice"—and Ray would hold dramatically on the word "ice," with a long conclusive tremolo, drawing the word into many syllables as he pressed his thumb and finger together and wiggled them in the air, as if they were vibrating with the beauty of the passage itself.

I'd been writing a series of quasi-modernist stories filled with unreliable narrators, portentous ellipses, and narrative slip-knots. Though not "experimental" in the sense that Ray practiced and promoted, any of these would probably have suited him fine. But the same imp of the perverse that made my poetry prosaic and my prose poetical rose up to conjure the inner Hyde once again. I submitted two pieces in a row in the prevailing mode of '80s-style realism, as remote as could be imagined from anything that could possibly interest Ray: flat declarative sentences, ordinary events, little epiphanies here and there, a scrupulous avoidance of any conflict or drama. The second of these pieces added the insult of going on for thirty pages to the injury of its middlebrow aesthetic, and as I read the story aloud in the workshop Ray hoisted each page of his copy riotously, fluttering it in the air above his head before turning it over into the next page, making a jolly show of his boredom. In the discussion of the story afterward, when a classmate compared it, much too kindly, to the work of Ann Beattie, Ray shuddered and snorted dramatically at the mention of her name. He was a man of little ill will, but if there was one thing that could raise his ire it was *New Yorker* fiction and all it stood for. I, meanwhile, found this scorn for things bourgeois a bit suspect coming from one who spent his weekends on the golf course.

Others in the workshop threw themselves with some abandon into the spirit of experiment that reigned, with submissions more notable on the whole for their uses of media than of literary form as such. One student who came to class wearing gray silk jumpsuits that were puckered at the waist turned in a piece called "Plato's Cave." It was written on the inside of a brown paper grocery bag, which readers were instructed to place over their heads; equipped with a flashlight, they were then enjoined to shine the light up into the bag, and read the words printed there. The writer could not control the order in which these words were read—that was the very point—but the gist of it all was something like, "Welcome to Plato's Cave. If you are looking for ideal forms you have come to the wrong place. It's the real world, bub!" Another submission consisted of about fifteen pages, each sheet distributed at random around the seminar table. On each page were ten lines or so, unpunctuated, and the first reader read the first line on her page, the second the first line on his, and so on around the table, working down the pages until all the lines were read. The idea was that no two readings would yield the same meaning. Indeterminacy was quite the rage that semester.

As much as Ray delighted in these exploits, his class favorite was Welch D. Everman, who used the middle initial when introducing himself, and whose experiments were more recognizably literary. Welch had already written a Federman-influenced critical study on the authority of authors, concluding that they had none, needed to imagine they had in order to go on writing, and should take pains to make sure they never really believed the pretense. He was working at the time on a sequence called "The Harry and Sylvia Stories," a Queneau-ish series of exercises about Harry's free-floating obsessions and Sylvia's apparently inescapable destiny as their convenient, all-purpose object. In sketch after sketch, Harry remained relatively constant, a self-centered shlub, treated with jokey indulgence, while Sylvia had a certain protean quality. Sometimes she was a nagging wife, others an unattainable sex-goddess; in one of the most memorable episodes, Harry lived alone but acquired a series of ill-fated pets in succession and named each one Sylvia. The conceit seemed a bit sadistic on the face of it, but the tone was always light, droll, whimsical.

A part of our sessions was usually occupied by colloquies between Welch and Ray, cogitations on everything from the latest translation of Blanchot to the liabilities of conventional form. The latter points were implicitly directed at me, I thought bitterly, since I'd been cast as the class traditionalist, with no way I could see to communicate the depth of my actual commitments. In spite of my jealousy of Welch, I admired how real his own writing seemed to him—and, *because* of my jealousy, derided it at the same time. He talked about his characters as if they were real people, and even more strikingly, he had the ability, over time, to draw others into doing the same thing. In one workshop a classmate observed, "I'm not sure this story is really being fair to Harry"—as if Harry were some wrongly maligned neighbor. Ray, meanwhile, would sometimes initiate their discourses by asking Welch jovially, "And how are Harry and Sylvia these days?" From time to time Welch himself would proudly announce, "I just finished a new Harry-and-Sylvia!"—as if they were already established in the Great Tradition, alongside the Pat Hobby or Nick Adams stories, as if there were untold masses somewhere, eagerly anticipating them, like the swarming mobs waiting at the docks for the next installment of a Dickens novel.

I couldn't even bring myself to mention the stories I'd written by name, let alone the characters, such as they were. Forced to talk about my writing in the workshop, I'd refer to "that story about such-and-such," instead of calling it by its title or even claiming it as mine. The stories I wrote did not seem "real" to me—but then, no fiction did, least of all the work I most admired, which reflected reality from a dimension far enough removed that the question became less what reality it showed than whose, and how, and what counted as real, and what did not, and why. My own experience had always been very "real" to me—probably too much so; I thought I understood why the modernists worried so much about the problem of alienation, but I cultivated a modernist's detachment mainly as a hopeful corrective to the intense immediacy of my own thoughts and feelings. In that sense I could not imagine ever being alienated from my self, and I felt so full of love in the company of so many others, or at the thought of them, that I feared for myself and withdrew myself, because I could not see how this love might be understood, or answered. The fact remained that I did not count as real. No gay person did, ultimately. I would have to deal with that.

I gave it one last try when J. M. Coetzee visited Buffalo and offered a seminar in fiction writing. Awarded the Nobel Prize in Literature some twenty years later, Coetzee was then gaining his early notoriety for such challenging, astringent works as *Waiting for the Barbarians* and *Life and Times of Michael K.* I had read both with admiration and little pleasure. What I admired was the severity—the refusal to indulge readers' frivolities. I happened to be in the main office soon after Coetzee arrived, when the brassy, crusty department administrator was grilling him on the proper pronunciation of his name. Coetzee wore bicycle clips at the cuffs of his pants, modifying his slight figure into an even more intense angularity. He gazed at the administrator for a long time before he answered softly and tonelessly, "You may say it however you wish."

The semester was a homecoming of sorts for Coetzee. He had begun his career in the early seventies at Buffalo, but as I understood it, the American government had declined to renew his employment authorization due to his participation in the anti-war protests. Despite his loathing of apartheid, he had then returned to his native South Africa. His work of that period was exacting in its allegorical logic. It was an unyielding effort to mount a critique of apartheid from outside, without engaging it on its own terms, a commitment that distinguished his work sharply from the more direct political critiques of socially conscious fellow writers like Nadine Gordimer, André Brink, or Breyten Breytenbach. It also opened him to accusations of quietism, but as one trying to articulate a queer identity with reasons of its own, unanswerable to prevailing doctrines to justify itself, and not simply constructed from the given terms—of which there were few that could be of use for such a self-fashioning in any case—I found much in Coetzee's seemingly remote writing that resonated powerfully.

If Carl's seminars resembled one of his tea parties while Ray's was like a roadside carnival, the atmosphere of Coetzee's was distinctly monastic. We spent the first two sessions working our way through the opening paragraph of *Madame Bovary*. Though all the trappings of a martinet attended his bearing, Coetzee conveyed an utter lack of will—so much so that it was not quite right to say that he conveyed it. He turned the same razor-sharp gaze upon everyone, on all occasions, and always paused before speaking, as if to register the inanity of whatever address confronted him. These were, admittedly, the mannerisms of an aristocrat besieged on all fronts by minor vulgarities, but their recurrence began to imply a certain imperturbability and, by accumulation, an equivalency. After a while it seemed that he looked at you that way not because he felt disdain, but because he was trying to see, and paused that way because he was trying to listen, and hear, to understand what you had said—though whatever it was could scarcely have lent itself to such intense considerations. These were ways of seeing and hearing that did not force you into their own rhythms if only because their rhythms were too strange, too out-of-synch, to be replicated, even assuming you could ever get used to them. Because of the appearance of disdain, one would hardly have called him polite, nor attributed much to him of the kind or the generous, perhaps. Still, for all the steely gazes and pregnant pauses, his manner was a courtesy of sorts, a way of being present, and withdrawing presence, accordingly, going silent, being still, letting many things be. He did not assume that his intervention was called for in any given moment. He did not wish to infringe on the fragility of your texture.

I submitted two stories with shades of Coetzee's own penchant for formalism. One was about a boy who accidentally burns his parents' house down while they sleep inside, then grows up to be haunted by their forgiving ghosts. The other was narrated by a man estranged from his older brother in childhood, who encounters that sibling randomly after many years in a distant city when they're both adults, and is led by him on a wild series of night-town excursions, ending in a church where the narrator discovers in a climactic scene that his brother, nihilistic in their youth, has become a faith-healer. I'd been sending my stories to Charlie back in Michigan, receiving encouraging but bracingly honest replies. About this one, he wrote:

> This morning I read your story with real pleasure and happiness in the stride you seem to have hit. It's a beauty. The sentences, one by one, are professionally turned out and very very beautiful. The story itself has moments—hell, it mostly is a whole sequence—of poetic imaginations, scenes that you can't forget: those wordless moments of flying down roads in the dark, the bars and prayer meetings and boxing gyms, as the whole story becomes progressively more elusive and rich. One would think of Kafka, but an American Kafka, but you haven't aped his styles or manners…

No letter I'd received since my acceptance to Buffalo had meant as much to me. Maybe I really *could* be a writer. But why had I been unable to tell, myself, whether the story was any good?

When Coetzee turned his own severe gaze on these stories, there was a troubling disconnect between how he talked about them in class and the written feedback. In class his tone was measured. He read a paragraph, stopping to observe a detail here and there, then looked to the class. "The prose," he said, "is very…*stylized*. Do you think it is…*too*…stylized?" The framing of the question seemed such that it would have compelled assent even among auditors disinclined to find fault. "This piece," he mused of the second submission, "has certain of the qualities of a…*bravura* performance. Is it *too* much so…would you say?" Yet his written comments focused on details, marginalia, with nothing to say along these general lines. I wished he would just come out and tell me whether *he* thought the stories were too showy, but he maintained his allegorist's posture of indirection to the end.

The stories I'd submitted were allegories themselves, in their way. Both were infused with a gay sensibility, I thought, but neither included any specific gay content, any more than most of what I had written had. Indeed, both protagonists were defined explicitly as straight, and I'd thought of the stories as intricate deconstructions of heterosexual attitudes. For my last submission in the workshop, I wrote a piece in the mode of `80s-realism I'd explored so disastrously in Ray's workshop, about a gay male couple, one of whom was suffering from terminal cancer. The point-of-view was that of the healthy partner, who (the reader was meant to understand) was dealing poorly with the situation—so much so that there was some indication that he might abandon his dying lover, until a final scene, rife with intonations of epiphany, suggested that he would stay. Even this piece had its allegorical side; I'd wanted to write about the ravages of AIDS but thought that topic was too close, or maybe too far beyond me. The genre of the "cancer story," more familiar then (in the work of an emerging writer named David Leavitt, for instance), seemed potentially within my grasp.

Coetzee returned the manuscript with this comment written in careful script in black ink on the last page:

> The present-tense narration does the trick—very good. I'm not sure the end of the story flows with the surprising inevitability it is supposed to have from the body of the story. Obviously you want to do [crossed out] achieve that without any emphasis, but it seems to me possible that the story could have gone another way just as easily. The problem is really very difficult, given the (correct) decision you have taken not to create a "plot" and to keep the crises small. Maybe if the story were pared down a bit, if the background detail were less full and the movements of the mind a little starker, the effect of the end would be more inevitable than it is.

As a reply to a novice writer's mildly promising effort, this seemed to me, itself, a masterful performance. Coetzee gave the impression of having fully entered the story—in a way beyond the commitment with which its own author had inhabited it—in order to think through the

5.
DISSERTATION:

"a lengthy and formal treatise or discourse, esp. one written by a candidate for a doctoral degree at a university; thesis." That synonymous "thesis" should have heartened me; I'd already written one of those, on Nabokov, back at Wayne State. Theoretically, then, I should have known something about the process.

But though endowed with a decent memory for facts, I was afflicted with a constitutional amnesia for skills. In the sphere of action I was always learning everything for the first time. A good swimmer, I still felt a moment's shock every time I dipped into water, a quicksilver sting of certainty that if I had ever known anything about how to negotiate that particular element, I had forgotten it. The old adage about recollection and the riding of bikes could never have been proven by me. Every time I made a fist I had to remind myself the thumb went on the outside, to prevent breakage on impact; I was possessed of the queer's instinct to tuck it away, beneath the folded fingers. Sitting down to write I'd be seized by a split-second's conviction that language was foreign and I'd forgotten how to make sentences or paragraphs, and that was before confronting the hunch that I really had nothing to say in the first place.

All I could do was to plunge forward, and trust—even if I did not know what it was I was supposed to be trusting.

I had framed a marginally manageable topic: late works and last testaments, texts that somehow summed up, whether consciously or not, a given artist's career. The works I was writing about struck the members of my dissertation committee as a puzzling hodgepodge. An opening chapter on *Dead Souls, Ecce Homo,* a few pieces of late James, *Finnegans Wake,* and *Between the Acts.* Then a chapter on Eliot's *Four Quartets,* a set of pieces in progress since the early `30s and published together soon after World War II, after which Eliot published no further poetry to speak of, aside from his verse dramas. A chapter on Nabokov's *Ada,* by common consent the writer's last major work. A chapter on Orson Welles's film *Mr. Arkadin,* a sort of shoestring deconstruction of *Citizen Kane* that, I argued, initiated Welles's late style—when the director was still under forty. I could see how they all fit together some of the time. All were gestures of finality, "late" works in an intricate dialogue with the artist's own earlier work. Each was in its way magisterial, and also at least a little ridiculous. Each had been declared in some not insignificant quarters a great folly or colossal failure. Each expressed a certain indifference to artistic mastery, and a certain confidence in its own.

Irving had never seen a Welles film except *Citizen Kane*, of which his memory was dim and not very favorable. He wanted to look at *Mr. Arkadin* before he read my chapter on it. Dutifully, but with a sense of foreboding, I led him across campus to the AV room to watch the videocassette on a TV monitor. As we made our way through hordes of students, he said, "I always remember what my mother told me when we walked in the city: in a crowd, just put your head down and keep going." I had no idea how to prepare him for the movie. By conventional measures it was often judged to be just plain awful, but I loved its steady glints of patchwork genius, its shadowy melancholy, its willingness to be absurd in the service of exploring kinds of filmmaking apart from standard practice. The first shot used what looked like a model to depict the title character's airplane in flight. "I used to make those out of balsa wood as a boy," Irving remarked. He had some trouble following the crazy-quilt plot and kept asking what had become of this or that character. Among the many set-pieces was a party scene during which, in one brief spark of Wellesian flash, a young woman holding a big white ball popped up into the frame, threw the ball at the camera, then ran out. At that moment, Irving gasped. When the film ended, he looked downcast. "Well," he said with a long sigh, "I liked when she threw that ball..." I thought if he could respond to such a passing instance of Welles's mercurial visual brilliance there was still hope that he would see more of it, but he remained unconvinced of any value I tried to claim for Welles or his sad, raggedy film.

The "modern masters" were still on the docket, though I now had the urge to humiliate as much as to honor them. The main problem would remain the elusive connection of mastery to self-consciousness. I'd cobbled together a hypothesis that there was something of an inverse relation. The highest aspiration of modernism was to achieve some apotheosis of self-consciousness, yet nearly every text in the tradition acknowledged that self-consciousness was fraught with liabilities—fixation and solipsism, to name two—that threatened the very mastery that self-consciousness was supposed to guarantee.

How, then, to achieve self-consciousness and mastery at one and the same time?

That was just the tip of the iceberg. There was so much I wanted to write about. Poetry, fiction, film. Mass culture. Gogol, Nietzsche, James, Joyce, Kierkegaard, Woolf, Barnes. Eliot if necessary, Nabokov to be sure. Welles, Hitchcock. Lateness. Bakhtin. Artistic ambition and failure. Old age. The Concept of Irony. Being and Becoming. Sex. Summation and mythologies of the self. Power and vulnerability. The strangeness of the world. The queerness of my self and its odd incommensurability with the strangeness of the world. Swan songs. Giving up and keeping going, learning not to care. Fascism. TV.

I had made the mistake of thinking that a dissertation was supposed to tell everything you knew. Instead of pursuing a set of ideas about my subjects, I felt as if I were enacting them in the process of composition. I could not figure out how the thing should look in whole, I was stranded in the parts, I was merely Becoming when I needed to have *already* Become. But how would such a thing be possible? There was always a sense of being ahead of myself and behind myself at the same time. Writing that dissertation was like trying to gain the farther shore before swimming the channel. I needed to be *Being*, inhabiting some ultimate space of self-consciousness and mastery, where—at least according to my thesis—those I was writing about seemed to think *they* were.

In a wing of a mall near where I grew up stood an aviary filled with exotic birds of all kinds and colors. It was shaped like a towering steel tee-pee, a big conical structure with thin metal spokes sloping from the tip down to the ground, making the frame octagonal and binding the wire mesh that confined the beautiful birds within. The birds rested on the branches of plastic trees or perched on little swings that hung here and there, or they flew gracefully about, chirping peaceably. I loved to watch them. It was one of my favorite spots. The whole time I was writing my dissertation I remembered it. I dreamed of it. I imagined myself inside the aviary, planted at the very center, my feet cemented into the ground. In these dreams, the birds were not peaceful. They squawked and swirled and swooped, they darted at my eyes. I understood that they were my ideas, given bird-form. I saw myself waving my arms frantically (think 'Tippi' Hedren), and I knew that I was trying to grab hold of them and to ward them off at the same time. Either way, they eluded my grasp. Day by day, writing, I came no closer to knowing what a dissertation was. But I knew what an aviary really was, despite the fine-sounding name. It was a cage.

Graduate school had seemed like a way to put off letting my life turn into a story. That had been one of its great appeals. For a long while that attraction held, or seemed to. My straight friends were marrying, buying houses, having kids, all the things that turned a life into a story before it had a chance to make up its own mind. I passed my days in a little cubicle in the Lockwood Library scratching out sentences, one at a time, that I hoped might still add up to something.

No story in that, I thought.

It could not hold forever. Once I'd finished my exams it had started to be clear that there *was* a story. Maybe there was always a story. Coursework, orals, dissertation—a compulsory trajectory, visible only in reverse, pitifully mimicking the obligatory route from youth to middle-age to dotage, that tedious template, the deep-structure, of every story. The past was not changeless. Subject to the discipline of narrative, it paled. *That eager young person—how little he had known.* And, of course, stories required constrictive feats of naming. It was to stories, after all, that we owed the existence of words like "dating," "wooing," "boyfriend." There would have been no need for them, if not to turn experience into a story. "Coursework"—what a dire designation. How could my nostalgia for that time stand in light of it? *Orals.* It sounded like some sinister combination of forensics and dentistry.

Finishing, I was aware that I had entered, at the age of twenty-seven, the grad-school equivalent of old age. It was what I was writing about. I was writing about lateness and finishing—about, it turned out, finding oneself beyond prevailing categories. Were *Four Quartets, Ada, Mr. Arkadin*, major or minor, naïve or self-conscious? There was a way in which (Bill's old catch-phrase) it no longer mattered. The works I was writing about interested me because I thought they illustrated, in some strange manner, Irving's ideas about the effortless. Irving never thought so, and discouraged that line of argument. But there was a way in which (once you got started it was hard to quit!) these works weren't even trying, despite the surface mastery. Or let us say that they were trying some things very, very hard, and others, the ones you might have thought, not at all. Each could have been seen as terribly overwrought; that was how Irving saw them. I thought I was trying to get at something else, how you *could* tell the dancer from the dance.

I spent a few weeks at the end of spring in Michigan. These trips had begun to feel less like homecomings, more like visits. Just before I would have to leave it, I was starting to think of Buffalo as home. I received a letter from Mary with news from Norwood. Distasteful uptown acquaintances, she wrote, were migrating down to the neighborhood: "Their moving into our area will be reason enough for me to claim myself exempt from all future 'round robin' dinners," she observed tartly. She went on:

> Now the second little incident is a bit closer to home. Guess where Friday night women's meetings take place in the summer? In the back garden, in various niches on the side of the house, and on the patio in the front yard. Mostly it looked like "intense" conversations, though I don't know what was going on out front. As I walked by on my innocuous little jaunt to the Bank Machine, it seemed I might have thrown the aura off. Carol does not really participate (or at least wasn't Friday past); she presides, tends the garden, and walks around blessing the needy masses…I returned from the bank and—IT HAPPENED! She *invited me to join them some time.* Now that I "have more free time." I looked at her bewildered and said I'd talk to her about it. What could I say? Of course I am never going to join them but I did not know how to say "I'm just not interested in your cosmic collective."

She told of trying to identify with the lesbian community in Buffalo but wrote, "I don't see myself in these places. The 'butch' affect, for example, puts me off...precisely because it must be put on...that is, I can't believe that being more masculine than other women comes along with being lesbian. I guess I'm interested in that idyllic identity outside of gender." She wrote of feeling restless, of longing for a life more settled. She wrote that the library had sent an overdue notice for me. I owed a dollar fifty on *Dinner Along the Amazon* by Timothy Findley.

I spent the rest of that last summer in Buffalo, finishing. Dan moved away, back to the city, to take a job in the public defender's office. Mary and Jean spent many weeks together in Europe. Our time was coming to a close. I had the Norwood house to myself for weeks, alone. All went quiet, everything still as blooms pressed between the pages of forgotten books.

I rowed in the mornings, wrote in the afternoons, and smoked pot and listened to Brian Eno in the evenings. Everyone was away, I felt lonely and unmoored. Jake, stuck working in a local restaurant, came by from time to time. He told me of his own loneliness, his longings for human contact. Straight as he was, I thought he should sleep with me. *I* was human. But he just wasn't built that way. I wanted a reckoning but put it off. There would be time, I thought, though things were speeding up. That was how it went, once a story was in the offing.

In the fall Bill came for a visit. He told us he'd been living on the streets, joked about it. He talked to Roy Roussel about coming back to the program. If he did, it would be the next year and we would all be gone. He was his old self—jolly, avuncular, seemed to be willing to give Jean a chance. The department offered me an advanced course to teach, and I did a class on the modernist novel. I chose books that "problematized" (as we said in the trade back then) the whole idea of stories. The focus, I decided, would be on how bad narrative was, as an idea and as a phenomenon. At first the students were puzzled. The first thing we read was a story, not a novel, Grace Paley's "A Conversation with My Father," a beautiful short piece about how stories deny the open destiny of life. Oh, thought the students—*that*. But it wasn't just that. Stories were deterministic, yes. More than half the time, maybe all the time, they were lies. They traded in the raw experience of life for a bunch of silly templates that could only falsify that experience, reduce it. They pretended things were linear. They left out far more than they could ever put in.

The students seemed to understand. Right away, they were more than willing to concede all of this. They wrote it in their notes. *Too* willing, I thought, so I kept on trying to persuade them. It was hard to do this and make them love the books at the same time. I was not sure I was succeeding but you could not do everything at once. Many of the books were scandalous—*Lolita, Naked Lunch. Eustace Chisholm and the Works* was only available in an edition with a lavender cover and the words "Gay Modern Classics" emblazoned on the front. "I hope that won't be a problem," I said. Nobody batted an eye. Overall I tried to neutralize the outrage so the real subversiveness could sink in. It might have been easier if somebody were outraged. *The Autobiography of Alice B. Toklas* was the only book we had read, I told them, that managed to escape the anxiety of narrative *and* to escape the anxiety of escaping narrative. That was why it was one of the only books ever written capable of expressing real happiness.

Charlie sent me the typescript of his first novel and I read it in one night, in one long gulp, from dusk to dawn. As the light broke and the story, told in reverse, reached its beautiful beginning, I wept. It *was* possible to be a good person and a great writer. But one did not get to decide. Which would I be, I still wondered—reader, teacher, writer? Which *could* I be, that is—I would always be a reader. Perhaps that would be enough. To be a teacher, to be a writer—for that I would need permission. The dissertation would not be the end of the story. That was the other problem with stories. They mistook beginnings for ends and vice versa. A job, if I could get one, would not be the end of the story either. It would start another. I applied for every job there was, a hundred or more. Then waited. Days went faster and faster. Every time Dan called from the city I was elated. A friendship could be life-long only if both parties agreed. Mary, Jean; Jake, Gwen, Karyn, Dave—I tried to hold them close. We would be elsewhere soon. My dissertation defense was a study in cheerful disappointment. Marty Pops said, "The thing about this, Tabby"—he called me Tabby, I reminded him of a cat—"the thing about *this* is that it's more than a definite pass, but—for the rest, for the rest, for the rest…it is really only *almost*." ("The trouble with you, Tabby," he had said years before, "is that you are in love with celluloid.") "As a dissertation," Irving said slowly, "it is more than fine, yes, *but* –" he turned to the others—"do you all remember Jim's early work?"

I got one interview at the MLA convention. In a hotel room, a round man with a shaved head and plucked brows that were teased into inverted V-shapes with dark eyeliner lolled on a bed and said, "So...tell us about *movies*." My voice broke; would it ever stop? Back in Buffalo I was told there would be time, other jobs were coming up in spring. Worse jobs, but a job was a job. All I needed was a job. Nobody seemed to get that. Others were getting jobs; why couldn't I? I'd done all the work and nobody cared. I had thought my dissertation would be weird enough to get noticed, but maybe it was just too weird. In the spring Mary was being flown around the country for campus interviews. I wondered if I'd be up to such exhausting travails, if they ever did present themselves. *Life can only be understood backwards, but it must be lived forwards.* I got a call from a Baptist college I'd applied to in the South. "This is delicate," said the man, before asking what my religion was. "Roman Catholic," I replied. That was that. When Jean got an offer in New York City, Mary contacted a department there where she was still a candidate for a position, to inquire about the status of her application. "We have hired," they informed her, "a young lady from Harvard." A few weeks later Charles B. Harris called from Illinois State University. I'd forgotten I had applied there. He offered me a one-year job, renewable up to five years. I tried to keep from crying; it felt like he was saving me. We rented a van and moved Mary fifty miles down the road, where she would be Assistant Professor of English at the University of Rochester. Jean was going to Fordham. They'd commute; it was settled. The contract arrived from Illinois State. I'd be doing four comp sections a term, in rural Illinois. It would be a spiritual penance to endure. But a job was a job; somehow I would still find time to read and write. At the last minute a one-year job in film came up at Wayne State, and they offered it to me out of what I thought was a combination of pity and hometown pride. Charles B. Harris understood, bless him. My old stomping grounds. Was it a backward step? Time moved only forward, and it was slowing down again. It was growing so quiet now on Norwood. Maybe you had to live with always being naïve and self-conscious at the same time. One year. It was still temporary. Nothing was forever. Once that was settled I could tend to the rest. You could not do everything at once. It was only the beginning, I thought. It wasn't over, there'd still be time. There would be time.

Buffalo Trace

JEAN WALTON

November 20, 1982 Buffalo

I got a letter from Samantha. . . And she hints that I might not be able to see her at Thanksgiving next week. I burst into tears. She has taken up residence within me somewhere, that's for sure. At times I feel myself to be the ridiculous figure of the romantic young lover, ardent, longing to be united with the distant fair one. Pining. Absurd. Young Werther, Frederic Moreau, the young narrator in *A la Recherche*, the male voices who articulate the medieval love lyrics we've been reading this semester. All of which makes Samantha such a distant and literary phenomenon. What do I desire when I think of her? I desire to write her poetry, to woo her with words.

If I cannot see her next week, I shall experience a sharp pain, but then I shall harden, find myself with three days in which to work and write, and my writing will be the compensation . . . I must be "missing out" on something in order to get anything done. Is it a kind of revenge I get—working while others play? How tedious to be so connected with everyone else. What a boring sound my own voice makes in my ears.

I am straining to hear a voice that is not mine when I write. Is it possible that I could surprise myself?

A project which would be nearly impossible to complete: to write 12 pages which could be sent to my grandmother as a loving letter, and handed in to Ray Federman as a paper on Proust, both at the same time. Who ever handed in a letter to her grandmother as a term paper? How on earth could I write something that was addressed to both these audiences, simultaneously? It would require a fictitious grandmother (the professor is *already* fictitious).

But, wait, I write to a fictitious grandmother anyway. The conception I have of her is so conditioned by Habit, and has been with me for so long, that every letter I receive from her startles me by its contradictory strangeness—I see my grandmother's mind, *composing*, in the same way that my own mind composes (how frightening to feel that her mind might be revealed to me). The package arrives, I recognize the handwriting, it is familiar Grandma, Gramma, yes, another holiday approaches, of course there is a package (Why this horrid, knee-jerk reaction—I take the package for granted: why can I not be surprised, immediately touched, as though by her hand on my cheek . . .)

I take the package into the house, tear it open, find scarf, toque and mittens, candy and a book of short stories. I am nonchalant; I put the box on the hamper in my room, thinking vaguely "I must thank her." It is not until thoughtful, careful Gus comes upstairs ("Oh look what I got from Grandma," I say, ironing, or brushing my hair, inattentive) and leafs through the book, that the film of Habit is punctured, and Grandma flies straight into my mind and heart.

"There are leaves pressed between the pages," Gus says, "and a letter."

I haven't even noticed the letter, her voice; I am a negligent spinning thing that will stop now, and look, will hold the page in my hand and think that I know what it is at first, have I not seen this script a million times, is it not innocuous to me? And then the handwriting dissolves away as the phrases make her presence felt, what is she saying?

"It was Halloween last night. It was fairly quiet in Surrey not too much mischief. I was at your Mom and Dad's for dinner—I baked a pumpkin pie for the occasion—there were quite a few trick and treaters at the door, not as many as other years. It is a full moon tonight and the moon is hanging in the sky the color of a pumpkin and it is a clear night. Looks beautiful from my glass doors. The autumn reminds me of a song we used to sing in school when I was a little girl. I still remember the words.

From gold to gray,
Our mild sweet day, of Indian Summer
Fades too soon,
But tenderly, above the sea,
Hangs white and calm,
The Hunter's moon.
Have to wrap the package now,
With much love, Gramma Em xoxoxo"

The moon? Like a pumpkin? All of this the strangest thing in the world to me. Maybe because I am alone in her presence and something is about to be revealed to me that will immobilize me, strike me stone still with its sheer astonishingness. But what is it? Who am I talking to here? What if I were addressing my Grandma; I cannot address her without being utterly innocuous. I think I fabricate a Jeannie that will please her in my letters. But it is a Jeannie of which nothing is really said.

My Grandma is true to me, truer than the most ardent lover, it showers down about me, wraps around me, tickles me. I put on the mittens she sent: a dollar in each one, my fingertips reach to where her fingertips reached to tuck each bill in.

What do I think I'm doing here, two thousand miles away from her? She assumes I am pursuing whatever it is I must pursue. Distance is inevitable when the grand-daughter strikes out to make a life for herself. What am I making? (What on earth is this wall I keep coming up against?)

I offer up this diary entry from so many years ago because it ranges over almost every longing and contradiction that characterized the near decade I spent in Buffalo, laboring vaguely toward a doctoral degree. My guilt at being so far from my family (condensed in the figure of my grandmother) made worse by the ambiguity of my life's pursuits; my preoccupation with Habit and its disruptions; the "fictitious" nature of my professors and myself; the irresolvable tension between work and play; and the multiplicity of my erotic attachments—here represented by a distant, idealized Samantha, and a close but almost taken-for-granted Gus. I had just reached the passage in Proust where the narrator, leaning over to unbutton his boot, is flooded with regret for his own departed Grandmother—a passage that had brought tears to my eyes, and thrust a dagger into my heart for its neglectful intermittences. No wonder I fantasized about bridging the gulf between my professor and my grandmother with this impossibly conceived letter. "If my writing cannot link," I concluded, "what is it good for?"

Sometimes I think I chose Buffalo just because it was not too far across the border. True, you had to skirt the periphery of a great lake before you could drop down into the States, but the Maple Leaf train from Toronto got you there in a couple hours, give or take some time for the border crossing. If things didn't work out, or if I needed to take refuge in the Great White North again, it was just hovering behind my back. It "had my back" as it were.

Something about Buffalo's Exchange Street Train station, its un-lovely brick building, the trash strewn tracks where I stepped down, knapsack in tow, the menacing shadow of the concrete freeway that overhung the train itself, putting us all in the dark—something about that eroded edge of a city that had seen better days, that had in fact, stopped trying to "better itself"—something about the very air I drew in, humid, rust-scented.

It gave me permission.

I had crossed over from Canada, where I had spent my teen and college years, back into the United States, where I had been born; from the land of peace, restraint, and conscientious social policy, to the land of belligerence, excess, and a who-cares attitude about what you want and how you're going to get it. Glass shards crackled underfoot as my new housemate, Gus, opened the trunk of a dull bronze Plymouth Valiant.

"From the salt on the roads, you know, in the winter," he said, in reference to an iron coil that poked up through the rusted floor. He was only a little older than I was, but looked at me shyly through a swatch of prematurely gray hair.

Buffalo was giving me its best performance of a Prime that had decidedly Passed: the days of heavy production were over in the steel belt of North America, and although this was true for Canada too, I hadn't felt it so acutely until my arrival in this place that called itself the City of No Illusions. I didn't quite realize it yet, but it was as though a switch had flipped in me, or a muscle relaxant was starting to take effect. All the ways in which I had held myself in, or abided by my own strict guidelines, I was quickly losing track of. Something had to crumble, for something else to emerge in its place.

The process had already begun in the "gap year" I had spent in Quebec City, where my high school sweetheart and I had traveled after getting our BAs in Vancouver's bastion of left wing radicalism, Simon Fraser University—built only a decade earlier on the top of a mountain. Leaving home for university had been as much about flight as about getting educated; in fact, looking back on it now, maybe that was when I got accustomed to the fuel that propelled my forward motion, that high-octane combustible known as "escape." No wonder so much of my subsequent displacement was marked by an urgency to leave something behind, as I moved from Vancouver to Quebec City, from English to French, from the rain fresh evergreens of the coastal West to the righteous separatism of the *Parti Québecois*, and finally, to America's once-upon-a-steel town, now in sad decline. If I lacked a "goal," it was no big deal anyway, it seemed to me. Goals were for business majors, not thinkers. I was a thinker. And you could not tell in advance what you might think up. And then, write down. I might not know what I was heading toward, in my series of decampments, but I felt very acutely the compulsion to leave.

I will share this first dream with you. It's typical of the kinds of dreams I had before I came to Buffalo. I had this dream while still sharing a basement suite with my boyfriend, at the foot of the mountain where we attended university. We were safe together there, for the moment, pooling our slender resources to pay the rent, huddling near the space heater in the damp winters, eating cream cheese and jelly sandwiches, reading our term papers out to each other, playing cribbage deep into the night. It was a Spartan life, but it was our own little charmed circle of two, where Thinking decidedly took place.

But my dream took me back to an earlier scene, the wooden A-frame on a noisy highway where my family had lived in my early teens. We had moved there from the States to take over my grandparents' motel, but things were not going well.

Mom has decided she will leave Dad because of his drinking. This is in hopes that he will stop and we can then come back. At first her plan is to make him leave, so that we remain in the house. It is morning time and Dad isn't up yet. Mom is explaining to us what we are going to do. When Dad gets up and learns our plans, his reaction is frustrated anger. He storms out, and I watch him get smaller and smaller as he walks to the ravine at the back of the field behind the Motel. I am watching through the back door and I am torn with anxiety and pain—I want to run after him and tell him everything is okay—but I know it will only hurt him—it is not in the plan. So he disappears when he reaches the back of the field and it's too late to go after him.

So far, the dream is a pretty straightforward reminiscence of a painful period in those years—my mother did begin to make plans to leave my father, I did feel anxiety about it, my father was distressed by these plans, which in the end, never materialized. But it was not the trauma of a potential break-up that made this dream a nightmare. It was, rather, the visceral way in which I experienced my own complicity with the plan of escape.

I am horribly frightened, and I make sobbing and grunting noises. A huge sow appears in the courtyard, rooting around, snuffling. It is almost as big as a small horse, and it is multi-colored—mottled. It seems to have a set of udders like a cow. It looks big and powerful and dangerous. I pull the screen door shut quickly and lock it so the sow won't get to me. The noises it makes seem to come from me also. Its head changes a couple of times. Once it looks like a lion's or tiger's head. All I can do for awhile is stand there and watch it through the screen door. I am sobbing I think, my tears obscure the sow after awhile. I'm afraid it might break through the screen door.

I am myself and I am a sow in our courtyard, huge and snuffling, displaying its obscene udders, I'm a sow like a cow, but dangerous, too, like lions or tigers or bears, oh my, and I sob and grunt, the sow grunts and snuffles, rooting and sobbing, I'm a big fat sow who stands between me and my father, forcing him away, through the weedy field to the creek at the bottom of the ravine, with all the other trash. We'll trash him and make a better life for ourselves, but how can you make a silk purse out of a sow's ear?

The dream was surely infused with the kinds of ugly accusations my father made towards my mother, and though the sow may have been his version of her, it was also myself, whose fearful blubbering sounded all too much like the grunting of a dumb, female animal, rooting around in the courtyard to satisfy its own fleshy appetite.

And so although that was the sort of thing I had "left behind," it routinely came back to haunt me, no matter how many times I crossed over to other sides.

I say that stepping off the Maple Leaf just south of the border, in Buffalo's Exchange Street Station, flipped a switch of relaxation in me. For if my years as an undergraduate were about economizing so that I could afford to live elsewhere than in my parents' home, it was also about economizing in another way, about living a life pared down to disciplined essentials: no smoking, little drinking, no TV (it rots your mind), no parties, conserving gas with an ancient Volkswagen bug. And most significantly, perhaps, the safety of monogamy, an unspoken pact with my partner-in-escape. Unconsciously, maybe, I sensed that abiding by a code of faithfulness would keep that sow from breaking through the screen door, exposing my own lascivious udders to the world.

All that was about to change.

The groundwork had already been laid in Quebec, where my boyfriend and I began the measured series of negotiations that were to lead to our amicable separation. The lure of separatism, hotly debated in the French Conversation class I took back in Vancouver, was as irresistible to me as the promise of complete immersion in a language that was not my parents'. While sharing an apartment with two *Québecoise* students, right in the center of *Vieux Québec*—the closest we could approximate to a European setting on our slender budget—we cautiously tried out non-exclusivity for the first time. The promise of Independence saturated daily life, despite a failed YES vote for separation in May 1980, just weeks before we had arrived. The *Parti Québecois* amped up its campaign in the new year, and we celebrated with our exhilarated housemates when René Lévesque brought the separatist party into power in the Spring of 1981. If Quebec broke off, we'd float away with it, like stowaways on the boat for freedom.

And so it was in that atmosphere that I met the Samantha who was still featured in my journals two years later. Though she was not the first woman who held an erotic attraction for me, she was the first to take me over to the fleshly side of what Adrienne Rich had just termed the lesbian continuum.

I had decided it was time to put into practice a new ethic with regard to intimate liaisons, sternly forbidding myself from coloring them with the conventions of romantic love, which is to say, the whole story of exclusive monogamy, engagement, marriage, baby carriage. Even though we had taken refuge in the safety of exclusivity, my high school boyfriend and I had already been practicing a stance of skepticism regarding our partnership, following our declarations of love to each other with a half serious, half joking hiccup of condition.

"I love you . . . for now."

I wasn't about to get caught up in all those outworn rituals of my mother's generation I believed to have been exploded in the world of my contemporaries, despite so much evidence to the contrary, as one after another of my high school and college friends, cousins, and acquaintances planned and executed elaborate nuptials. (I brought my camera to these ceremonies, treating them like the quaint local community events I had used to cover for the weekly paper in my teen years, documenting them in the most flattering way possible, and sending the prints to the bride and groom after I had absented the scene. I would agree to give them these sumptuous reflections of their wedding—if they in turn would not be offended by my continued refusal to get hitched myself.)

And so though I "fell" for Samantha, I was also ripe for her initiation into the art of not quite "falling" after all: her mode of being in the world, an unapologetic and irresistible mix of desire and self-anatomizing, was so akin to the inchoate ways I had been trying to fashion myself as a sexual and feminist being, that I matched myself to her, as though we were Lucy and Harpo, doing their routine in the doorway. I don't mean that I imitated her actual gestures—but for instance, I never felt the slightest impulse to puff on a cigarette until I saw her peaches and cream complexion, her button nose, her oversized aviator glasses wreathed in the smoke drifting up from the inevitable butt clipped between her gesturing fingers. Suddenly, I too carried around a pack of Marlboros, despite having harangued my boyfriend throughout high school and university for persisting in what I thought was a filthy addiction. Now I had somehow gone over to the other side, as if in demonstration to myself of how irrational pure desire could be. I was trying to make it a matter of mirroring, maybe, rather than a matter of pining.

I adopted her phraseology as well when it came to bedding down this one or that: it was how our mutual seduction had transpired in the first place. If I had written, in one of my bland letters to my parents, that I had gone to my friend's for "tea and muffins" after a movie one night (was it one of the Godard flicks Samantha was watching for a cinema course at Laval?), I did not mention that, after blowing smoke out the side of her lip, as much to avoid getting it in my face as to express her contempt for this "last one" of the evening, she looked me in the eye and stated that it seemed there was some sexual tension between us, and did I agree? Nor did I write to them that, having agreed, I enthusiastically complied with her suggestion that we dispel this tension by going to bed together. I kept my confusion to myself about whether I really wanted to "dispel" anything, as though getting it out of the way would somehow regularize our encounters into a non-tense platonic friendship. As though sexual tension was just a minor annoyance to a companionship that was otherwise *très sympat.*

It should have been a sign to me that Samantha invited me into her bed in just this way—since maybe for her, the so-called "sexual tension" was, indeed, an annoyance. Our physical encounters were few in the end (she soon took up with a *cuisinier* from Brittany), but they nevertheless charged my impressions of her with the character of a forbidden fruit briefly tasted, then evermore withheld. And as she recounted in her subsequent letters to me, she seemed to repeat this "dispelling" of sexual tension many a time with others she encountered after me. And so I adopted this way of addressing sex head-on with those whom I wished to bed—just present it as this tension we could dispel, if we put our minds to it, by acting it out "in the flesh," as it were. That way, if I didn't feel like doing it again, I'd have an alibi—the original impulse— well, it had been dispelled. Dispersed.

Establishing a new policy of multiplicity, on my arrival in Buffalo, was not as easy as I had hoped. Some part of me insisted on settling down into a familiar and comforting groove, as though it were the only condition under which my other parts would be allowed to wander. I was thrilled to be accepted into a shared living arrangement that still had the air of a seventies co-operative. My bedroom on the second floor of our yellow double-decker looked out over a tree-lined brick road just a block or two from SUNY's main campus, where I could catch the Bluebird Bus to Clemens Hall, nestled within the sprawling concrete rabbit-warren out on the suburban campus. I wrote home excitedly about our dinner arrangements, happy to have reduced the labor of cooking to a single day of the week, and being served by my housemates on the other days. Everyone should live this way, I professed, since dividing domestic tasks left so much time for life's higher pursuits. But this communal living very soon became merely the backdrop to a coupledom that seemed to creep up on me out of nowhere, or out of convenience, as the very Gus who had fetched me at the train station rapidly became the unassuming erotic companion in my busy schedule. It was just so easy—allowing my body to be pampered by his gentle attentions when I returned from my exertions in the classroom or took a breather from the rickety card table that served as my writing desk; slouching on the bench seat of his gas-guzzling Valiant as we rattled around the streets of the city—no public transit for me anymore; attending potlucks with other grad school couples, or hanging out in the kitchen together on our respective cooking nights. I lacked the decisiveness, it seemed, to dispel the sexual tension with a housemate and then assert my social autonomy, as Samantha had modeled for me. Unable somehow to undo what had been done, I made it palatable to myself by clarifying to Gus that ours was not to be an exclusive relationship, he must understand that, and simply accept it as part of the deal.

Scribbled on the cover of one of the journals I had started to keep again, after a several years' hiatus, was the phrase "someone being necessary, but not sufficient, to someone else." I recognize this as the fragmented bits of a logic course I had taken as an undergraduate, re-purposed now into a tentative philosophy of human connection: that the person you seemed most intimate with might be necessary to you, but they were after all not in any way sufficient. And so it was that Gus became my "lover-of-record" for the next few years, as I willfully introduced sexual intimacy into as many friendships, acquaintance-ships, and mentorships as I possibly could, out of curiosity, as I put it to myself, the kind of curiosity that you could only satisfy through direct bodily friction and exchange. I was only half right when I interpreted the nightmares I kept having about my imperiled childhood cat as guilt dreams about my family; it is curiosity, after all, that kills the cat, and my curiosity was insatiable. Sufficiency was the endpoint I could never reach, no matter how many additional people I added to the necklace of syllogisms that became my life.

Anyone who came to grad school was finding there more than one kind of education. There was the official one, of course, which would grant you your degree and with luck, a tenure-track job, and then there was the "*éducation sentimentale*" that unfolded differently for each of us, depending on what forms of "self-actualization" (the favored term of a sociologist friend) we had chosen. For me, that involved carrying out experiments on my affective sensibility, even as I mediated those experiments through the intellectual concoctions that only a program like Buffalo's could offer, with its chaotic and flammable mixture of deconstruction, psychoanalysis, and postmodernism. The picture might look different had graduate school been happening for me in the following decade, dominated as it was by the new lexicon of queer theory. But it was as yet still only the eighties, and so the multiple closets I shuffled in and out of were defined not so much around an overt straight and a hidden queer. I wanted nothing more than to emerge as some sort of truly complex and emancipated sexual being. But it wasn't as simple as unveiling a hidden interior. It felt more like an end-stage I could only reach by passing through some ill-defined apprenticeship, or as I said, a scientific undertaking of which I was the main subject.

A warning to the reader: if you seek in these pages an accurate portrait of the talented and influential professors who taught at SUNY Buffalo in the eighties, you will be disappointed, and maybe even disapproving. I haven't reread the term papers I wrote for them, nor the dissertation I eventually cobbled together, and only glanced briefly once more into the books that they published while I was there—Rodolphe Gasché's tome of deconstruction, *The Tain of the Mirror*; Charlie Bernheimer's psychoanalytic reassessment of *Flaubert and Kafka*; Ray Federman's metafictive *The Twofold Vibration* and Claire Kahane's and Bernheimer's co-edited volume of essays on Freud's famous hysteric, *Dora*. No, I'm relying rather on the unsteady archive of the journals I kept in those years, those repositories of my Buffalo Traces, that is to say, of the affective traces left on me by these professors, both in and out of the classroom, by the free play of the signifier and of my social companions, by the pot-scented parties, the bar-room poetry readings, the raucous nights at Rude Boys, the afternoons of colloquy at one or another of our mentors' suburban homes. But I'm thinking also of traces in that other sense, as in the side straps on a horse's harness, as though I were being ridden by a lazy Faulknerian farmer, who gently slapped my haunches with the leather now and then, to keep me progressing.

My journals were not chronicles of the real as much as they were a machine for churning the Father's rational discourse into the Daughter's contrary fantasia. Imagine what you might get, for example, if you put together a French lecture on whether one may escape our prisonhouse of language, delivered by Michel Serres in all his Gallic sophistication, with a dream in which I'm "pedaling a tricycle, as hard as I can" while a man stands on the back bumper. "I hardly get anywhere, because I'm not strong enough to pedal both of us up the hill."

Gallic sophistication—that was, in part, what I sought, though I would not have expressed it quite that way. Putting geographical distance between my family and myself was also necessary, but not sufficient. There had to be a linguistic shift as well, hence the move to Quebec. I had my eye on Paris, in the long run, and hoped somehow to make Buffalo my ticket there. Denied the opportunity for study abroad as an undergraduate (since I was a foreigner in a Canadian institution), I returned to the States in part as a way to remedy that glitch. I think I hadn't even realized how much Buffalo was itself a kind of Paris of the rust belt, but it was. It had, in part, to do with its overlapping English and Comparative Literature programs, featuring as they did total immersion in the whole gamut of French novel-writing, from Stendhal to Marguerite Duras, French deconstruction of course, including in-person visits from Derrida himself, and the Frenchification of Freud's psychoanalysis as encountered through Lacan's cryptic texts. Later there were the French feminists, translated for American consumers or, if you could get your hands on them, the original texts in which le sexe was parsed in the mother tongue. Even Edgar Allan Poe was somehow French in this context. And the Beef on Weck sandwiches we devoured while whiling away an afternoon over the pool table at Anacones were, for me, reminiscent of what had been my favorite restaurant comfort food as a child: the enchanted "French Dip Sandwich." In fact, although I was officially taking my degree from the English department, I could just as well have declared myself a Comp Lit specialist, with a slight shift in coursework. Why didn't I?

As an English major, I had considered myself a superior product; but were I to specialize in French, it seemed I would always be ill-clothed—I mean, if your use of language was how you appeared in the academy, it would be as though I had always "mis-be-buttoned" my gown. French was fine if I were not going to be "graded" on it, but merely expected to survive and earn my living in it—as during that gap year between college and graduate school. My French was the French of the hotel chamber-maid at the Quebec Hilton, I spoke it well enough to *bavarder* at breakfast with my *Québecoise* housemates. I preferred the Dictaphone typing tasks of my first temp clerical job to the more rigorous *dictées* of the French classroom. A bad grade in an academic setting horrified me more than possibly losing a job in a world where I was, after all, only posing as an office worker.

My interim life in the "real world" was the life of an imposter; I was only simulating a chambermaid, a rent-a-car agent, a secretary—and so it did not matter that my language skills were imperfect. If anything, I thought my stumbling French contributed to my disguise as one of the common people. I must have felt that I returned to my official identity (if not my true identity) when I enrolled once more in classes at graduate school—everything that occurred in that setting was in earnest. It all counted. So I never submitted my written French for scrutiny. It would have been more vulnerability than I could tolerate.

Lucky for me, there was an author I could study whose own crossing of national and linguistic borders qualified him as a kind of faux Frenchman—an Irishman who abandoned his native tongue to adopt French as his passport to alterity—belatedly, I could see myself as having followed in his footsteps insofar as the severance from home was also a crossing into the language of the great French novelists, poets and philosophers.

I had read Beckett's most famous play, *Waiting for Godot*, as an undergraduate, and had liked it well enough. Then in my first year at Buffalo, when Ray Federman plunged us into Beckett's fiction, I was transfixed. It was partly the way Beckett's prose was performed for us by this genuine Frenchman, who would read aloud his favorite passages sometimes in Beckett's original French, sometimes in a heavily French-accented English. (It was only much later that I realized that of course, Beckett himself spoke with a faint Irish brogue. I had for a long time superimposed Federman's Parisian inflection onto Beckettian prose). But even more importantly, under Federman's tutelage, hypnotized

by his telegraphic black eyebrows, his comic grin, his monkish cap
of silver hair brushed forward into a kind of widow's peak, we came
to understand the dramatic unfolding of Beckett's writing career
as the story of "how one becomes French." Ray was a Frenchman-
turned-American now bringing to Americans this Irishman-turned-
Frenchman—a story of self-transformation that was irresistible, and
readily transposable to oneself. I could have decided at once to write a
dissertation about Beckett—but there, too, it seemed as though a slow
apprenticeship was in order, while I picked up, and put down again
different authors, different genres, even different literary historical
periods. One could not rush into a thing like a dissertation, since it
was to define you, I thought, for life.

But the Beckettian voice was always murmuring in my peripheral
vision, coloring, in shades I couldn't quite name, the prose of my journals. And on the cover of the first journal I began to keep in earnest, in
my second Autumn at Buffalo, was a reference to another French post-
modernist. On one of the Key-tabs I had brought with me from Canada
I had filled in the blanks as follows: Name: Djinn, Subject: Djournal,
as though giving myself a *nom de plume* that was, all the same, my own
name after all. It was a *"nouveau roman"* by Alain Robbe-Grillet I was
quoting there: a kind of textbook disguised as a *policier* he had published in 1981. It began with a chapter in the simplest present tense,
using easy vocabulary, and progressed through the *passé composé*, the
future, the subjunctive in each succeeding chapter, getting more and
more complex, until the English speaker had, without hardly noticing,
transformed into a French reader, though without solving any myster-
ies along the way. The novel's title, *Djinn,* was also the name of a mysterious figure around whom its male narrator circulated incessantly, but
who never took on a palpable identity. An enigma, this shape-shifting
Djinn eluded the narrator's grasp at every turn. You couldn't even tell,
at first, whether it was a mannequin or a human, a male or a female.
The narrator had thought, at first, that he was to meet a Monsieur Jean,
because in French, of course, Jean is after all a man's name. But it turns
out that this Jean, got up in trench coat, sunglasses, and felt slouch
hat was an American, and therefore, a woman. And so, in this French
textbook that takes inter-linguistic ambiguity as its plot material, the

name must be spelled out as the titular "Djinn" to emphasize that the "J" at the beginning must be pronounced as in English, with that hard aveolar "D" sound before the fricative takes over.

If I identified with Robbe-Grillet's "Djinn" it was partly because of the delight I had taken for years in the very thought that if you put me in a French context, my name made me a man—*Jean*—and maybe conferred upon me all of the privileges thereof. And then, by identifying myself as "Djinn" on the cover of my "Djournal," it was a way of translating myself back into a woman again, but a different kind of woman, a woman who was also a magical creature, the Djinn of French Orientalism, supernatural and all powerful, a Djinn that would confront you. I was ready to cash in the Bimbo "I-Dream-Of-Jeannie" image from American television of my youth for this more gender-ambiguous Djinn of the *nouveau roman*—and yet, even that Jean-Djinn was so entrapped in Robbe-Grillet's already passé narrator's voice that identification was a stretch.

Some pages into the novel, the narrator complains about modern "girls" who are "no longer the way they used to be. They play gangsters, nowadays, just like boys. They organize rackets. They plan holdups and practice karate. They will rape defenseless adolescents. They wear pants . . . Life has become impossible." This seems very quaint to me, and would have then too—to read in 1981 that girls are not what they used to be—in part because they wear pants, as though the era of the enforced skirt had not disappeared thirty years earlier, even before my mother's generation. Was France really so backwards that a woman in trousers would cause such consternation in the narrator of a postmodern novel? And what about that absurd idea that the modern girl will seek to "rape" an adolescent? This was making the *nouveau roman* seem neither new nor novel, at least not where sexual politics was concerned. And yet, Robbe Grillet seemed to be asserting sex as the new arena for world struggle. His narrator, abashed at having this woman, Djinn, for his boss (imagine that! A woman as a boss! well, he'll go along with it, despite its unorthodoxy) shares with her a thought that he has been harboring, that "*La lutte des sexes est le moteur de l'histoire*" or as the English version has it, "The struggle of the sexes is the motor of history." In this new era, apparently, Marx's dictum about the class struggle was to be translated into the battle of the sexes. The sexual was, after all, the focus of my own politics, even if I had only the most rudimentary training, and almost no mentorship in this area; and at the same time, *j'ignorais* the class conflict that hovered beneath the surface of my interactions with the academic professionals who were about to define my future world for me.

How striking it is to me, looking over that last sentence, to see that as I revisit the whole ambience of "Frenchness" and what it was to me, I slipped into one of my old habits of those days. You saw that interjection of the French word for an English one that could have served perhaps just as well. It wasn't just that I adopted the affectation of peppering my English with the odd word *en français* (though I'm sure I did that often enough)—it was, rather, that certain words were like "switch-points" for me, between English and French, but also between other ambiguous binaries that marked my existence. Words like "*ignorer*" as in the sentence above, for instance, with its willful sense of not paying heed to something in English, "to ignore," but its less voluntary quality in French, as in being merely oblivious to something, to be ignorant of it, those were the switch words, carrying with them the double load of their sense in both languages. To say that "*j'ignorais*" the class conflict at school, to express it like this would, at that time, have been an unconscious mode of self-preservation. Something in me, I see now, wanted to ignore willfully what would do me no good.

And so to sign my "Djournal" as "Djinn" was to acknowledge that my own name was one of these switch-words, with multiple versions of itself depending on how you pronounced it or how you spelled it: Jean or *Jean* or Djinn or *Jeanne* or Gene, back and forth I went from the masculine to the feminine, the foreign to the familial. I was myself a switch-point, with a compulsion to cross, but no clear idea of which track to take.

This adoption, if only briefly, of Djinn as my djournaling name was a sign, too, of how self-conscious I felt as I made my tentative move to resume the keeping of a regular diary. In the summer before Buffalo, while still in Canada, I had made a false start, scribbling a few pages before leaving the rest of a notebook blank. Canada was in the throes of a protracted mail strike, and the U.S. postal workers were threatening to walk off as well, so I portrayed my attempted return to journal-keeping as though it were the only option left to me where correspondence was concerned. "Who to write to when there is a postal strike—maybe in BOTH countries, North and South of the border?" I posed it like a conundrum.

The obvious answer of course is to write to oneself—and that is precisely what I intend to do. Especially since it has been so long since I've heard from myself. You Jeannie—why haven't you written in so long? Why I remember when you wrote regularly, once a day, in a notebook just like this—at least 2 or 3 pages a day. And why did you stop?

I wearied almost immediately of the conceit, "But this is absurd," I berated myself. "Who am I, addressing myself to Jeannie like this? I'm Jeannie myself—I'm both guilty of not writing and forlorn at not receiving."

It was almost as though I needed to be cut off from my usual correspondents, my mother and father, my sister and brother, my Canadian grandmother, my Coloradan grandmother, my college professors, my Vancouver friends, new friends and lovers whom I'd hooked up with in Quebec before they returned to Toronto, Chicago, Argentina—I needed to be literally deprived of the ongoing conversations I had been having with them all before I could lend an ear to my own voice.

And it wasn't that I was melancholy or lonely, in need of a therapeutic outlet for my pain. The first subject I seized upon, in this return to journal-writing, was a mysterious sense of well-being that I could not explain. "Sometimes," I wrote, "in fact often, I am struck by a sensation of complete and peaceful happiness. Like a perfect contentedness with myself, with where I am, what I'm doing, the very objects by which I'm surrounded."

It is exhilarating and irrational, inexplicable, and happens often when I am alone. At the same time, I am aware that it is a fleeting sensation—or rather I suspect that it is a trick of youth, that it is the disgusting complacency of being young and finding that one can indeed survive.

This sensation was "the opposite of depression, of tedium, of impatience, of anxiety, of claustrophobia, of fear." I'd be walking, and suddenly I'd be "filled with a sense of fearlessness—and yet that can only be illusory since at any moment I might be mugged or raped or struck down by a passing truck. So why should I feel so fearless?" I wondered. Why did the prospect of dying not seem to make any difference to me? And then, as though to ward off an evil spirit, I undermined this happy feeling by imagining myself befallen by a calamity:

You see, I'm just going to forget dying altogether, and then it will all explode. Somebody will die. Or get sick. And that's when I will look back with contemptuous disgust and scorn on my former self who thought she was so fearless. It's easy to be in love with the world, right from the dirty wrappers on the cracked sidewalk to the rustling of the trees in the afternoon, from the ringing of the refrigerator to a cat's eyes gleaming in a ditch—when none of it all has ever been cruel to me.

I decided that I must not be "too smug about it all, keep my mouth shut, and bear in mind that charm is temporary, misfortune is bound to strike sooner or later and *then* we'll see what I know about living."

If I hoped to make journal-writing as regular a practice as my letter-writing routine, then it wasn't so simple a matter as asserting myself as a regular among the recipients of my correspondence. While those who had been too long "hidden from history"—women, people of color, gays and lesbians—struggled to find their literary voice, and to make it heard around the world, I had declared that I was "straining to hear a voice that is not mine when I write." And I wonder if, somehow, my prodigious letter-writing was related to this hope that I might surprise myself with a voice that I did not recognize. I wrote all those letters to stay connected to be sure, but it was also a way of anxiously mollifying a past while attempting to fashion myself into someone else—or rather, into a being defined not by one alliance only, but by so many alliances that I could never be atrophied by familiarity. So even as I wrote, in the balmy early days of October, that Gus and I had dressed up and gone out for Italian food at *La Stanza's* to celebrate the one-year anniversary of our "first kiss," I had also just posted letters to a dizzying array of others with whom kisses, and more, had been exchanged over that same year.

There was the European journalist whom I had met within a month of having arrived in Buffalo, during my first and only visit to the campus Gay and Lesbian Drop-In center. I had been astonished at my luck that night, to have locked eyes with a freckled Scandinavian Beauty almost as soon as I came in the door—let's call her Ingrid, after Ingrid Bergman, about whom I'd had many an erotic dream. We nibbled a cookie, then she whisked me out of there and off to Buffalo's only women's bar at the time, M.C. Comptons, where she promptly cut her finger on a bathroom door. We did not let the rest of the evening waiting for a tetanus shot at the Emergency Room deter us from whiling away the next few nights together, swigging white wine, and then tumbling onto my mattress in a daze. Each year, we'd meet up again when she returned to the Buffalo suburb where her family lived, and cheer on Martina during the US Tennis Opens, or sunbathe with her sisters and mother at one of the nearby Lake beaches, or burrow under the covers in her childhood bedroom, before she returned to the European world of journalism where she had made her life.

I also corresponded with three or four different friends from my Vancouver past, guys with whom there had been an attraction when I was in college, or who had been my friends, or who had graded my papers as a teaching assistant—now I was the one on visits home, during Winter or Summer break, crossing over into a fleshly knowledge of these people whom I'd refrained from drawing near when I was staying true to my high school sweetheart. It was all a belated adventure with these friends, a sexual "do-over" for each one, though I never intended for any of it to lead anywhere. Still, with most of them, too, there was an extension, in letters, of what had begun in bed. "Either I see no one at all," I wrote during one visit to Vancouver, "or everyone all at once or in rapid succession. There is at least one new one every year until I have more people in my heart than I know what to do with."

What made it even more difficult was the proximity of my mother through these visits. My official story with her was, of course, that Gus and I were in a "stable relationship" together—the rest were only platonic friends. But she couldn't help but wonder at my busy social schedule. "Where is he going to sleep," she asked about one unidentified guy—I don't even recall the circumstances, nor my answer to her—but

I dwelt instead on what her question meant about her desire to know me, and my inability to allow her that knowledge. "See," I wrote, "she suspects that he, too, is a lover of mine—it's the not being able to tell her everything that bothers me maybe. If she knew how much in the sensual I live, how 'accessible' I am, how entangled with so many other people . . . she would worry about me and disapprove." I wondered to myself why I needed her approval, but was it perhaps myself I was trying to convince? I had been contemplating a more conventional settling down with Gus, but then interrupted this train of thought: "No—I want to keep my own room, my own place. I love many different people in many different ways and I am true to my feelings towards them. Sounds hollow. What about 'Trust me, but don't depend on me,' and is that not what I do with other people?" I couldn't convince myself, so how could I convince my mother?

As always, the drama in my personal life seemed shadowed, or even abetted, by the literary thematics I kept encountering in my classes. During this same year, my second year of intense course-work, the complex intellectual terrain populated by my professors began to show its contours. First of all, I think I was only partly aware of what it meant to be in such a "male-dominated" environment. If our professors were offering us a model of academe, then the ratio of phallus to invagination was not an encouraging one. For every Claire Kahane or Carol Jacobs, there were a dozen men, bearded or clean-shaven, stooping or stalking, clad in jeans or sporting a tie: just off the top of my head I recall Leslie Fiedler, Bob Creeley, Rodolphe Gasché, Ray Federman, J.M. Coetzee, just to mention a few luminaries, or Charlie Bernheimer, Norman Holland, Jim Swan, Dave Willbern, to list some of the psychoanalytically inclined, or Bob Daly, Ken Dauber, Marty Pops, Neil Schmitz if you want some Americanists, or Bruce Jackson, Roy Roussel, William Warner, Henry Sussman, Art Efron, Irving Feldman, Dick Fly, Irving Massey, Howard Wolf, Fred See, Mark Schechner, Alan Spiegel, Bob Edwards . . . but I see I've already exceeded my estimate of twelve to one. The same was not true for the graduate student population, where I had my pick from about an equal count of male and female classmates alike, whether it be for friendship, study group, romance or hijinks. Where were we destined, then, all these "co-ed" doctoral candidates?

Were we expecting that departments like SUNY Buffalo were suddenly going to change their hiring patterns? I could count only one female friend who frankly admitted to having entered grad school in search of her "MRS" degree, and she seemed like an anomaly. The fact that, as things panned out in the end, most of the women I knew found quite acceptable niches in the academy, all across North America, was not in any way something we could have known ahead of time.

And so, as you might imagine, I was not going to be getting a feminist education, beyond my one course in "Women and Literature" with Claire Kahane, which is not to say that questions of gender and sexuality were absent from the courses I took from the array of male professors that far outnumbered their women colleagues. This was the case, for instance, in the Virginia Woolf seminar I was taking with Charlie Bernheimer.

An essay on *To the Lighthouse* was due within days, and I had barely begun to sketch it out. "Odious, odious period," I wrote, "when the paper hasn't even been conceived yet, and time has run out so alarmingly fast. I will muse about it to myself here, where anything is permitted, so that maybe the rushing together of things, the conviction will come even on this page." Pages and pages followed, still with no conviction, as I posed myself questions about what one was to do with the novel's "world of women versus men" and our "different expectations for both of them." But that didn't seem to be the crux of the matter, I decided, this opposition of women to men. "Is there a division more important than this one? There are those who ask for sympathy, and those who give it when asked." It was the men who seemed to have the right to ask for it, and the women who were expected to give it, of course. And so I thought maybe I ought to investigate every instance in which Mrs. Ramsay, the mother of the novel, administered to some kind of need. For her son, she was a "transformational object," since she "held the promise of a desired metamorphosis" and embodied "the adventure of going to the lighthouse." Having put into play this concept cribbed from the psychoanalytic article by Bollas we had been given, I then tried to decide whether being this transformational object was good or bad, whether we approved or disapproved, because it seemed we were required to "come to a judgment in the end, a judgment of Mrs. Ramsay." But why was it all about judgment?

*This is the track I've been put on by Charlie Bernheimer—who ap-
proaches this novel by asking "How do we feel about Mrs. Ramsay?"
He describes how he feels, how his feelings have changed. First he
liked her, would have desired her as a mother. Then he changed his
mind, and didn't like her. Why? Because she manipulates people in
order to gratify a need in herself (to be reflected flatteringly). Her
narcissism is one that feeds off other people.*

Now my hackles were up, as was almost always the case in the seminars I took. For whom or what had she "fed" off of, I wondered? I
recalled that my professor had pointed out her "mania to marry everyone off, when this is clearly bad advice." And somehow, her "feeling
of well-being—of having created the thing that endures—at the end
of the dinner. A feeling which comes upon her in solitude as well, but
which she has SHARED this time"—that is, shared through the or-
chestration of the sumptuous evening. That, too, had somehow been
evidence of her narcissism.

I don't think I connected this image of Mrs. Ramsay reveling in her
"feeling of well-being" with those similar episodes I had recorded in
my own diary. But having conjured that passage for myself again, after Bernheimer had drawn attention to it in class, that scene at night,
when the rhythmic stroke of the lighthouse flare conjoins with Mrs.
Ramsay's sense of well-being, or what we now called her "*jouissance*," in
keeping with the theoretical wash we were soaking in, having recalled
that scene again in lining up the ways she "fed" off others—I suddenly
turned in my tracks. "Never mind Bernheimer's discomfort," I wrote.
"Maybe what we are looking at is:

*A. Having the vision, feeling the eternity, the moment, the aesthetic
completeness of it all, alone—and not having communicated it to
anyone (for indeed—how would she? Women can't paint, women
can't write. Charles Tansley's observation has taken permanent
lodgings in her mind)*

*B. Creating the vision, the moment, the eternity caught in the sur-
roundings, by so arranging and connecting things that everyone
else feels it too. If the feeling of well-being that everyone has at the
table is an illusion, then so is the art object an illusion. Boeuf en
daube is a drama—a ritual in life.*

It was not necessarily an original reading, but it was getting me closer to something I could think of as a feminist reading—taking the emphasis off Mrs. Ramsay as a mother, and putting it rather on Mrs. Ramsay as artist. For what were we learning about mothers in our graduate seminars? That you could never be a good-enough mother (Winnicott); that when mothers failed to function as transformational objects for their children the analyst could compensate for it later because his "reliability. . . unintrusiveness. . . use of empathic thought to meet the requirements of the analysand, are often more maternal than was the actual mother's care" (Bollas); that someone would always be trying to make up his mind about whether he liked you or didn't like you, and of course, he'd probably be thinking of his own mother, not really you, even if you were just a character in a novel.

This wasn't where I took the paper, exactly—though it did end up being a kind of defense of Mrs. Ramsay, doing the best she could with the existing "materials" of her art, the art of bringing people together, of extending sympathy where needed. Virginia Woolf was trying to "expose the flaws" in an ideal of womanhood, I decided, and thus the way to do it was to set that ideal woman in motion, and see what would happen, as in a French naturalist novel. If the "ideal cracks," I concluded, "it is not the fault of the woman who plays the ideal role's part: she is in a way a pawn." What's more, her "sense of well-being" is found "in spite of the role destined for her."

If I accuse Bernheimer of working out his own Oedipal angst in that class, it is not without some suspicion that I, too, was working out mine. This whole question of judging mothers was a vexed one for me. Or rather, if I felt compelled to defend Mrs. Ramsay from a judgmental professor who imagined himself as her son, it was as much due to fears I had about my own unconscious aggression towards my mother as about my emerging feminist consciousness.

Within a month, I was to regret the impossibility of writing a letter to my grandmother that would double as a paper for my Proust seminar; but I think it was even more distressing to me that most of my affective life was cordoned off from my mother. As already evidenced, I presumed that she, like Mrs. Ramsay, would be most pleased if I could reassure her that the security and familiarity of marriage was in my not-too-distant future. The hostility I felt against marriage, and every-thing it represented, was tantamount to hostility toward my mother—or so I thought. Today it seems strange to me that I was so convinced of my mother's convictions about marriage, since she certainly never urged me to marry, never hinted that she wished for wedding bells, never expressed longing for a grandchild. She was never anything but enthusiastic, supportive, downright proud of me. When I had written to announce that I had been accepted to Buffalo, with the whopping stipend of $3500 a year as a Teaching Assistant, she replied that she had to keep "biting her tongue" so as not to brag about her "brilliant daughter" to everyone.

But as I revisit that letter, I see that her initial excitement, as she had put it, was "dampened this week by some terrible news" about the daughter of one of her friends, who had been walking across a fast food parking lot, and

> a car came in out of control and smashed her up against another car. . . . I don't know the extent of the injuries yet, but they have am-putated one leg, after trying to save it, and I heard last night that she lost all of her teeth and she has internal injuries. It sounds like her entire body was badly broken up. I still feel like crying every time I think of her.

That these details had been preying on my mother, raising the spec-ter of what she would suffer should a similar fate befall one of her chil-dren, became evident in the next line. "Anyway, I know there is no use worrying about my kids just because they are far away," she concluded, because her friend's daughter had "lived in Greece for six months and nothing happened to her, but now this happens just a few blocks from where she lives." No use worrying—and yet, I knew she worried just the same. There it was, hanging over us, that shadow of death. That thing that I could not take seriously when I was experiencing those sensations of well-being; that thing that I had to remind myself would strike one day, putting an end to my naïve enthusiasm. In a P.S. my mother urged me to "phone Immigration and find out what happens to your Landed Immigrant status if you work or go to school in the U.S." She didn't say it, but she wanted to make sure that I could return to Canada, maybe even return home, after my sojourn in the States. There was the danger, after all, that Canada might cease to be my official "home" once I had begun working and studying on American soil. I would no longer be "landed" north of the border anymore.

I didn't call Immigration, blithely preferring to take my chances, I suppose. I was going to Buffalo no matter what, so why bother checking up on what the possible technical implications would be. But a nightmare I had within a month of announcing my news betrayed a deeper sense of uneasiness about my decision to prolong my absence from home by crossing an international border. I dreamt "that my mother was murdered and I was somehow responsible." Her throat had been cut, so severely as almost to decapitate her, though I kept hoping, throughout the dream, that she might not be dead after all.

But why was I responsible? I don't know. Perhaps I could have prevented it but didn't. . . And also I was connected with the knife (there was blood, and a loaf of French bread cut in two). After her death (I knew where she was, but waited for someone to find her because I didn't want to be suspected of having murdered her), I knew I had to go see my father—a meeting which I dreaded.

A priest showed up with a rose from which he plucked the petals, arranging them before himself in the shape of another rose—was this a gesture towards the process by which reality must be picked apart and then reassembled into representation? This rose, or this image of a rose, was connected with the murder, and both the priest and I got to keep some of the petals. One of us pronounced that

death was also a recommencement (yes we used the French word), only, rather than taking comfort from this idea, I felt false and cynical about saying it—because it seemed to me that both the priest and I were profiting in some way from my mother's death, and it was to our advantage to perpetuate the theme of death as rebirth. I said "you learned that from religion, and I learned it from Shakespeare."

The rest of the dream consisted in my finding ways to discount what had actually happened, to reverse events, and bring my mother back to life. Undo what had been done.

I lacked the tools, on waking, to make sense of this horrifying vision of matricide; all I could say about the dream, which I had recounted in a letter to Samantha, was that I didn't know what to make of it. Didn't know where it could have come from. I didn't seem to notice the significance of "French bread" (the Frenchness that had already distanced me from my mother) or the multiple resonance of "*recommencement.*" As a French word it, too, was one of those switch-words, for more reasons than one. Literally, it meant to re-begin, of course, a trivializing of my mother's death that I could not abide—the idea that a fresh start could be made from a gruesome murder. But that word had packed into it some additional double-trouble related to its use in academic settings (like the one I was about to take up again now in Buffalo): I had always been confused when the term "commencement" was applied to one's graduation ceremony; shouldn't it describe the inaugural moment of one's education, not the end? And so to "recommence" switched not only between English and French, but between beginning and ending, between setting out and arriving and then setting out again. But not, after all, returning to one's starting place.

This anticipated meeting with my father in the dream, did I "dread" it because he would find me guilty of killing my mother? Or of being somehow "responsible" for her death, by not preventing it? In waking life, it was my father who was the perpetrator, and my mother who suffered at his hands, though it was true that I was not there to intervene in that suffering, that I had fled the scene altogether. But that had all gotten muddled in the dream—or perhaps it was some sinister version of the fears I had sometimes expressed in earlier diary entries, that I would "turn out" like my father, some of whose less likable traits I seemed already to share. Instead of my father, however, I meet up with a priest—a strange substitute, given that my only truck with religion had been sporadic attendance of Unitarian churches in the various locales where we had lived. Unitarianism was, I had believed as a child, the religion for atheists, and priests belonged to a whole world of superstitious belief that I disdained. The closest analogy I could make was to associate religious consolation (death is also a rebirth) to literary insight. Religion had taught the priest to rationalize death; I had learned it from Shakespeare—which stood in, of course, for my whole literary education. Was this the crux of the matter? My fear, whether founded or not, that my literary pursuits were somehow dangerous to my mother, even as these same pursuits provided me with mealy-mouthed alibis, like "death is also a rebirth?" And that devotion to literature meant being in cahoots with its high priests?

And so, here I was two years later, defending Mrs. Ramsay, who presided over the whole of modernist literature as the Mother par excellence, defending her as much against my own aggression as that of my professor, and writing rather condescending letters to my own mother about how glad I was that she was so involved in the public speaking organization she had joined, which meant that she was finally developing interests outside the sphere of her unhappy life with my father. Feminism for all, and all for feminism!

When I had finally finished my paper on *To the Lighthouse*, I remarked in my diary that it was a disappointment, somehow reductive in comparison to the inconclusive but suggestive pages I had written in my diary. At the same time, I was taking a seminar in which we were encouraged to write open-ended responses each week, structured more like free-associational meanderings from the couch than arguments leading to a well supported conclusion. This was the famed Delphi Seminar, instituted by Norman Holland back in the experimental sixties, when Buffalo's Center for the Psychological Study of the Arts was just getting started. Like the cooperative house I lived in, this seminar had that air about it of belonging to a recently bygone era, when ideals of freedom, community, letting it all hang out could still flourish with only a modicum of irony. The premise of the Delphi Seminar was that in order to know literature, you first had to "know thyself," a principle transferred to the realm of letters from the training model for psychoanalysts. By submitting to the talking cure with an already trained master, one would eventually come to know the peculiarities of one's own neuroses, blockages, blindnesses, and thus be less likely to reproduce these shortcomings in the treatment of one's clients. Here, the clients were literary texts, and our goal was to know ourselves through and through, as the necessary groundwork before we embarked upon interpretations of novels, poems, plays. Each week, Norm Holland himself, who presided over the proceedings like a kindly *pater familias*, handed out a stack of photocopied articles on fetishism, or the uncanny, as well as a sampling from the literary world, and sent us off to free associate for a few pages. These pages, what Norm called our "squibs," were, in turn, photocopied for every member of the group and provided the bases for our discussion in the following week. Halfway through the semester, we had reached the Delphic Turn, which meant that now each week, we were to read the collected squibs of one or two of the Delphic participants, to which we would write yet another squib, free-associating this time on the personality that seemed to emerge from our collected Delphic oeuvre. Norm was working on a giant tome titled *The I*, whose thesis, as I understood it, was that each of us had a core identity that was expressed thematically through our uses of language, our activities, our habits. Though there might be variations among these expressions that defined us, they amounted, nevertheless, to "identity themes," and always pointed back to this core that remained unchanged. After the semester's Delphic Turn, our goal was to ferret out each other's core identity, by subjecting those squibs we had written to the Holland-trained interpretive tools we had developed.

Wanting always to be the best student in the batch, despite my doubts about the quality or legitimacy of a given course, I took the premise of the Delphi Seminar as a personal challenge. If the methodology was to free associate, I'd free associate, no matter where it might lead, even if it meant that there might be some casualties along the way. Even if it meant I might myself turn out to be one of the casualties. If those were the rules, I'd play by them, I'd push them to their logical extreme, come what may. This did not put me into direct confrontation with my Professor most weeks, but when Norm included, alongside essays by Freud and Winnicott, a sampling of his own professional writing (I forget what it was) it was as though a gauntlet had been thrown down. A ruthless self-examination produced an outburst in my journal:

> *Realized that if I really wrote down what goes through my mind as I read Holland it would go something like this: Resistance, irritation, hackles up. Mixed with—a vision of myself as posturing macho man "Oh yeah? Ya wanna fight? Put up yer dukes, old man." Father complex. Mr. Holland is a successful academic: he has written WORDS and WORDS and published them all, and he's*

even having us proofread another work about to be published, that mammoth volume sitting on the desk in my office, The I (I, Norman Holland, I Djinn?). So what does Jeannie wanna be? Jeannie wants to be a successful academic TOO. Jeannie reads and reads, like Mr. Ramsay reads, as though she is working up an argument, pinning something down, expressions of challenge, then gloating (when she thinks she has found a weak spot) flitting across her face. How can I concentrate on what Norm Holland is saying when I am too busy trying to dethrone him—no—trying to shoulder my way into the world of printed ideas, too, and well aware that my shoulders are pretty puny next to his because a) I am a young, ignorant upstart so obviously going through my stages and b) because I am a woman, whose fantasies are "mainly erotic," as the Father of fathers says, Mr. Freud, and not "ambitious" (as Mr. Holland's of course are).

This last bit about erotic versus ambitious fantasies I had gleaned from Freud's essay "Creative Writers and Daydreaming"—was that the article Norm had given us this week? In this little treatise Freud had reiterated his idea that if the motive forces of our phantasies are unsatisfied wishes, then all our phantasies are but the fulfillments of these wishes, and that though they varied according to each person's "sex, character and circumstances" they could nevertheless be placed into two main categories: "They are either ambitious wishes, which serve to elevate the subject's personality; or they are erotic ones." Moreover, and this is what galled me, of course, he found that the "erotic wishes predominate almost exclusively" in young women, since their "ambition is as a rule absorbed by erotic trends." For men it was the opposite: "egoistic and ambitious wishes come to the fore" though there might be erotic wishes underlying these primary wishes, like the portrait of a donor to be seen in the corner of an altar-piece. Look in the corner of a man's ambitious fantasy, and you'll find the "lady for whom the creator of the phantasy performs all his heroic deeds."

I was so obsessed by this gendered opposition of ambition and eroticism—arguably the double-dynamo that propelled my own forward motion—that I drew up a little chart, a sort of logical parsing of the sentences, where I tried to work out the missing implications. There were two columns to my chart: under "Ambitious" I wrote "Male fantasy which serves to elevate the subject's personality" and opposite that, under "Erotic" I wrote "Female Fantasy [lowers subject's personality?]. But under "Erotic" there seemed to be an exception to the rule (that this was the woman's realm of phantasy)—and that was "when [the man] dreams of 'the lady for whom the creator of the fantasy performs all his heroic deeds.'" But there didn't seem to be any "exception" for women under the Ambitious side, that is, no instance where you would find her having an "Ambitious" fantasy. And finally, at the bottom, in the Ambitious column I had written "His majesty the ego—Nothing can go wrong" meaning presumably that nothing in the fantasy could go wrong. Whereas on the side of the Erotic, I had written "Her majesty the ego" and wondered if "everything can go wrong."

I knew I had ambitious fantasies, of course, or why else would I be in graduate school? It should have been easy enough to dismiss Freud's outmoded pronouncements about women versus men, and in fact feminists were doing just that. But I persisted in working *with* such texts, not in simply jettisoning them. I suppose it could be argued that I was required to do so, after all, in order to make my own ambitious daydreams come true. But it wasn't just that.

No, there was something about this opposition between the ambitious and the erotic, between rising up in the professional world and sinking down in the world of bodily pleasure, between work, in short, and play, that had me in its grip.

For the time being, I postponed a deeper plumbing of this apparent binary, and finished off my diary entry by shifting off into a slightly different direction. "I try to console myself," I wrote, "by noting (or taking satisfaction when someone else notes) that Norm Holland is past his prime, has written his best, is on his way out, being edged out already by the new and improved versions of psychoanalysis, has been pigeonholed by more than one other critic, summed up in so many words, his limitations neatly demarcated, and dispensed with (hands dusting themselves off, a complacent smacking of the new, improved theoretician's lips; he has just polished Holland off)." If I dared to submit the whole rant as my squib for that week (and I *did* dare) maybe I thought I had gotten away with it by portraying the demolishment of the father by a male rival, portraying myself as a bystander, though not a very innocent one. As if to add a little further self-protection, I turned once more to Woolf's *To the Lighthouse* for some help in my final image:

> *Here I am, Cam in the sailboat between my Father and my brother, both of them pressuring me to side with them—the father wants my sympathy, my flower, wants me to be tickled by his story of the puppy, James, the brother, wants me to remain true to my pact to resist Tyranny to the end—not give in to Daddy. Either way, it is a man who demands something from me. The real tension is between the men, they are the subjects and I am some kind of mediator.*

The question of ambition, rivalry and mediation had already been circulating among the Buffalo intelligentsia for over a decade, ever since René Girard had taught there in the first half of the seventies, in the wake of having published his treatise on triangularity, *Deceit, Desire and the Novel.* I had no doubt been imbibing it, second hand, from Girard's former colleagues, but by this time, I may have been reading directly his compelling account of how everything we think we want, as though from the depths of our heart, really comes to us through the mediating principle of someone who went before us, and who had already infused our cherished object of desire with a value that it would not otherwise have had. If it was a case of a man who resented bitterly the competition of his rival for the attentions of a young lady, then what had to be admitted, in such a triangle as that, was that the charge of emotion, the truly significant connection was that between the two men: the alluring woman was only the excuse for the connection, or perhaps an alibi. I liked the way Proust had put it in his *Remembrance of Things Past*, one of the novels Girard had used to lay bare this structural pattern, replayed again and again: "In love," Proust wrote, "our fortunate rival—otherwise styled our enemy—is really our benefactor." This rival could be counted on to add an "immense value" to a woman who had originally aroused merely an "insignificant physical desire" in us. "If we had no rivals, physical pleasure would not develop into love".

I was struggling in my Delphi squib, perhaps, to come to terms with where a desiring woman ought to be inserted in that model of triangular desire: I had cast Norm Holland as my professional rival, and was willing to admit that the object of my desire was pre-defined by his own investment in it: success as a literary critic, an academic career, public recognition for authorship of a book that would command a readership. And yet, everything I read seemed to suggest that it was somehow ludicrous to present myself as a "rival" to my professor—hence the caricature of myself posturing like a macho man—a comic image meant to put you off the scent if you suspected that I was serious. So I replaced myself with male rivals, and stepped aside—but that only meant I slipped into the position of a daughter, playing the secondary role of a mediator for those other players—Woolf's Cam in the sailboat, caught between her father and her brother. This was not quite what Girard had meant by mediator, of course, i.e. that role played by the more powerful or older or more established male competitor. No, as female graduate students, as doctoral aspirants to the degree already attained by our male professors, our mediating role was to offer the semi-eroticized territory across which their battles would be played out.

Even my Comprehensive Exams were somehow structured by the libidinal preoccupations of the moment. At Buffalo, what we in the world of doctoral studies call one's "Comps Exams" was a strictly oral affair. For several months, you read books from three areas you had defined in consultation with your committee members, in my case, the entire oeuvre of Samuel Beckett with Federman; then a secondary field that seems ridiculously broad and ill-defined to me today, but which just shows me where feminism was at the time: a list with Claire Kahane that we called "Women and Literature" and which included a survey of British and American texts from the 18th century to Modernism, from Aphra Behn to Virginia Woolf. For my third area, I had chosen Medieval literature in English, and translated from French and Italian—justifying it by Beckett's own preoccupations with Dante, I suppose, and spurred on by the expertise of our Director of Graduate Studies at the time, Medievalist Bob Edwards, with whom I had studied the Medieval love lyric. This conglomeration of periods, genres, and national traditions was in some ways the epitome of the kind of eclecticism that reigned at Buffalo. I don't know if my experience of the exam itself was typical, but it astonished me how little was involved in testing my knowledge of my chosen areas of expertise. It was, I mused afterwards,

Like a long discussion of women as desired objects, desire and writing, women as writers, Dante and Beckett, why I chose those three

areas, etc. No one block of time devoted to one list, but we floated around to all of them. Emphasis probably on Beckett, or he was a kind of focusing device.

After two hours of this, I was sent out for five minutes, invited back by Ray, "a twinkle in his eye," and told that I had passed. I declined his invitation to go for a cup of coffee afterwards, eager to flee the scene. It was funny, I concluded, that I had "slept fine the night before," but that it was "the night *after* that I had insomnia, thinking about what I didn't say, what I could have said, how I mispronounced concupiscence . . ."

Concupiscence, indeed. For there was always the possibility, lingering like an ever-present aroma in the air, that the literary foreplay in the classroom and the lecture hall might lead to a not altogether Platonic consummation elsewhere. Oh, not in Norm Holland's Delphi seminar, perhaps—he was pretty conscientious about maintaining the fatherly distance, tolerating even my unseemly provocations with his gray mustachioed chuckle. But there were other seminars where this was not altogether the case, and I either took for credit, audited, or dropped in to a lot of them.

We had occasion to mingle with our mentors in more relaxed venues as well, mostly parties hosted by the graduate students in our rented houses and apartments, up and down Elmwood, or in our own neighborhood closer to the Main street campus. These were smoky, boozy affairs where, as Mrs. Dalloway had put it, one had this feeling of being something not oneself, and that everyone was unreal in one way, much more real in another, because of being taken out of their ordinary ways, or putting on clothes you would not normally wear. There was the married professor who showed up, sans wife, in a festive sixties polyester shirt, for instance—I remember him leaning up against our kitchen table, littered with empty wine bottles and corks, holding forth to a few of my classmates. Was it true, as I heard later, that this retro paisley had been worn at his wedding, and that he got it out for parties now these many years later? I drifted away into the dining room where we had shoved the furniture aside for dancing, and couldn't believe my luck when one of my fellow Delphic squibblers agreed to a slow number with me, her electric hair tickling my nose while I tentatively pressed the small of her back. Or there was the time, at someone else's party, when another professor leaned in so close to me I thought he was going to impress his dress-up tie on my bosom, indeed, he seemed eager that I should appreciate his tie for some reason, or if not his tie, then his curriculum vitae, which he promised to show me if I would come by his office later, where it resided in his filing cabinet. Another professor intervened at this point, and began to mock the dress-up tie, and I was to understand that this new interloper preferred to wear a denim shirt, it was more in keeping with his social consciousness, and did Professor Dress-up Tie have any socially conscious entries on his curriculum vitae? Pot smoke drifted in from the other room, as though urging me to take my leave from this pleasant banter, and off I went to partake with some friends, the joint passing from the lips of students to the lips of their educators and back again, in a free exchange of ideas. Someone may have left with someone else on any given night, it was always a possibility.

Not that I left with any of the Professors on those nights, but I could have, the groundwork was certainly being laid for getting laid. I was of two minds about all this: did I add in a Professor to the growing constellation of sexual partners I was acquiring? Or should I keep a critical distance from them all, subjecting them instead to my rapier critical faculties? I had copied down Woolf's advice, given to the contemporary woman writer in *A Room of One's Own*: that she should "learn to laugh, without bitterness, at the vanities—say rather the peculiarities, for it is a less offensive word—of the other sex. For there is a spot the size of a shilling at the back of the head which one can never see for oneself. It is one of the good offices that sex can discharge for sex—to describe that spot the size of a shilling at the back of the head." Her advice, I wrote, "has been underlying my work this semester, I guess: it is at the bottom of the first Woolf paper I wrote (hence the emphasis on the men's obnoxious behavior), it is no doubt what I imagine myself as doing in the Delphi seminar." But much as I loved this encouragement to write satirically of the "other" sex, it seemed somehow out of keeping with Woolf's other pronouncement, that "the best writing is done when one is not 'consciously' aware of one's sex. To focus on that spot," I mused, "requires that one write *as* a woman, doesn't it?" It was a paradox, it seemed.

Moreover, where Proust was concerned, Woolf's advice did not seem somehow relevant. "Proust still escapes me," I wrote, "—somehow I think he saw the spot at the back of his head, and at the back of mine too." Was this because his queerness somehow exempted him from qualifying simply as the "other" sex? After all, not only did I conclude that it would be impossible to write the paper on Proust that could also be sent as a letter to my Grandmother, what I did write about Proust was out at the furthest possible reach from what I believed could be admitted to my grandmother's limited sphere of reference. Though the queerness of Proust was not the aspect that Ray Federman emphasized for us—caught up as he was in Proust as a predecessor of Beckett, the Modern that would lead to the Post-modern—it was nevertheless the Queer Proust that I most wanted to explore. And so I zeroed in on the narrator's covert surveillance of the Baron de Charlus and Jupien, as they engage in a mating ritual compared to that of the orchid and the bumblebee. Somehow it seemed imperative that I write about the transformation that takes place in Proust's observing narrator, as the moving image before him appears one way, then suddenly, as he realizes what he is seeing, is transformed before his eyes into something altogether different. "It's like looking at the trick picture of two profiles facing each other," I wrote. "Hear someone tell you it's a vase, and suddenly you see a vase, not two faces at all. Yet nothing has changed. Only the way you perceive. This is what happens to Charlus when the narrator sees him flirt with, then make love with Jupien." All you had to do was look around you, realize what you were looking at, and the reversed sexual world, its men-women and its women-men, its secret assignations and its coded signifiers, they would be revealed to you after all. It was nothing less than the dawning of sexual knowledge for Proust's narrator, and perhaps for me too, but a dawning that could only occur if there were a serious rupture in one's habitual perceptual apparatus.

Breaking the habitual was something that had come to obsess me at this point, and it was to the triumvirate of Beckett, Proust, and Woolf that I turned for some pointers on the matter, as I tried to craft an ambitious term paper on the commonalities among their takes on Habit and its disruptions. On one occasion, though not for this paper, I was to cast the whole question of Habit in terms of sexual ennui. A professor

to look at a page of a rhyming dictionary bigger than a pillowcase. He's not yet aware that I don't adore him.

Or another dream in which

I'm clutching a towel around myself and shouting for him to get out. Then I try talking softly and reasoning, telling him I'm very attracted to him and I think he's very nice, but I just don't want to sleep with him. In point of fact, I sort of do, but there is some reason why I shouldn't.

Or yet another, where

I am with a group of people—women colleagues? In a house where a man is showing us tricks of some kind—balancing, with a bicycle. . . I'm running around in a flimsy nightgown, or sometimes nothing at all. At one point I've got two men following me around the outside of the house, I'm going to show them where the loose wires are.

Meanwhile, in the daylight hours I'd sit in on classes like Bill Warner's "Love and Romance in the Novel" where I watched him "draw a diagram of the self and the other, entering into a timeless state of love, as the self makes the other into a mirror of itself, and the other does the same, and each of them make themselves into an image that can be loved by the other. A kind of hermetically sealed specular relationship, a double mirroring." It would go on like this, Warner said, "until the first fight, at which point it is suggested that at least one of the parties has an alibi—i.e. a reason other than the beloved for being in the relationship, or motivations other than pure love—investments in the outside world." I then noted that some "Lacan and his mirror" and "the name of the father" were thrown in—at this point, I wondered if I should have taken a thesis guidance with him, but reasoned that it was just as well I didn't since "they say he's too bossy and coercive."

But for this paper on habit and its disruptions, I was trying to transition into some more existential territory, and had been floating for many pages of my diary on the suggestive waters of Woolf's *The Waves*. This novel, with its several characters seeming to speak in isolation from each other, mulling, murmuring, reflecting each one on the others, but disconnected from any identifiable plot—it was a transitional novel for me between Proust's triumphant repurposing of "things past" for a literary future, and Beckett's jadedness about it all. Was there a progression there, I wondered, and could they help me out with this whole question of translating life into story? Even as I decided to focus on the character of the aspiring writer in *The Waves*, a "phrase-maker" called Bernard, I felt immediately self-conscious. Wasn't that too obvious? I thought for sure "everyone else" chose to write about Bernard, imagined myself one among a herd of "inveterate phrase-makers" all "so sheepish about our little notebooks, yet we trot dutifully at Bernard's heels as he does the same thing." I felt a "painful, inescapable consciousness of going through my phrase-making stage—or my defense of phrase-making stage, or my pretense of laughing at phrase-making . . ."

I noted that Woolf had remarked, a couple years before starting *The Waves*, that Proust would influence her, and I wondered if the influence had to do with a parallel I had detected in their way of thinking about writing and habit. What if you put these two passages side by side, for instance. First Proust:

> This work of the artist, to seek to discern something different underneath material, experience, words, is exactly the reverse of the process which, during every minute that we live with our attention diverted from ourselves, is being carried on within us by pride, passion, intelligence, and also by our habits, when they hide our true impressions from us by burying them under the mass of nomenclatures and practical aims which we erroneously call life.

And then Woolf:

> I . . . suppose that the shock-receiving capacity is what makes me a writer. I hazard the explanation that a shock is at once in my case followed by the desire to explain it. I feel that I have had a blow; but it is not, as I thought as a child, simply a blow from an enemy hidden behind the cotton wool of daily life; it is or will become a revelation of some order; it is a token of some real thing behind appearances, and I make it real by putting it into words.

Whenever I read "habit" in Proust, I marked it with Woolf's "cotton wool," and vice versa—they were the same as far as I was concerned. And in both cases, it was the writer's responsibility to put life's shocks to good purpose, and to produce a glimpse of something other than the "cotton wool" that is life's habits. Was storytelling the desired end in itself? "For Proust, yes seemingly so," I thought. After all, his protagonist's life had been "a vocation—preparation to write his story. And write it he will, in defiance of death. It is a kind of immortality." But I couldn't be certain of Woolf's Bernard, for whom there was no assurance the story would be written, "because of course he is *not* writing it, but merely recounting it once more to his dinner partner."

At this point, it seemed that I had to bring Beckett into the picture. I recounted a whole train of thought I'd had, leading from Woolf's modernist Bernard to my post-modern Irishman:

> *I come to the part about Bernard fantasizing he is lying in a ditch—immobile—sick of neat phrases which land on their feet—disillusioned with the easy strand of continuity he can create, like another habit. And I write "Beckett" in the margin—it sounds to me like Beckett—but I'm not sure why. Maybe just the cynical weariness of the whole writing enterprise—the phrase-making which has taken over like a compulsive, self-asserting action repeated . . .*

I had already marked up this passage in the ditch when, the next day in class, Charlie Bernheimer made "the same remark about the same passage—asks us who this ditch business reminds us of, and I exclaim Beckett, and he says yes (it's scribbled in his margin, too)." And yet, I still wasn't sure what to make of all these apparent correspondences.

Beckett had written a small but pithy volume on Proust, and in particular on this same topic of habit and its disruptions. No doubt I read Beckett's *Proust* before I began Proust's magnum opus itself; in any case, this was the Beckett I now turned to as the culmination toward which all the ambivalence about phrase-making was heading. After those long quotes on habit and cotton wool by Proust and Woolf, I copied out a third by Beckett:

> *The fundamental duty of Habit...consists in a perpetual adjustment and readjustment of our organic sensibility to the conditions of its worlds. Suffering represents the omission of that duty, whether through negligence or insufficiency, and boredom its adequate performance. The pendulum oscillates between these two terms: suffering—that opens a window on the real and is the main condition of the artistic experience, and Boredom—with its host of*

tophatted and hygienic ministers, Boredom that must be considered
as the most tolerable because the most durable of human evils.

Woolf had seemed hopeful that her "shocks" afforded her the clarity to see through life's habitual cotton wool, and to write about it. Beckett's take on it was a rather bleak oscillation between the suffering that resulted when Habit failed to perform its duty, and the boredom that ensued when Habit was successful. There seemed to be no middle ground. By now, it was Beckett and Proust I was really caught up with, despite my longing to ally myself with the woman writer ("why on earth do I want to frame V. Woolf with two men" I lamented, "and in a course where the approach was supposed to be feminist?"). "Compare these," I instructed myself:

If there were no such thing as Habit, Life would of necessity appear
delicious to all those whom Death would threaten at every moment,
that is to say, to all Mankind. (Beckett)

But:

It is our moments of suffering that outline our books and the inter-
vals of respite that write them. (Proust)

If Beckett disparaged Habit as that which prevents us from finding Life delicious, because it obscures our apprehension of the "Death" that threatens us, this seemed in direct contradiction to Proust's observation that we could do with a little "respite" from suffering. Beckett's Death and Proust's suffering were on one side of an equation, with Habit and respite on the other, and so a paradox seemed to emerge: the disruption of Habit might allow a view of the "real," or more particularly, of Death, but it "tends to petrify us into stasis," I wrote. "We are afraid, and cannot act. Hence Proust's recognition that the 'intervals of respite' (from suffering, from disruption of Habit) are necessary for the writing of our books. Things cannot be apprehended and represented directly; they must be recollected—or indeed, re-invented (with the illusion of remembering)." In other words, Habit stuffed us round with Woolfian cotton-wool and thus prevented us from seeing well enough to write; but Habit protected us with cotton-wool—or in Proust's case, a cork-lined wall—so that we could feel well enough to write. And besides, I concluded,

If Life appeared delicious to all Mankind, would there, indeed, be

any need for Art? What is Art, but a reminder of Death, a disrupter of our Habit, an appetizer, concocted to make us find Life delicious?

That was me, not Beckett, not Proust, not Woolf. I seemed to have written myself into a corner by this point, for if Art is nothing more than an appetizer, why bother to engage with it in the first place?

In some ways, I suppose, this impasse I had reached was typical of a certain kind of Buffalonian trajectory: whether you were working on British Modernism, or French naturalism, or American Transcendentalism—for some of us, all roads led to nothingness. It was inevitable. I have already described Warner's mise-en-abîme of mirrors between the married couple. Then there were Rodolphe Gasché's lectures, "describing how Flaubert tries to write a 'pure fiction'—how he is already Mallarmé—in his novels about 'nothing.'" Or when I finally got around to reading Freud's *Interpretation of Dreams*, I suddenly understood why my friend Dennis "kept talking about artichokes to me when he read it—I have a picture of him," I wrote,

> *going up the stairs of Clemens while I'm going down, or vice versa, and he asks me what's in the center of an artichoke? The heart I say. But is there really a 'heart'? he asks, or does it just go on and on, leaf after leaf, until there is nothing?*

As we traced out the double-helix of that stairwell, one spiraling up, the other down, we tried to picture Freud's interpretive method, its layers peeling away until nothing is revealed at the end of the process, our voices echoing in the column of emptiness rising up the middle of the concrete steps.

This is what it meant to be getting one's doctoral degree, in this suburb of Buffalo, in the anonymous windswept ten-story building that was dubbed Clemens Hall, after one of America's most iconic writers. Designed by Ulrich Franzen, known for his Brutalist style and his "fortress-like buildings," Clemens was a rectilinear beehive of intellectual inquiry—form adhering to function in this sense perhaps: that our surroundings would be minimized to the bare but adequately heated necessities—metal desks and book-cases, filing cabinets for holding Curriculum Vitae, Delphi squibs, and photo-copied essays, a fluorescent-lit hall, with the Professors' offices on one side, skittering snowflakes side-swiping the plate-glass behind their venetian blinds, and the shared Graduate Student offices on the other, where no windows diluted the pool of ambience you could create if you brought your own desk lamp from home. The life of the mind flourished, undisturbed by any beautifying architectural or design elements, as we criss-crossed the hall, knocked on each other's doors, shared a smoke or surveyed each other's books, kept appointments, or missed them. Many a night, Clemens Hall structured the architecture of my dreams, when I seemed trapped in the interior wasteland of an anonymous high rise, unable to tell whether I wandered a hotel or a hospital,

> and at one point it even seems to be the academic building where my professors' offices are housed . . . I go up and down the elevator . . . a naked woman is wheeled onto the elevator by two nurses . . . she is writhing on the stretcher bed . . . I am surprised they don't have her in bed clothes . . . I get out of the elevator . . . I wind up back at the elevator . . . I try to carry it off as though it is the fashion and I am very casual about it, but in truth I can't remember where I left my shirt . . . up and down in the elevator . . . no main hallway . . . I feel there are professors around too . . . so many ups and downs on this thing.

A fit setting for the professional pursuit of nothingness, perhaps, especially in the months and years after we had finished our course work, gabbed our way through our Orals, and matched ourselves up with mentors to engage in what we called the "Thesis Guidance."

It was during one such Thesis Guidance session that I had been babbling for some time in the office of J. M. Coetzee, recounting details from a recent biography on Beckett, until he pulled me up short with a terse observation about the verb "to write." I had, it appeared, been using this verb transitively—"like it had a direct and indirect object—that Beckett writes *something* for *someone*." He wanted to remind me of the verb "in its intransitive form: 'to write'—not necessarily something for someone" and I asked him "were we supposed to consider writing as intransitive verb aside and apart from publication? For obviously Beckett writes to be published," but in his characteristically minimalist fashion, Coetzee declined to entertain my questions. And besides, why was I bothering with all that biographical detail, anyway? An undertaking like the biographer's "would, to him, seem like a betrayal of my project as I have set it out now." It always unnerved me, I wrote, "when he refers to my project like he has a very specific idea in mind about what it is I think I'm doing. And of course, I would have felt silly asking him to elaborate on what my 'project' is—what would I be betraying?"

Unsurprisingly my own stabs at creative writing aspired to the meta-fictive ideal of nothingness, as witnessed by attempts that never got past the outline stage.

"A choir director announces to a choir," for instance,

that they will be doing a modern piece next, very difficult, very challenging, but it will allow them to grow as a choir. He hands out the score. There is not a single note on anyone's score—though all the dynamics are there: crescendos, diminuendos, sforzandos, there are even key signatures and time signatures. Just no notes. Only rests. The piece is made up of silence—but a very tightly scored silence. The choir is to work on this piece for 8 weeks, in preparation for a concert. It is the most difficult thing they have ever done, since all their experience has been in controlling their voices, never in controlling their silence. The director waves his arms as usual, gestures to the altos when it's their turn to come in with a silence, cocks his head to hear if all the silence is in unison at one point, walks around the room to hear each individual's silence, and to see if anyone is faking it. In the last week, the choir has rehearsals with the orchestra, who also plays only silence, and the maestro takes over, to make sure the choral silence is synchronized with the orchestral silence.

Or there was the Blanchot I was reading, following Federman's advice, "Literature and the Right to Death," which I summarized as "all about writing, and how you write from nothing, with nothing to write, yet the necessity to write . . . the duplicity of language which is not something to mourn but the writer's only hope." It was just like Beckett, with his *Fizzles* and his *Ill Seen Ill Said* and his *Texts for Nothing*. Federman and I had a whole meeting in his office one day, during another of those Thesis Guidances, about this writing about nothing, which I faithfully recorded in my diary later.

Yes, we talked about what it means to write a book about nothing.

First, what it is—an entity that hangs in the air, unattached to any-thing outside it. Beckett's The Lost Ones is this book, Ray says. But what motivates one to want to write this book about nothing? The desire to avoid all meaning, Ray says. But why that desire? I ask. Why, one wants to—there is always the danger of interpretation, Ray says. Danger? I say. Why is it a danger? And Ray laughs and says yes he guesses he used the word danger. We didn't take it any further for the time being.

If you think I sound like Freud here, letting my patient off easy for the moment, until our next session, you are not far off the mark. Or rather, I was starting to enact, perhaps, one of the fundamental ideo-logical rifts in our department, as was evidenced by my next remark: "I guess I want to get at that sense of fear," I wrote, "that danger. And is it through psychoanalysis that I do that? Or is even psychoanalysis a fallacy if it tries to explain what the danger is? Does philosophy explain this sooner and in a way that sort of heads psychology off at the pass?"

It did not seem that I was to solve the dilemma anytime soon, and the paper on Habit and writing, with Woolf sandwiched between Proust and Beckett, had not coalesced into anything definitive either, but amounted to a series of rambling associations, tugging one way then another, but leading to nothing. Even the title seemed to say two contradictory things: "Breaking Habit Making Phrases," which could either mean that I was breaking a habit by making phrases (writing as disruption and discernment), or that I would have liked to break the habit *of* making phrases. Moreover, although I saw the wisdom of Proust's insight—that respite from suffering was the only state in which one could produce a book, or in my case, a dissertation—I didn't seem to be able to establish any protective habits that would afford me a regular writing schedule. If anything, I was exponentially multiplying the constellation of individuals with whom I kept crossing over into nakedness, as though it would be limiting to occupy just one corner of a triangle, no, I wanted to range freely over all the connective points in a vast geodesic dome of desire.

I wanted to mingle words with caresses, putting my body to the test with the bodies of others, pressing my foot on a classmate's foot under the table, meanwhile pouring a beer for his girlfriend topside, the pool balls clicking behind us. Or I'd have erotic dreams about another class-mate, let's call her Annie, until one night, after a pitcher or two, we end up in front of her place at two in the morning, and she invites me in, and there we are on her bed, marveling at the way our breasts feel when we move in towards each other. A blizzard had blown for days, muffling everything up, disrupting school the next morning when I went out to walk home, making a detour first to push my way through the thigh-high blanket of snow outside her bedroom window, carving a heart the size of a VW and waving to her as she pushed aside the curtains.

Annie was the second person with whom I tried to engineer a *ménage-a-trois* with the ever-tolerant Gus, who was into his second or third year of following my dubious lead in the realm of sexual ar-rangements. The first time, I don't know how it happened, or whose house we were in—it wasn't the cooperative house where I lived—and Laurie Anderson was playing at top volume, breathy machinic vocal pulses underlying her two-toned electronic voice, telling us we didn't know her, but she knew us, and had a message to give us, we'd better get ready. I was mesmerized by the other-worldliness of this voice that seemed now male, now female, enveloping us with a galvanized buzz that thrilled the nervous system, infecting me with the recklessness of the *avant garde*, as I reached out to the friend I had spirited over to this place, and put my hand ever so gently on the nape of her neck. We could come as we were, Laurie Anderson sang, and after kissing me my friend kissed Gus, too, on the other side of the couch, and before we knew it, we had decamped to someone's attic loft, where we stripped off our jeans and tried out a few futuristic combinations with each other. It didn't last long, in fact, not beyond that first encounter after which we were just casual friends again.

Then with Annie, I longed for a *ménage* of intimacy among the three of us, her, me, and Gus, but it somehow turned to enmity between the two of them, periods of truce broken by bad feelings, a day of reconcil-iation, then "resentment, smiles, tears, frustration all in one night. We only see tips of the icebergs now and then," I wrote, "and are appalled at how deep and bulky they seem to be beneath. There seems no way for things to work out—there is going to be loss, and hurt, and lingering resentment." I don't know what I had hoped for; it seemed that I was attempting to force a sexual intimacy between the two of them, for I remarked that I felt "like a pimp." Things seemed to work out better when I just kept my friendship with Annie apart from my domestic arrangements with Gus, and she and I became what in the next decade we might have called "Fuck Buddies," mixing up our *tête-à-têtes* on "writing about nothing" with occasional rolls in the hay with each other, and once, with an acquaintance we picked up after an evening of pogo dancing at Rude Boys. "Does Annie desire me?" I wrote one day.

I know she did at certain times. Why do I want her to? Is it because I desire her? Yes—at least at certain times. Yet I'm inhibited for fear of wearying her. And then there is the unfinished work, sitting on my desk with its hands on its hips like an angry mother. Everything turns into a battle between pleasure and work, until the pleasure becomes like self-torture, because it grows into "that which keeps me from finding myself in my work."

Or as I put it succinctly on another day, "I should get an award for time-wasting this year. Whoops, there's Annie at the door. Runner-up."

Was it this tension between work and play, the ambitious and the erotic impulse, that I was trying to reconcile when I started up yet another intrigue in one of the Clemens Hall offices? It was a winter afternoon, perhaps, or maybe a Spring morning, when I got up from grading papers in my windowless office, and wandered up or down the hall, crossing over to the other side, noticing the door was ajar to someone else's office, let's call him Professor X, since I've been pretty discrete about people's names here, if not about what I was doing with them. I knock on Professor X's door, or maybe he's walked past my office and asked me over for a chat, I really can't remember. But there we are, in his office, and somehow the door has closed behind me, it must have been closed, or how else could we have ended up locked in an embrace? It was not something I recorded in my diaries at first, and I have no recollection of what we must have started talking about, and how it could have led to a clandestine affair, kept secret for reasons having to do as much with professional protocol as with Professor X's married status. It must have been our first encounter that happened in a motel on a strip of highway, out towards the airport, the stereotyped sleaziness of it all affording me great amusement, as though we were just acting out the roles of adulterers for some hilarious sit com. Until I took my shirt off, and Professor X gazed in the mirror at my ratty Playtex cross-your-heart bra, grayed from so many washings, and said he knew it would look like that, even before he saw it. What was he accustomed to in bras, then? Was he comparing my bra to his wife's? Or to the bras in underwear advertisements or movies? For me a bra was just an article of underclothing, chosen for its practicality and durability, but his comment somehow made me acutely aware that another woman might have dressed up special for the occasion in a lacy push-up affair, the better to show off her assets. That kind of packaging of one's breasts was, to me, a relic from some unenlightened past era, the era to which Professor X belonged perhaps, despite his apparent delight that he had found someone as negligent about sexing up as I was.

Only some episodes into this liaison did I comment on it: "I must be crazy getting into all this," I wrote. "What *is* the motivation anyway? It hardly seems to be lust. It's not a natural kind of desire. It has more to do with curiosity—the desire to know, to experience—and there exists an ever-present irony in everything I say or do now that gives the day's events a certain irreal quality." I couldn't decide whether my fright outweighed my intrigue in it all, even as I told myself that the whole affair was "so banal." One afternoon he took me to Circle of Thieves where we had a "long talk over meaty sandwiches . . . then I suggested we go for a ride in the 'country.' So we went beyond the campus, toward Lockwood, pulled over in a deserted looking wooded area, took a short walk and found ourselves in the backyard of an abandoned burnt out house. Dallied. Got back to campus around 4:30." There were so many ways to dramatize the secrecy. As I transitioned from one cahier to the next, I commented on the opening page that I was in an "evasive mood here," not wanting to "embarrass myself on page 1. This will give the snooper time to get bored and give up before reading on to anything more important." But then, I reflected, it might not matter how deeply I had buried any incriminating evidence, "Shelley Winters, of course, just grabs James Mason's Lolita diary and starts right in the middle—and all is revealed right away. She knows! Then, poof, an accident and she's dead. Knowledge kills." Notably it was Humbert Humbert I identified with, not the violated young girl. I was a danger to myself and others, a guilty old pervert with secrets to hide. Then as if I'd forgotten all about the warning I'd just given myself, that "knowledge kills," by the next page I was reflecting on a series of bedtime stories my mother used to make up for me, entailing a good and a bad Jeannie, no doubt each with its little moral. Was it that I had "warring Jeannies" in myself, one wanting to harm me, the other to help? "No. It is not as clear-cut as that, for when can I ever say anymore what helps and what harms? I am just driven to pursue certain things, by neither a good nor a bad Jeannie—but by what then? The desire to know? To know and to know more and to know it only the way one who has experienced it can know." I longed to find the amoral framework from which I could elaborate the ethic of my sentimental education, but it kept eluding me.

Although my Orals were long over, I was still attending a seminar on literary theory, and composing an essay on the French Medieval writer, Christine de Pizan—a long overdue term paper for a course that had already terminated. "Anxiety creeps back in," I wrote upon my return from a winter break spent in Canada. "Bob Edwards glowering at me in the hall, waiting for a paper. He left a *blank space* in place of my grade. Now we must 'discuss' it."

The wonder is how I got any work at all done, given how successfully I had suspended myself above any groove of habit that might mire me in the cotton wool of boredom. "I feel constantly on the edge of it all," I wrote one day, "of true and total commitment to the academic enterprise."

Do I really want to do all the necessary things to establish myself, to "further my career?" Perhaps I'm just fooling myself when I think I haven't yet become one of "them"—that I still have the choice of withdrawing from it all. I have a little fantasy about dropping out, disappearing into a mundane, banal occupation—then all my thinking and "projects" go up in smoke; it's as though they never existed. A person says "how's your work going?" and what is really being asked is "does it still exist in your imaginary realm of expectation and self-projection? Are you nursing your illusions well?"

The pull of the "temptation to escape" crystallized one day, when I was called into the office of the Director of Graduate Studies, the same

Bob Edwards for whom I was writing my Pizan paper, and given a sort of "counseling session" as I called it in my diary. I didn't know if that was standard procedure for him, or if I had been singled out for some reason. "He was trying to let me know just where I stand and what my options are," I recounted, "beginning of course with the unquestioned assumption that I take my 'career' seriously and really want to get a teaching job soon." The way I put it so casually, "get a teaching job," tells me that I had only the vaguest idea as to what was entailed if I intended to pursue a life in academia. First he broached the question of the near future: it appeared that I was up for a fellowship from the university, a generous award that would almost triple the minute stipend I had been receiving each year. I had hoped that, having failed to win a Fulbright to Paris, I could use this Fellowship to go instead—its lure for me was stronger than ever, since Samantha was there now, enriching her theatre skills at a Parisian mime and clown school.

Well, Paris was a possibility, Edwards told me, but only for one semester—we'd have to make a compromise. What he really wanted to stress, he said, was that "my priorities should be to build a visible profile for myself—concentrate on getting published, on working out a dissertation topic a.s.a.p., on interviewing at MLA next year." Moreover, it appeared that I had much more of a profile already than I realized.

He knows all kinds of things about me—what papers I have written and for whom, what my teaching record is like (he referred to it as a "solid" teaching record—where does he get this from?). In fact he was full of praise for me—intimating that the department (meaning him?) would try to make things as easy as possible for me to succeed here . . . Don't know what to do with all that. But I feel a little like I'm being bribed into taking myself seriously—I've got to banish those fantasies of throwing everything up and taking off.

Apparently, tabs were being kept on us all, in ways I had not quite fully realized. What I had taken for granted as my own business, or at least, the business between myself and my professors, myself and the undergraduates whom I taught as part of my Assistantship, was in fact the business of the institution, stowed in one of those Clemens Hall filing cabinets. I can see it now, come to think of it, a very particular filing cabinet in the Office of Graduate Studies, had I pulled out the drawer once, to check up on myself, or am I just imagining that? We were not graded in our graduate seminars, rather, our Professors wrote statements about our work, ranging from a hand-scrawled paragraph in green ink, to two or three neatly typed single-spaced pages, depending on the inclination of the Professor. These statements were collected in a manila folder, and tucked away in that Graduate Office file cabinet, available for perusal to anyone with the proper authority. Knowledge of that file had hovered vaguely in the back of my mind, but now its significance, as well as the significance of other systems of evaluation, was being made acutely explicit to me. I was not, as I had thought, a private individual, beetling along through a network of passageways of my own choice and construction, sometimes above ground, much of the time hidden in a sandy underworld, in solitude with my thoughts, or sharing with maybe one or two other companions. Or rather, I couldn't tell how many of my comings and goings were a matter of institutional record, visible to entities unbeknownst to me, and subject to evaluations that would further determine where I'd be going next, and how I'd get there. If Buffalo was to be my passageway to Paris, then some deals had to be made. I had to professionalize.

I had a dream in which I was "some kind of creature that thinks it can fly, but really it's too heavy for its wings." In the dream, I began "running along the beach, trying to flap my wings. I'm thinking to myself that maybe I can't fly, but I should be thankful that I live so close to such a beautiful beach. But part of me is too stupid to appreciate that." Flying, of course, was the way I'd be getting to Paris, so far away from Buffalo's inland beaches of great lakes and minds. Or, I dreamt I was a "laborer with a bunch of other women at a Hotel—we're all maids or something and I am just starting. But when we go for inspection, the 'inspectors' turn out to be hired thugs who terrorize us—by disheveling our uniforms and pouring soap all over our crotches." Eventually it dawns on me that most of the women are also prostitutes, and that I'm expected to "put on a tight top and go out to find a customer." Or a dream in which I'm waiting with many others for a train, "we are going one by one through a *guichet*," (another of those switch words— here *guichet* was a turnstile, through which we passed into French, perhaps?) but "the waiting train pulls away, only half full, while we watch in despair and frustration, silly bureaucratic rules." Happily, a group of radicals comes along and "they take over the whole operation at the *guichet*," and we are told we can "do it by putting money in a hat." There were many dreams like this, in which I was only one among a population of people all caught up in some sort of institutional setting, the pronoun "we" appeared as often as the pronoun "I" as I wandered amongst my fellow compatriots, as we were all processed, trained, surveyed and groomed. "We're in a big building," I wrote, "full of people who have been 'arrested' or 'detained' and brought here."

> We have been told to wait with our pants pulled down because presumably they are going to give us a rectal examination. So we are all squatting on the floor, trying to cover ourselves out of modesty, but not daring to pull our pants back up. I am conscious that we are instances of something that has already happened in history.

I pause at these images of the missed train, of the gathering of undressed detainees, waiting for their examination. Although I did not comment on it after copying out this last dream, my remark that we were somehow an "instance" of an historical occurrence that had already happened resonated with a ghostly presence that always hovered in Clemens Hall. I'm thinking, of course, of that "unspeakable" chapter in the history of the Western world during which the parents and grandparents, the aunts and uncles, even the brothers and sisters of some of the very people who lectured to us, who read our awkward prose, who listened to us grope for words in their offices while the wind howled outside, had been taken by train to gathering places that were not so conducive to literary inquiry, instructed to remove their clothes, and then herded into gas chambers to meet their death. If the Holocaust was the historical "moment of suffering" par excellence, where one's book was outlined, then Buffalo was the prolonged "interval of respite" during which it was being written. There was a context for all that nothingness we found at the center of our interpretive artichokes, and yet it was a context, in my case anyway, that was as yet so ungraspable that it never emerged from the dream-life of my unconscious as something I could have made the object of scholarly inquiry.

It was already the object of Ray Federman's exuberant, wrenching metafiction, *The Voice in the Closet*, which had come out only a couple of years before I arrived in Buffalo, and in which he recounted, though obliquely, and in a prose fractured and punctuated by its own French cross-over words, the experience of a boy protagonist much like himself who desperately tries to catch up with his family, but misses the train that has taken them to the camps, and is transported Southwards instead into the French countryside, eventually ending up in America. That was the part of the story I left out, when I described our Frenchman turned American, our Beckettian Federman; I neglected to tell you that the transformation was accomplished through the exigencies of a complicated escape plan, in which Buffalo was the eventual destination for a twelve-year-old who had missed the train for Auschwitz. Were my dreams, then, the symptoms of a sort of pedagogical transgenerational trauma? The inheritance of an unimaginable experience, not from our fathers but from our father figures, not in a familial but in an institutional setting?

A few days after the dream of the missed train and the *guichet*-turnstile through which we could not pass without paying, I found myself at a Beckett conference in Austin, Texas. It was an extravaganza of Beckettians, the whole club seemed to be there—that's what Beckett Studies seemed to me, a kind of society of best friends of the Master of Failure, a society that seemed both exclusive and banal to me—a club that might not admit me, but even if it did, would I want to join? I was staying with Barbara, one of my undergraduate professors from Vancouver, at the house of some friends of hers in Austin. We were going to make a road trip of it afterwards, with stop offs at the Alamo, Nuevo Laredo, and the beaches of Corpus Cristi where we'd take a Spring Break dip into the surf. But first, I was to hang out at what must have been my first academic conference, take in the talks, get a bead on the latest in Beckett Studies and maybe network a bit, in anticipation of my eventual trip to Paris. I was giddy with excitement on the day of my arrival, but by the end of the first series of panels, my enthusiasm was already wearing thin. "One paper after another," I wrote. "Sometimes it just seemed like I was hearing the same old things about Beckett's work—self-reflexive, impoverishment of content, of language, of style, paring down to essentials, is he comic or is he realistic? Blah, blah, blah."

Yet, despite my sense that I was finding nothing new on the Beckettian cutting edge, I could not shake my customary shyness around all these scholars of renown, whose articles and books I had been reading all year. With his usual jovial expansiveness, Ray Federman was introducing me all around, but all I could do was look "quiet and demure, kind of stupid and tongue-tied all the time, conscious that I am just a graduate student and not even a local one at that, so why have I come so far—just for a conference?" I still don't know whether my unease was founded on an impression given to me by these academics I was meeting—preoccupied as they were with schmoozing among themselves— or if it was just another symptom of the painful self-consciousness I brought with me to all professional encounters. It was partly a class thing, I realize now—my not having imbibed, from an early age, the taken-for-granted assumption that my opinion was as valuable as the next person's, and so I might as well voice it whenever I got the chance. I still carried around this sense of needing to subject myself, humbly, to a long and arduous apprenticeship, even though I was a good three years into it by now, before I could utter my little peeps. But it was even more a matter of gender, I see now, as I consider some of the other comments I made: for what did I imagine to be the suspicions these people harbored about me? "Were they wondering," I asked myself, "if Ray had a little tart on the side?" Was it my own sense of culpability that led me to speculate this, since I was, after all, sleeping with a professor? Or was it in fact something that was being conveyed by some of the people I met? In a conversation with one of the keynote speakers, whom I found "very friendly, easy going, a little lecherous perhaps," I confessed my desire, in the near future, to go to Paris. "Why not? He asks. Meet Beckett. He likes to talk to young women. Oh boy." My pithy "Oh boy" at the end of that entry did not express my excitement at the prospect of meeting Beckett so much as an exasperated realization that if Beckett ever agreed to meet me, it might have more to do with my feminine wiles than with my literary talents. And although Ray made sure I sat with him at a lunch table that included more literary giants, Marjorie Perloff and Robert Coover among them, I was struck by how much their conversation had to do with the cotton wool of life, as I "listened to gossip about other academics' private lives—friends

his own mistaken impression of external obstacles that prevented him from going through the door. And me, what was preventing me from walking through? And had I even found my own door yet?

For I hadn't even decided on which century I'd write about for my dissertation, never mind which author—despite my continued truck with Beckettians. For weeks I had been working on my Christine de Pizan paper, and it was finally shaping up into something that seemed worthy of being typed into a computer. With the acquisition of something called a "floppy disk," and attendance at my first "word processing lesson," I had entered "the world of computers, the 'wave of the present' as Professor X called it. My children will be astounded that I was initiated at such an old age—'what did you *do* before that, mommy?' they'll ask me. Perhaps they'll have floppy disks for journals!"

Before this, all my term papers and my Delphic squibs, even many of the letters I wrote, had been scrolled through the portable electric typewriter my parents had given me when I made the transition from high school to college. I'd hand write my essays, moving back and forth from the exploratory notes interlarded with dreams, diaristic observations, and aborted attempts at fiction in my journals, and more formally composed paragraphs on loose notebook paper. Only when I had finally compiled a stack of messy sheets, with sections cut and taped onto some of them, as I arranged and rearranged my argument, did I finally type out the fair copy on my Smith Corona. My friends and classmates worked in a similar manner, though with varying stages of messiness before the typed version: there was Zoey, for instance, who spread out hand or typewritten scraps of paper all over her living room floor, in an effort to see the entire paper at once, in all its sections and subsections, which she would rearrange, snip into smaller pieces, or tape to the wall when the floor space ran out. It took her weeks to shape this chaotic collage into something that she felt could be tamed into a typewriter. In contrast to that was one of my housemates, who sat cross-legged on her bed for a few hours and composed the whole paper in her loopy handwriting on the consecutive pages of a spiral binder, slapped it shut, then came out and stretched, saying she'd finished, and was ready to type it up. I compared my own process one day to the experiments of a doctoral student in the sciences who lived next door to us:

He makes crystals with chemical compounds. Then he must wait weeks for the crystal to grow big enough that he can see whether it is cracked or not. Many crystals were cracked this semester, and he had to abandon his project. A long, frustrating process. Are my notions about a text like crystals? I let them grow—in my mind, in the writing—and cracks appear, time after time. But in this discipline—one can cover over the cracks—set up the words in such a way that the cracks do not show—or distract the reader so that she overlooks the cracks.

By the time I was working on my Christine de Pizan paper, I had reached something of a cross-roads where academic writing was concerned. Looking back over the seminar papers I had produced, I remarked that I felt like I had been writing

unambitious little studies of single literary works, and there has been a kind of tacit agreement between my professors and me that my motivations for choosing to do one thing rather than another would not become an issue. We call it "academic freedom" I guess, and I'm allowed to hack away in my cozy corner as long as they are allowed to hack away in theirs.

I had been trying to make these projects more "theoretical" by auditing yet another literary theory class, but I struggled with how I was to make the theory relevant to a "crystal" that might take shape in the Petri dish of my cogitations on a given novel. "It's all so abstract and ethereal," I wrote, "I never know exactly what they're talking about."

That sensation of having my head in a steam-room, with concepts and notions and ideas and people's opinions swirling all around me, and I try to read the fleeting steam-formations, try to recognize the other bits and pieces of naked bodies I catch glimpses of through all the billows and swirls, and all the while I'm talking, talking, talking—as if by filtering all these impressions through my little sieve-brain I will catch a few morsels to call my own.

This image of naked bodies in a "steam-room," as though we were all enjoying the pleasures of a cleansing sweat together, our professors, our fellow students, the theorists we read, catching enticing glimpses of each other's flesh through the cottony billows—was this my unconscious attempt to transform the deadly gas chambers of the past into the communal *schvitz* of the present, where relaxed colloquy might lead to intellectual insight? That was all very well, except that I never seemed to be able to make it all add up to something. "I'm a slave of the particular," I decided. "The general either bores me or terrifies me."

The Pizan paper was beginning to take shape, a page in early February, four more by March first; by April I was up to twenty-one pages, and three weeks later, I announced that I had "26 pages out of the computer now. I can scribble changes on them." I was delighted by the prospect of being able to see my composition as a "printout" that I could further edit without having to type the whole thing up again. My half-finished paper could be "held" in the floppy disk while I continued to work on it, then printed out again and again—as many times as I wanted. It was a revolutionary time-saving device. Ah, if only the labor of typing had been the sole reason for the slowness of my writing process. Truth be told, I found writing itself excruciating, the way it seemed to poison what might be otherwise pleasant daily routines with an undertone of distraction and self-flagellation.

> *I am in the continually excited and hyper state that comes over me when I'm writing a paper—food is tasteless, all activity meaningless or at least I'm indifferent to it—reading newspaper, eating dinner, playing Scrabble, riding in car, making conversation, constant feeling of my throat being partially shut so that it is difficult to swallow. Blank expression on face most of the time except when I screw it up into a half hysterical grimace and pounce on the bed or something. Then, I sit down to write and the ink flows without pause for an hour or so. I produce another page or two. Then an interruption, I jump up, run away thinking I'm escaping it.*

And now that I had introduced computers into the composing process (since they were not in my house, but somewhere on campus, and thus not always available when I was ready for them), new periods of agitation would sometimes present themselves. I'd get into "one of those unendurable restless states," as on one evening, when I had

> *finished all possible work on the paper but couldn't do anything with it till I got to the computers. Kept feeling like if only I were somewhere else, with someone else, I'd feel better. Or at a large*

party, wandering amongst all the people, making remarks, flirting, flitting, farting secretly, getting high . . . then I might feel better. But I realized no, probably not. I was just caught in it.

The paper had started out as an exploration of memory in *La Cité des Dames*—Christine de Pizan's fourteenth-century feminist treatise on the necessity of educating women. I had been meditating on my own memory just a few weeks before I started the paper, commenting to a friend that I was

convinced that I can't remember anything about my youth except for the things I have remembered once before, at least once before. And then, I'm not sure if it's the actual thing I'm remembering, or if it is the memory I'm remembering. There are many things I re-member, of course—but I try and try and can't think of an image I haven't summoned up once before. They all seem rehearsed, too well thumbed.

I decided that these were not actually memories after all, since they were habitual and came dutifully when I summoned them. "Perhaps a *real* memory would have to come upon me suddenly," I reflected, "un-beckoned, like in Proust's tea and cookie." In the end, I took my "defi-cient memory" to mean that I should be recording as much as possible in my journal, so that I could consult it when memory failed me in future years.

Memory was one of the conundrums that was visited and revisited in my Buffalo seminars—starting with this involuntary memory I had just conjured in Proust, an experience more like complete transpor-tation to a moment of the past through a sensual trigger—the famous *Madeleine*—and an inhabitation of that moment to the obliteration of one's present surroundings. Proust had built a masterpiece of a novel around the fault-lines of memory. On the other hand, when a woman failed to remember a childhood trauma, real or imagined, it became the occasion not for her own masterpiece, but for the birth of psycho-analysis itself. I'm thinking of Freud's hysterics here, who if they "suf-fered from reminiscences" it did not mean that their memories caused them pain so much as that their failure to remember produced symp-toms that only the doctor could read. Memory, thus, had been pretty problematized where women were concerned, by the time I happened across Christine de Pizan. Bob Edwards had been teaching me about the literary conventions of the middle ages, when it was customary to rely on already existing source material to fashion one's own poems, narratives, and treatises. Originality was measured not by how "new" your plot was, but how you repurposed a plot that was already tried and true. Chaucer's *Canterbury Tales* were all inherited from elsewhere, for instance, and refitted for the cast of characters who made up his pilgrimage. Christine de Pizan's *City of Women* (which I was laboring to read in the original French as well as the English translation) was no exception to this rule. Like Dante, in his *Inferno* and *Purgatorio,* Pizan was creating what I had come to understand as a "memory house"— that is, an architectural structure that would contain all manner of significant historical, mythical, literary figures. But whereas there were only "three female inhabitants" in Dante's world, "Christine's *Cité* will be populated ONLY by women," I wrote.

> But her borrowings from Dante are only the beginning. Her whole
> work is a tissue of hijacked material. The effect of this? Appearing
> to pay homage on the one hand to her "masters"—instituting her-
> self as carrying on in their tradition. And yet she re-models what
> she takes to make it suit her purpose.

I relished the special literary term given to this "remodeling" tactic. If Pizan's narrator, for instance, found that a pantheon of male writers had maligned women in their texts, she would practice something called "antiphrasis:" a rhetorical operation whereby such pronouncements would be interpreted to mean the opposite of what had originally been intended. The most obvious example of this was "her borrowings from Boccaccio, whose Illustrious Women, also a compendium of women, she borrows from and supplants." Pizan's *City of Women* was a rewriting of every "slander" of women that had graced the pages of the manuscripts of the masters. I don't know how conscious I was of finding, in this 15th century woman writer, a figure for the intellectual woman of my own generation. Pizan was, I reminded myself,

> A woman writing in a tradition in which to have any authority, to
> have a voice, one must gather in all the other established authori-
> ties and show that they are echoing throughout one's own work. If
> you are arguing a point—the fuel you need comes from all those

other voices before you who have established themselves in the public forum.

Thus, she imported into her text the "renovated" tales of women she had inherited from scores of other texts; she borrowed the very architectural structure of her book from others who had gone before. But with some crucial changes: in her case, the structure was itself a kind of fleshly edifice:

> *the city functions like a giant body— is made up of women's bodies and Christine's ink. The city is the place where female body and writing are combined—into an impenetrable structure.*

Not only was her city a giant mnemonic device, preserving for posterity all the brilliant and illustrious women worth remembering, it was also a fortress against further incursions by the purveyors of misogyny. Was this "antiphrastic architecture," as I called it in my title, something I could deploy in my own attempts to fashion a dissertation that would stake out new territory even as I appeared to "pay homage" to my predecessors? And perhaps even more importantly—how could I construct a text whose perfect logic and impeccable precision made it virtually "impenetrable?" For I desired almost nothing more than to armor my prose, defend it from the critical advances of my imagined detractors.

Even before I had printed out the final draft of my Pizan paper, and deposited it with huge relief on Bob Edwards' desk, I had turned back to my post-modern preoccupations, becoming "completely and happily immersed" in the essays and philosophical stories of Maurice Blanchot, and determining to settle the matter once and for all of just who or what would be the primary object of my investigations. Two of his texts obsessed me in particular, his "Literature and the Right to Death," which I had annotated diligently, brought to my sessions with Coetzee, parsed with Ray Federman, and taken on several trips out of town, and his story *Death Sentence* (or *L'Arrêt de Mort* in French) that described a woman's illness and death from the point of view of a male narrator. At the time, I was oblivious to the precise context of Blanchot's writing immediately following the war, when France was attempting to come to terms with its recent history of collaboration, occupation, *la Résis-*

tance—and where any given writer's loyalties had been during the war. The question of death and writing was actually quite a concrete one for Blanchot and his contemporaries, in the wake of the execution of a French writer, Robert Brasillach, for his Fascist collaborationist publications. But I was somehow unaware of these historical details, and read Blanchot instead as a companion to Beckett, trying to parse out his parables about the function of literary language and its relation to reality. I went over again and again the idea that when a word was written, it "abolished" the thing to which it referred—the world of things seemed to disappear into the insubstantial, and yet powerful, tissue of language that was a text. For me it was another allegory for Proust's characters who themselves were merely fodder for the book his narrator was in the process of writing. Or, as Coetzee had put it, Blanchot was writing about what Beckett's disembodied narrator of *The Unnamable* was experiencing.

The way Blanchot figured this process, however—of world disappearing into word—seemed ripe for an investigation of its gender implications. For what was his example of how this happens? "I say, 'This woman,'" Blanchot wrote, "and she is immediately available to me, I push her away, I bring her close, she is everything I want her to be, she becomes the place in which the most surprising sorts of transformations occur and actions unfold: speech is life's ease and security." And to be able to say "this woman" Blanchot had to "somehow take her flesh-and-blood reality away from her, cause her to be absent, annihilate her." Death was very much in the air, and not just any death, but the death of a woman at the hands of a purveyor of language.

> *Of course my language does not kill anyone. And yet, when I say 'This woman,' real death has been announced and is already present in my language; my language means that this person, who is here right now, can be detached from herself, removed from her existence and her presence, and suddenly plunged into a nothingness in which there is no existence or presence . . . . My language does not kill anyone. But if this woman were not really capable of dying, if she were not threatened by death at every moment of her life, bound and joined to death by an essential bond, I would not be able to carry out that ideal negation, that deferred assassination which is what my language is.*

I don't think I knew at the time why this should have had such a compelling hold on me, and kept drawing me back throughout the Spring of my Pizan paper and my Beckett conference, the summer of visits to my family, to Samantha, and to the small town in rural Pennsylvania where I drove with Gus to visit his parents. Something suggests itself to me, though, as I reread the tortured accounts I gave of a rare trip to Boulder, Colorado, where my mother and I met up to spend a week with her sister, mother and aunt—all of whom had returned to this town of their youth. I loved the Colorado mountains, where I had spent part of my own childhood, and had been looking forward to this vacation for ages. But something about this proximity to my female relatives, even though they were the dearest to me of all my kin, turned me into a sort of monster. "What is this surliness I fall into when around my grandmother, Aunt Ethel, Bobby and Mom," I asked myself, thoroughly perplexed. "I just seem to go along with them where they're going, wait ages for plans to be made, cars to be parked, more plans to be made, banal discussions of banal things to be carried out— but why should they seem so banal to me? Aren't I rather banal myself? So I'm just silent all the time and try to smile conscientiously when I'm looked at, but really I'm itching to go ride into the hills on a bicycle, or go read a book, or go . . . I don't know. Go."

Of course, as an aunt myself now to a young woman on the cusp of adulthood, I'm experiencing it all from the older generation's point of view—and am thoroughly aware of how boring my sister, my partner and I must seem to my niece, with our own planning, parking, excursions "en famille." It is the normal course of things. But on that trip to Boulder, I took the inter-generational dissonance very hard, convinced I should just be able to snap myself out of the incomprehensible mood I'd fallen into. I'd wake up in my Great Aunt's adorable Victorian house (we called it the Gingerbread House), sit with my coffee and my diary, and barely speak a word to her,

> rather taciturn, as usual. She mentioned it this morning, asked if I was interested in anything besides literature, then threw up her hands and said she didn't know what to talk about to me. My lame answer—I'm not very talkative in the morning. The door clangs shut once more. I feel like I'm the odd fish on this vacation—the

surly, frowning girl who doesn't seem to be interested in anything—
does she have loftier things on her mind? No, we don't know what's
wrong with her.

And that was just my aunt. The night before I had felt "horribly de-
pressed before I went to sleep" since, although I had spent an evening
alone with my mother, I had hardly talked with her at all. "She seems
so utterly mortal to me," I wrote,

> *and I'm afraid of not loving her enough while she's living. I just*
> *make little sarcastic or wry comments to her all the time, or say*
> *nothing at all. And all the time, I imagine I am lonely for some-*
> *one my own age or something—or for someone who 'understands'*
> *me—which is a crock of shit—no one 'understands' anyone else.*
> *There are unbridgeable gulfs everywhere—but I guess the hardest*
> *one to cross is between oneself and one's Mom.*

And all along, I had been reading and rereading Blanchot's repeated
phrase: "my language does not kill anyone," followed by his avowal,
nevertheless, of how "this woman" is threatened by death "at every moment of her life." If I wanted speech and language to be my "life's ease
and security," did I need to put myself in the position of the murderer?
It seemed I was still in the world of that nightmare I'd had, years before,
in which my mother's death was somehow bound up with my literary
pursuits—figured by a priest with whom I had plucked apart, and then
reconstructed, a living rose into its representation. Blanchot's scenario
in which a man "killed" a woman with his speech—it was all too familiar to me; my father had been chipping away at my mother with his
drunken monologues all our lives. Was I experiencing my presence in
Boulder, with my mother and her sister, and her mother and her sister—infinitely regressing funhouse mirrors of female relatives—was
I feeling my own compulsion to write while I was there as a "deferred
assassination" of them all, even as I longed to communicate with them?
"It is accurate to say," Blanchot writes, "that when I speak, death speaks
in me. My speech is a warning that at this very moment death is loose
in the world, that it has suddenly appeared between me, as I speak, and
the being I address".

Unsurprisingly I brightened up on my visit to Samantha in Toronto, where she was staying at her parents' place on her return from

the Parisian clown school. "Funny," I wrote "I feel more at home here than I did staying with Grandma or Ethel in Boulder. Maybe because no one makes a fuss over me, and I won't offend anyone by crawling off to a corner to scribble." While Samantha herself rebelled against her parents' entrenchment in academia, it was probably this very trait that made their house so welcoming to me. Or maybe it was that the deep thrill I felt at being in her presence again momentarily displaced the burden of my unwritten dissertation. We spent the whole day "just goofing off,"

Bits of conversation, exercises, bicycle-riding, muffin-baking. I find myself unconsciously walking like her, lighting my cigarette like her, shaking out the match with her flick of the hand.

This automatic mimicry, now that I was in her presence again, was perhaps a way to compensate myself for being denied a physical intimacy with her. Our relationship, I told myself, was "restored to a realness, an everydayness—as opposed to the dreaming and longing and romanticizing I do in her absence." But even as I matched my gestures to hers, I became

> more aware of my otherness than ever before, of the stubborn core
> of me that will not be like Samantha, which therefore makes Sa-
> mantha so much the other that I desire to have with me. I try to
> explain to her what I like about what I am reading—it all seems
> too theoretical and useless to her, though she trusts I know what
> I'm doing with it. Meanwhile, she juggles, does handstands, mimes
> a person being pursued, wonders what she wants to do next.

While I won't say that the "sexual tension" had finally been dispersed between us, since I did after all still experience "desire" for her, it does strike me that our friendship had somehow become a safe haven, a holding place for the "stubborn core" of me that cared only for reading, writing, cogitating about abstractions. Samantha was all about the antics of the body, spectacle, kinetic connections with audiences, but I felt a "trust" radiating from her that my inward-turning preoccupations with the likes of Blanchot and Beckett were not entirely pointless, despite my own uncertainty about what I would be doing next. This "desire" then, born of our "otherness" from each other, functioned as an affirmation of the "me" I was becoming; unquenched, it turned itself into an object of contemplation in my diaries, one strand of a network of filaments connecting me to others—each with its own singular sensations.

Back in Buffalo, I had an idea for a paper one morning while lying in bed, "thinking about Maurice Blanchot," and the example he uses to "show how his word 'kills' the thing it designates."

> One could construct a kind of dialogue between Blanchot and "this woman"—become her writing pen and have her re-invent herself—"I say I—and as this woman I may lose the I I was before I wrote, but I become the I that flows from my pen. Can Blanchot erase this I on my paper, can you put to death an entity that lives not in life (with real possibility, certainty, of death) but on paper, where a certain immutability is attained, a certain immortality?

By the logic of Blanchot's example, I had decided the obvious: that the only way you could save a woman from being absorbed into the writing of a man was by having her take up the pen herself. He utters "this woman" and she disappears; if she utters "I" instead, she might still disappear, but into her own linguistic creation, not his. If death was to "speak in me" the moment I myself spoke, let it kill not my paternal rivals, not my vulnerable mother, but my former self, the self I relinquished as I rose again on the written page. I never wrote this paper; it was one among a hundred unrealized projects. Blanchot in fact never made it into my dissertation. But some ground was being cleared. An impasse was beginning to budge. Or perhaps it would be more accurate to say that I was moving ever so slowly to the end of my apprenticeship, and in the world of desire and rivalry, was about to meet my match.

At the beginning of that summer, I had been granted the graduate fellowship for the following year; this meant that Paris had become a reality, though I would not be permitted to go until after I had taught a course in the Fall semester. Forced to sketch out a proposal once and for all, I settled finally on a single-author study of Beckett's fiction, resolving to get to the bottom of that question I had left dangling with Ray Federman, about why one would want to write a novel about nothing, and the danger of interpretation. Whether I was to draw from the tool chest of philosophy or psychoanalysis was still to be determined;

maybe it would be both. In any case, the timing of the following year was dangerous for me, offering as it did yet another excuse for delaying my dissertation, for how could I start writing if my research trip would not even begin until the following Spring?

The complicated web of intimacies I had woven around me expanded in one direction, contracted in another, but became no less a source of distraction from the kind of routinized existence that might be more conducive to a sustained writing practice. As the summer wore on, my Scandinavian lover came and went again, spending the night with me while Gus was on nightshift at the job that kept him afloat while he worked on his own dissertation. I don't think I could fully admit to myself how little she and I had really connected over the years, despite all appearances of attraction between us. Things had remained the same—white wine and bodily intimacy during her visits to Buffalo, followed by a series of affectionate trans-Atlantic letters—but we never had "the talk" about whether we should enter into a more permanent arrangement, once I had reached the dissertation stage, and was ready to make "life plans."

Meanwhile, it looked as though the fling with my Professor was going to reach a conclusion, since he was leaving town for an extended period of time. I had no regret about this, realizing that if I "faced facts," I would have to admit that I had never had a "big attraction" to him.

What did I think it was in the beginning? Why is sex sort of ho-hum with this man? I like him lots—and I'm certain he's extremely turned on by me and gets an enormous kick out of the whole thing. But there's no . . . electricity. No fire. So what am I in it for? The intrigue. Or maybe it's the "authority syndrome" as Ann Landers so glibly pointed out to the woman in love with her choir-master.

I had hoped for electricity and fire, but had to settle for the *frisson* of intrigue—not quite believing in the advice columnist's category of the "authority syndrome." I didn't want my sex life to be summed up as *any* kind of "syndrome" in fact, since it would reduce my affective experimentations to a mere psychological condition, a compulsion over which I had no control. But in the absence of a language or model for what I sought, I continued to experience a fearfulness about where it would all lead. Despite the ground rules I had set from the beginning with Gus, that monogamy would not be a part of our arrangement, it had become evident that he hoped, from one year to the next, that I'd have a change of heart, though he never put it in so many words. And so from time to time, I'd resolve to do some "thinking about Gus, about my secrets from him, and whether I want to go on in this way. It seemed to me last night, while I lay awake in my insomnia, that I was endangering myself somehow with all my expeditions into strange nakedness with other people." By "thinking" I meant resolving to end the current state of affairs, and yet I never managed to do it, one way or another. "I guess I'm getting so that I *have* to lead a double life," I reflected.

I'm no longer satisfied with one, open, familiar self. There must be another one that lives simultaneously, face turned away, lips lifted slightly in a partly exasperated smirk. There must be something which is secret from everything else. Only then do I feel present and whole in the everything else, only then do I not try to escape from the everything else, because the something secret is always there, apart, aside, shoring me up, allowing for unexpected pockets of irony.

It was appropriate that I put it this way, perhaps—in an intellectual climate that fostered the dogged pursuit of "nothing," I cast myself as needing a secret "something" that would help me cope with an otherwise intolerable "everything else" that consisted of the usual round of social events—potlucks, picnics, movie nights—to which I showed up with Gus, one couple among others. Gus himself seemed disinclined to take a definitive stand on the situation, preferring a kind of "don't ask, don't tell" policy, haunted by an undercurrent of quiet discontent. And I suppose, too, that he was always a sort of "Plan B" for me. For there were two versions of the fantasy I had of one day abandoning the arduous and uncertain path toward the professional life of the mind: one was vague and ill-defined, in which I'd disappear in a foreign land somewhere, and begin a life anew in some unspecified exotic set of circumstances. It would be a chosen adventure, a reinvention of myself where anything was possible. But the other version took over as a kind of default scenario, should I fail at everything else: in this fantasy, I'd marry Gus, knowing he'd take care of me, he always had, and we'd settle down, have kids, and I could finally give up that constant striving and yearning for the unknown. I'd make my peace somehow with the "written" self that I hadn't been able to bring to life. I might not "speak," but no death would speak in me either.

Professor X had once said to me that I was a person who needed to cross boundaries, or rather, who needed boundaries to cross. This prompted me to recall a snapshot of myself, at three years old, climbing over a chain link fence near our mountain home in California, "a fence three times my height—my little fanny sticking out as I lean over the top and plan my descent on the other side." I liked that he had noticed that about me, that I'd "always go beyond the point of prudence." But as I think back on that photo now, it could just as well have depicted a child who had gotten stuck at the top of the fence, unable either to retreat or to descend to the other side. Not "fence-sitting" exactly, but "on the fence," to be sure. I went so far, and then waited for someone else to take charge, to decide my fate.

Indeed, I had taken up this question of fate on more than one occasion in my diaries, as when I tried one day to rationalize what seemed to be the motivelessness of one's life choices:

The only way to have a purpose in life is to make up one for your-self. If the choice seems arbitrary at first, it will become less so as time accustoms you to it, and one day, it will seem like your fated destiny. You will discover that a million factors were intimately involved in your decision, pointing you inevitably in the direction you took, so that you could not have turned down any other path.

And on another day, I sketched out the plot for an unwritten story, in which a woman wakes up one morning with a purpose, "a detail of business to be taken care of on the other side of town which, once settled, would be the step towards the launching of her life, and the control of her destiny." But there are a series of delays throughout the day, most of them "acts of generosity" for other people who are themselves "pursuing their purposes with vigor and confidence." She is not obliged to help any of these other people,

but a certain passivity inevitably guides her actions, and takes precedence over the original feeling of purpose. In the evening, when it is too late to carry out her original errand, she has forgotten about it and her mind is preoccupied, instead, with the business of her neighbors. Just before going to sleep, she remembers that she had meant to start her life that morning.

If I was unable to take "control" of my destiny, it was lucky for me that someone finally arrived on the scene who was willing to intervene in the ill defined clutter that had become my life, and to make it her business to knit our two fates together, come what may.

As summer decanted into fall, a series of coincidences brought me into the orbit of a graduate student who had been in the program for a year already, but with whom I'd never spoken more than a word or two. I'd go to a movie, and her glossy black curls would appear two rows ahead of me; at a poetry reading, she'd be sitting at the next table with the red-headed guy that was her housemate. Of course, I saw various classmates all the time at one event or another, it was the normal course of things in Buffalo's graduate community. But something about the glances that passed between us suggested that I was about to add another individual to my collection of intimates. The term hadn't quite made it to my vocabulary yet, but we were definitely "cruising" each other.

The first mention I made of her in my diary was near the end of August, after we'd connected at a Potluck. "I had the longest talk with Mary Cappello," I wrote. "Little, brunette, intriguing Mary Cappello who's on the verge of capturing my heart." I tossed off pronouncements like that all the time, of course, even as I truly meant it about each person who drew me to them. "We talked about cats and their meaning (for her, they are too sensuous and mysterious, so she thinks she's developed a psychological allergy to them) and about why I like to undercut romanticism in movies. She probes me. Maybe that's what I like."

A few nights later, at Nietzsche's, a favorite establishment where Gus and I had come for a few drinks with friends, I found myself on the dance floor with this Mary Cappello, letting the raucous music coordinate our limbs into a *pas de deux* that left little in question. I didn't think much of it for the moment, or rather, had categorized it among the dozens of other times in which provocative dancing had promised further fun, but had in the end led nowhere. But later, when her flushed and bespectacled face showed up next to mine in the Ladies Room mirror, I knew something was up. "You're funny," she said, as though launching a serious indictment in my direction. "Funny ha-ha, or funny strange?" I asked. It appeared that she found my behavior contradictory, since although I had danced with her, I had also danced with that gray-haired guy at my table. What was up with that? I dance with a lot of people, I said. Yes, but you've been finding your way into my poetry, she said. So she was the type who wrote poetry.

"She seems so vulnerable all of a sudden," I reflected later, "and I'm so, my life is so complicated and spread out. These are not things I said to her. But I suddenly felt that a door was wide open for further development between us—an endless vista of possibilities."

Early in September, on the night of a full moon, I had her over to dinner while Gus was on his nightshift. "Who knows what will happen," I wrote in anticipation of it. "Who knows if I want anything to happen—or am I just looking for trouble as usual. She's probably too poetical for me, and I'm probably too caustic for her." But apparently, we were the kind of opposites who attracted. Because by October, we had not only started sleeping together, but were already having long, complicated conversations about what we wanted from each other. This lead to much frustration on her part, and much defensiveness on my own, since I had shown no inclination either to leave my relationship with Gus, nor to put an end to the other involvements in my life, about which Mary was learning more than she cared to.

One day, to my horror, she came into my office to confront me with a bit of gossip she'd just heard from Marty Pops, a professor with whom she'd become friendly, and who was in the process of trying to woo her. Was it true, she asked me, that I had slept with Professor X? Because in trying to persuade her to get involved with him, Marty had shared this detail with her, convinced that it would deter her from any further truck with a bad person such as myself. Once I overcame my shock that Professor X had obviously confided in someone about his infidelity, despite having sworn me to strict secrecy, I experienced huge relief that someone else finally knew. It was a revelation to me that the pleasure of confiding in Mary far outweighed the rather lonely irony I had been enjoying as one of the side-effects of my duplicitous life. And as far as she was concerned, Marty had involuntarily brought us closer.

She probes me, I had said, on the very first mention of her. And how I struggled against that probing, found it simplistic and naive; how dare she call into question my desire to flout the conventions of monogamy, how dare she accuse me of being "afraid of being loved." All those triangles, she said, were just "a way of avoiding real involvement with one person." Oh, yes, I could see that one coming, I wrote, but it seemed so unnecessarily dichotomous to me: "Either/or: either you love one person directly, OR you get into a triangular situation to avoid involvement with anyone. Or the fact that you are *in* a triangular situation is evidence that you are afraid of the real, full love you would (presumably) have in a non-triangular relationship." It was all too limiting, I felt. And besides, what did love *mean* anyway. Wasn't I being "reckless and irresponsible" in even using that word, when I was "not convinced it really has a decidable signified out there?"

But at other times I'd have to admit that all my extra and complicated relationships were "bound up partly in my trying to get away from a healthy, productive relationship to my work. If I get myself into an emotional mess then how can I be expected to write a dissertation? So I create emotional hazards to distract me." I wandered out into the hall after writing these lines, and lit up a smoke, looking through the window at the lamp-lit street. "The leaves hanging from the tree across the street seemed to be forming little Eiffel Towers. They had been reminding me of Eiffel Towers all night, but this was the first time I realized it."

Paris, of course, was beckoning. I'd be taking off in just a couple of months. You'd think that this prospect of a sustained separation would encourage us to pull back from any deeper involvement with each other, but on the contrary, it seemed to propel us even more headlong into each other's arms. At the end of the semester, I went to see family and friends in Vancouver, struck by how routine my visits there seemed to have become, full of "nostalgia, claustrophobia, anxiety about the future and death, frustration at myself for only being half alive." I felt impatient at not having received a single letter from Mary, after having sent her three, and chalked it up to the slowness of the Canadian postal service. I returned via Toronto, where Mary met me for a weekend in the city before we returned to her empty apartment in Buffalo. Gus must have been at his parents' place in Pennsylvania, because I spent the next few days with her there, "and in complete privacy she plumbed my depths, to use a trite cliché. Got beyond all sense of distance or difference between us. Mainly my barriers down finally, and so then the most concupiscent, oodly wonderful love-making for five nights in a row—Mary's garlands of orgasms, and my one big one in the middle of them."

A blizzard blew relentlessly, "burying all in snow, wind still howling today and chill factor at 20, 30, 40 below." You would think that such forbidding weather would be reason enough for me to decline when Gus showed up, ready to drive us both back down to his mother's place, and then to JFK to catch my plane. But I left with him, overwhelmed by a sense of estrangement, which was just a symptom, I reflected, of how "alone I've always been, opaque, impermeable."

But then, "Mary Cappello," I wrote in the next line, as though her name alone belied what I had just written. Even as an overnight jet-liner sped me in a sleepless daze over the Atlantic, I was still taking shelter on the third floor of a Victorian house in Western New York. "I miss Mary—snow-bound Mary, stuck in the middle of the Buffalo blizzard—how fun it would be to be stuck with her, all alone in her apartment, just the two of us in her steaming bathtub with the wind and the snowflakes battering the windowpanes, and we just sit there in the hot water up to our breasts, and I put her toes into my mouth . . ."

I'd tell you about Paris in the Springtime, my long afternoons in the *Bibliotheque Nationale*, how I looked into the "washen blue" eyes of Beckett himself, and my further adventures into nakedness with yet new additions to my geodesic dome of desire, but all that is material for a different story. Suffice to say that so many things could have conspired to wipe out the fragile strands that had begun to connect me with Mary, and yet, inexplicably, we started with each other again when I returned the following Autumn. Things warmed up so dramatically between us, it was as though we dispensed our very own climate change into the frigid air of Buffalo itself. Why else would November turn out to be so freakishly warm? We'd been having dinner in her apartment, talking over post-cards I'd brought back with me, then retiring to her room to make love. "Debussy," I wrote, it must have been a tape we'd popped into the cassette player, and then, sometime after midnight,

We go down into the warm wind and decide to ride our bikes to the lake—black streets and yellow leaves sliding slantwise across them, under our wheels, the Ferry street Bridge, trembling in the wind, then the river itself, almost frightening in its speed and power, one man bent over the rail, his fishing line plumb down into a corner of garbage and foam; a couple gets out of a car nearby, walks a short distance, returns. We decide to go to Compton's where there's hardly anyone there and half of them men, but we dance anyway, alone, on the dark dance floor, and a fast, funky piece comes on and I see Mary dance like I've never seen her—this time all her movements informed with the supple bone and socket curves and angles of a break-dancer—she is complimented by a boy who has been watching, "My mother would be proud of you," he says. Cool off, ride home even sweeter, warmer, more silent than the ride out, the near naked trees, the piles and scatterings of leaves, the pink-orange streetlights, the wind a ceaseless rustle all around.

And even as the trees had shed their leaves, I had, one by one, shed the other lovers from my life, almost without knowing it, unconcerned to see them whisked away on the warm breeze set in motion by my persistent partner's dance moves. "It's happening to me and I care less and less," I wrote of our growing intimacy. "Whoever that was so stiffly protesting back there has been shut off behind bars and carried far away—I don't even know if she can still watch from there."

I saw it then, and I still see it today, as a matter of destiny after all, and even began another unfinished story that seemed like an admission that something definitive had, after all, occurred.

When I saw her, beneath the neon florist sign, I didn't know she was to be my destiny. But how can one talk of one's destiny, as though one is already in that corridor beyond the room where destiny took place, or standing on the rim of the filled cup of destiny, rather than drowned in it? Yet I can say that she "was to be my destiny" when I saw her beneath the neon florist sign, and that she "is to be my destiny" even now as I say this, for my destiny happened before I saw her, while I was seeing her, and at this moment, and will happen again and again in hours and days beyond this one. And she is to be my destiny, though I did not bump into her, face to face, did not fail to look away, avert my gaze, as I was passing her where she stood beneath the neon florist sign. I saw her there, I saw her face from a distance and then I did not know she was to be my destiny. But as soon as I looked away, at the pavement beyond where she stood, so that I could walk safely to that empty place on the pavement instead of smack into her face, as soon as I had passed her, making a slight kink in my otherwise straight trajectory, like the bubble in the upper line of the Libra sign, I knew then that she would be my destiny.

Because your destiny is always that which you have just swerved to miss, your destiny is what puts the kinks in all your beelines, what prevents you from seeing what you have direct-ed your eyes at, for you haven't directed your eyes at anything at all but merely away from your destiny. There are those who are foolish enough to think that the battle against destiny can be won in only one way, that the best strategy is to look fear-lessly into the face of destiny and to walk there, boldly. To this theory I have only one thing to say, that it is mistaken. Destiny will call your bluff, if you are bluffing. And if you are not, it will make a kink of its own to avoid you.

Where did I learn this? When I was ten years old my bicycle hit a rock and I fell to the ground, scraping my knee. I cried to my mother, and my father came to give me advice. When you are riding, he said, and you see a rock, you must look away from the rock, fast, to where you want to go instead. If you do not look at the rock, you can't hit the rock, your hand will steer you where your eyes are looking.

You will go where you want to go and you will not fall.

My father's advice was harder to follow than I had imagined. Because rocks, like all objects, have a mesmerizing power, they draw your gaze to them, and especially when they have the potential to destroy you. I rode on my bicycle looking for rocks so that I could avert my gaze from them, test my father's theory, see if my hands did indeed steer where my eyes looked. But as soon as I saw a rock, even somewhat out of my path, I began to steer towards it. Then I'd look away. To avoid it. Yet could I ever be sure I really saw a rock after all, perhaps it was a mark on the pavement, or a snail.

I work outdoors, in all kinds of weather. While drills, picks, cement mixers transform the road behind me, I hold up my hand and wave a flag to the traffic that passes before me. I make sure they swerve, detour, put a kink in their beeline to and from work, so that they will not run into our construction team. I wave the flag to catch the attention of each driver, I am compelling him to look at me, then I wave my flag to make him look away, for I do not want him to drive his car into me. We drive where our eyes are looking. My job is a tricky one, to get people to see me, then to look away from me.

She was not waving a flag underneath the neon florist sign. She was not waving an eyelash. But I looked at her and looked away so that I could walk past her. As soon as she was behind me, I knew she was to be my destiny. She had been holding a bunch of roses in a green funnel of paper.

My Secret, Private Errand
(An Essay on Love and Theft)
MARY CAPPELLO

"Yet this adventure [in theft], by strange paths, brings together two souls which may otherwise never have met…Oh, Jeanne, to reach you at last what a strange path I have had to take."

Robert Bresson,
opening inter-title and closing line of *Pickpocket*

I.

My friend Marty Pops, at one time my teacher, but no, he'd never stopped being my teacher even if we would leave what he called each other's "orbits" for years at a time, my teacher whose friendship was from the start a defining, inseparable feature of his tutelage, a mentoring in this case dependent on a fantasy of egalitarianism and confraternity, all things being equal, taught me the power of pause (poetically speaking, *caesura*), and sudden linkage; of subtly formed associations; and of words as restoratives that could be medicinally applied to individual persons or cultures, some words being better for the constitution than others. Together we might nix phrases like "post-traumatic growth," but argue for other words to come back into circulation, like "brio," "godspeed," or "fondamenta."

By what strange paths any of us finds the other.

And by what strange paths, if we're lucky, we find each other *again*.

When I met Marty Pops, I was coming into queerness, and yet we flirted. I was 25 years old and he was, what? 40? 50? I still don't know. Or pretend not to know, or better, prefer not to. He certainly did not seem at a Dante-esque mid-point, lurching unshaven into a dark labyrinth of the soul, though in his lectures he was keen to point out that Melville thought his life *began* at 25, "From my twenty-fifth year," he'd told Hawthorne, "I date my life"; and that his bud had drooped by 31, after he wrote *Moby Dick*, whereas Ahab, at 58 (who knew Ahab existed in real time?), was "supremely equipped for his final battle." I maintained, in the meantime, a seriously narcissistic identification with Keats who had written his best poetry by 23, and considered all I need know was that truth was beauty and beauty truth. At 25, the truth of the matter is that we're ageless, and that is beautiful, and so was Marty.

In those days, the early 1980s, when the life of ideas and desire and flirtation were all bound together, never neatly severed, when *ingénues* sleeping with their English professors was *de rigueur*, when so many of the male professorate were on the prowl and English department parties ended with drunk professors literally chasing female graduate students around the table where the party fixings had been set, I remember being cornered by Marty among a crush of people in a crowded room. He sported a combination of down-to-earthness and élan as he coursed through the crowd, balancing his small drink high above his head so as not to spill it on his sneakers, T-shirt, or jeans. To this day, I fail to recognize what could have drawn him to me, what physical signal he had read that said, "This Way." Could it have been my oversized aviator glasses? Before the age of "retro," merely throw-backs to the 70s? to something I hadn't caught up to yet, and so, my innocence and disembodiment, for surely I was disembodied. Or, conversely, a petite-ness that made us kin, the small people with big minds, our bodies a type in common, for we were both compact, put together (I didn't say nicely), well-proportioned. We were both contained. I'm not sure either of us could pass for "sexy," but I felt the moment he sidled up to me that our bodies could and must *fit* together, lock and key.

We talked, and from the corner where we found ourselves, eventually slunk away from but not exactly above the crowd. We found a place on the floor—but there was no one else on the floor—where he sat *a la* John Lennon in half-lotus position but with the difference of a foot encased in a terribly cute sneaker, while I crouched in black square-toed boots *a la* Sonny Bono, nursing a non-alcoholic drink, probably Root Beer soda, *a la* Lolita. He wanted to know more about the ideas I was consorting with—had I really said that? Did I really think this line of thinking would hold? Was there something there, there? "Ah," he kept saying, "ahh," as though he were a patient, rather than "hmmm, hmmm," like the doctor that he was.

Not long thereafter, under the trudge and blur of Buffalo skies—a suddenly bright break in the clouds occluded by a bumble of hail or squall turned tranquil again—he ushered me into his interiors and gave me full access to his libraries and to his galleries. I know this sounds like something out of Henry James, and it was, for his house was not so much a domicile as a place where, with each squarely, sparely, carefully planned room, he staged a series of *hommages* to the ideas that captivated him. One room was oriented around the way an enormous jade plant spoke to the ethereal geometric formulae of a painting by Juan Gris; another by the creation of a black and white diamond pattern that defined the floor—could it possibly have been a kitchen pantry or a bathroom?

Marty had hired someone to scrub each millimeter of the floor with a toothbrush until it resembled the domestic pavements in the paintings by Vermeer that he had studied, those rudimentary absorptive planes that reflected the yellow or brown orbs of a collar, a paintbrush, or pearl earring. In one room, nothing but the plush patterns of an oriental rug on which he learned to read before he learned to crawl. There were no paintings in this room, and no furniture to speak of, but the walls were lined floor-to-ceiling with books.

Like a girl in Henry James being given the grand tour of Europe, I entered Marty's rooms while he bid me to see what I could see there. I didn't exactly take notes, but stored impressions, like the feeling that immobile things have no shape in themselves but are creators of the space that give animate creatures their volume. Slowly, Marty's orange tubby tabby roamed past while the snow outside beat steady.

SUNY/Buffalo's English program, or, "Buffalo," as it was known to converts who hailed it as the "Berkeley of the East" was, at that time, a hotbed of Deconstruction. In place of a romance with master narratives, we would be asked to court radical uncertainty, to ferret out historical grounds, differences, and contradictions. Nevertheless, in Marty's hands, from Marty's lips, I could still be seduced by the force and swell of grand pronouncements; tempted to discover my own *modus vivendi*; moved by the prospect that reading and writing could alchemically incite "lasting transfigurations." Melville's Ahab, according to Marty, was a "culture hero and a self-seeking culture bum." In Ahab, Melville had created an "epic anti-hero who did for society what society could not do for itself." We were novitiates, and what was Melville doing but forever finding ways to recast tales of novitiates and their development?

"*Moby Dick* was a whale of a book," he never tired of saying, and we never tired of nodding and laughing, only half-understanding the sinister nature of the book's "uncommon bulk," knowing full well that Marty meant to say the book would, as the whale did to Ahab, "heap us," and "task us." The whale was the wall behind which Ahab toiled, Marty went on, an assonance that did more to frighten than to please. And who could match Melville for his coinages? To have described the whale as "an antemosaic" would require a book in itself.

By his sentences, ye shall know the shape of his thoughts; in molding rhythms, you ignite the dance of the intellect. One sentence folds inside the other, then is turned inside out, revealing a new form inside of which the original sentence resides. The rhythm of his lectures was liturgical; of his scholarship, winding and accretive; but when he *essayed*, as in a book he called *Home Remedies*, his rhythms were punch-like, lending truth to the analogy he liked to make between literature and boxing. Life in a story, he'd say, was like life in the ring; it was life intensified. So his sentences move—one two, one two, one two, left hook, and then leap and turn—boxing as ballet. At first you feel their punchiness as telegraphic or staccato, but there is always linkage, a swaying bridge to hold the chin atop the hands and the head atop the body. There is always linkage, even if it be invisible as the forces of physics that enable an acrobat to land safely on his feet and restore an audience's breath to bodies.

"The two most visible 'solutions' of the sixties were provided by those specters at the psychic edge: the hippie and the militarist," Marty had written in *Home Remedies*:

> For the hippie the way free was through drugs, hair, and clothes—the beatnikery of the fifties exacerbated. Drugs widen the margin because they extend the boundaries of the psychic being; hair widens the margin because it literally extends the boundaries of the physical being. As collage restores three-dimensionality to a two-dimensional plane, drugs and hair restore 'dimensionality' to one-dimensional man.

You begin to hear what I mean.

"He taught me generously and freely" is how Robert Bresson's Michel in *Pickpocket* describes the lessons learned, the sleight of hand, the elegant, outlandish tricks of the trade gifted to him by a fellow pickpocket who appears suddenly in his doorway, beckoning with a glance and a whistle-less call. The transference of illicit trade, and with it the implication of erotic ways and means and climaxes, might color all good teaching at a core. All lessons worth learning are learned in the dark.

"Well, you've made a great difference for me," Miss Tina offers poignantly to the unnamed predator-narrator of Henry James's *The Aspern Papers*. Being changed, being touched, being taught exacts a cost, and the difference made in this case was not reciprocal. Her "well" and its elliptical comma is pregnant with meaning, as if to say, "well, even though I'd like to murder you," "well, even though you've cut me to the quick," "well, even though you've been meaner than mean to me," because of your instruction, I have come into my own. The difference you made for me was one of differentiation.

Each life contains such a host of teachers (if we're open to instruction, and if we're lucky) that the issuance of a self—its never final form, its beautiful immanence, its ungainly growth—collects inside the range of types of teachers and what they did for or to us. For me there was the fountain bringer, the diver, the adventurer, the inspirer, the releaser, the de-railer, the leavener, the crush; the violator, the rain maker, the sparring partner, the mixer (she who fruitfully mixes one up), the thief.

Those for whom we bloom must enjoy a separate category even though blooming isn't always required in order to learn. But it is momentous; it is intense, and it feels like a sacred share.

One day, on a lunch date with Marty that seemed no different from other days we shared, he sprang a question. We were discussing whether a good relationship could be gauged by how a couple kept pace with one another in an art museum when he offered me a gallant-sounding synecdoche that went: "I want to have a relationship with you. Do you want to have a relationship with me?" Or maybe the operative verb was, "I'd like...would you like?" The question required that I tell a truth without confessing, and in that, suggested we perhaps were not as intimate as we had thought, so I answered Marty, generously, freely, that I had found myself drawn to other women, and to one woman in particular with whom I felt I was in love, a fellow graduate student named Jean. Lunch turned disastrous—I'm sure we'd both stopped eating if we'd even ever begun—as he proceeded to tell me what a mistake I was making, and how I didn't know what I was getting myself into, I had no idea what a "bad" person this woman was whereas he knew, he knew, and then he told me she'd recently slept with one of his married colleagues. He knew because his colleague told him. He knew because everybody knew.

I suppose we shocked and stunned each other equally that day, and our relationships survived the dislocation. For Jean and me, it incited a turning point in our young relationship, and drew us closer. Angry with Marty, I told him this, but I don't remember his response. I only remember a separate incident on a separate day on which I found myself alone inside his university office.

What was I doing in his office you might ask? I was enjoying the privilege of my exception, because the curious thing was that I'd never really, never formally, "taken" a class with Marty even though he was among the teachers from whom I was learning the most. I'd sat in on one of his upper level undergraduate classes in Nineteenth Century American Literature and Art, but that was all.

Marty was on sabbatical that semester and he gave me free reign of his office which was so much larger than my shared graduate student quarters and which also enjoyed a window. No doubt the snow kept up its banal repetition through that misty portal as I surveyed the more interesting spectacle of his shelves, for he had always given me access to them—to his books. I wasn't looking for anything in particular when I made my discovery, when I struck upon the ruby in the crest of the crown: not any book, here was Marty's personal copy of the book on Melville he had authored, *The Melville Archetype*. I opened the book to the thrill of his penciled marginal notes, and remembered a story he used to tell that made the book more dear: a student in one of his classes asks him following the presentation of one of his luminous exegeses, "Did you make that up, or did you read it in a book?" And Marty answers the astonishing question,

"I read it in a book." Pause.

"And I wrote the book I read it in." Punch.

A teacher need know better than to bring a student into his confidence, to entrust her with the keys to the castle, to allow her liberties. Before I knew it, I'd determined to *take* the book. Not to borrow the book, but to keep the book, to make it mine. It was stealing pure and simple, with or without stealth. It hadn't been pre-meditated; it had just, as criminals are wont to say, "happened." In one part of my mind, I considered that I wasn't stealing. It was a pact, the creation of an invisible bond, except only one party could know about it. In another part of my mind, perhaps I contemplated revenge: Marty and I often shared what we were writing with one another, though, needless to say, I more often read his work than he, mine. One day I gave him the typescript of an essay I had written about my burgeoning aesthetic as an essayist. All that I remember of the essay was that in it I compared writing to dropping a live and ruddy lobster into a boiling pot. When I asked him for the essay back, he told me he no longer had it. He'd thrown it into the trash after reading it, as he did with all notes, scraps, bits, pages, or anything that might clutter his otherwise pristine quarters. Didn't I know—but of course I did!—*always* to make a copy of my work?

My act, though, was not to be confused with a tit for tat gesture of revenge. Taking the book was more like the Private stealing the Captain's epaulettes. It was about wanting to feel in advance what it might feel like to command a troop of words on the page. To steal meant to hold fast; to take the book was to exert a hold on my friend, till death do us part. I wanted him to know I loved him, and this is how I'd show it.

"Claiming to discover the dark side at fifty or fifty five is a bit backward," Marty had written in one of his loosely autobiographical fictions, quoting a friend who chided him for his mid-life fascination with the perpetration of a petty crime. But I was 25 not 50, so perhaps this was for me about the discovery of my "Shadow," what Marty had described, paraphrasing Jung, as the "not or not sufficiently lived side of [the] psyche...the dark mass of that stuff of experience we have never admitted into our life." Or perhaps, in a Jamesian vein of Modernist neurosis, the theft of the book was my "secret private errand," guaranteed to keep me repressed.

I climbed the three stories to my graduate student hovel, so unlike the replete world that Marty had made of his interiors, and began to read. Blocking any thought of there being something wrong about my claiming this book, in a solitude I could call my own, inviolate, I read about Melville's whale from Marty's point of view, "his deadwall face, his spout, his sickle jaw, his flukes," and I took note.

Don't ask me about the *art* of the steal because I know nothing about it, though, like you, I have stolen and been robbed repeatedly.

Our lives are but a history of our loves, thefts, illnesses, meals, wounds, and shoes. Tell me what you've stolen, and I'll tell you who you are. Theft makes the man. I'm not talking about grotesque malfeasance, the corruption on a grand scale of the 1%. I'm talking about your record—which is not quite the same as your batting average—that record that we long for as a sign of our existence. I'm talking about the petty pot-shots of any one day and its particulars, the bits of beach glass that accrue at the ebb-tide of being, of taking and took, that make a more variegated inlaid design than guilt or innocence can convey.

But you've never stolen anything, you say, never in your entire life. Once, in a writing seminar, my class and I decided spontaneously to go around the room and announce one thing we'd stolen in our lives. I remember being especially intrigued by the person who had stolen a traffic cone because she'd never seen anything else in the world that was that purely orange, and the lengths she went to stuff the ungainly thing into her car. One *ingénue*, however, drew a blank, and when pressed, said for her there had been nothing that she'd ever claimed that wasn't hers for the asking. When I suggested this meant she was a freak, she went home to think about it, and later wrote me:

Dear Professor Cappello, Just wanted you to know that, after class today, I was thinking about stolen things, and then ended up spending the long drive home trying to remember things I had stolen! So far, I've come up with: various artifacts taken from the backs of memorable classrooms, an essay copied from a classmate in the second grade, art supplies taken from a school closet in the fifth grade (apparently I was more daring in elementary school), two books mistakenly stolen from two different high school classmates, two shirts stolen from a former boyfriend, and a different former boyfriend who WAS the stolen thing (long and awkward story)…It took me a while to think of these things probably because many of them were unknowingly or mistakenly stolen, not stolen by design…I'm now thinking that my next piece might be about mistakenly stolen things.

"Mistakenly stolen things could be a great premise for an essay," I replied, "even more intriguing, or at least also worth pursuing, might be the copied essay from 2nd grade. Especially since you've grown up to be a writer."

My own accounting would have to include an instrument from a doctor's office that I can only write about in the third person:

*To the pickpocket: never steal the gleaming instrument, part tube, part light, part battery, part eye, that a doctor uses to examine the ear, nose or throat. "You've **got** to be kidding me!" the words made the thief flush more fully than her 102 degree fever, when she opened her black leather jacket to reveal the stolen goods to a friend. Now she was the sort to steal watches and flash them from inside her greasy coat in the market or on a street corner for you to buy. Not really, though, because this was the only object she'd ever stolen (or so she said), and she didn't know why and she did know why and she didn't know why. Theft is always about indignity expressed through objects. The day before seeing the GP at an emergency clinic, her gynecologist had left the speculum in for an inordinately long time all the while asking her about the classes she was teaching. Then the doctor thrust a semi-opaque, plastic jar half-filled with bloody contents in front of her to say she saw a polyp on her cervix and had "snipped it" without telling her, without asking her. "So you see it was the speculum I really wanted to confiscate not the ear-piercer." But when a flu came on later that night and she was bleeding to boot and couldn't get on a plane as planned, she learned that she couldn't get her money refunded without a doctor's note to prove her incapacity. Sweating, supine, she roused herself into a winter's day to be felt up roughly by an anonymous GP who wanted to give her drugs she didn't need. "I just need your signature on the form," she smiled wanly, and he left to work on someone else for a full half hour but he also left his instrument in the rumpled sheets beside her sore wrists, and stomach, and thighs. He was gone for so long that she had "a lot of time to think" about this object-theft—she took it, put it back, took it, put it back again. I exist, I don't exist. Here, there. Here, gone. Present, absent. Taken, took. Never steal the object that is a doctor's instrument because there's no pleasure if you don't know how to use it, and it cannot be returned.*

My therapist referred to my act as an "abridgement of judgment," leaving me to consider constructing a poem out of the phrase, but I mostly felt caught in a trap of my own making, feeling, as I did, the need to return the, no doubt, "expensive" instrument, and imagining the patients who wouldn't now enjoy the "benefits" of its use, but not knowing how to return the thing without exposing myself. Admit the crime is all we ask of our fellow man, confess and you'll be free—but we know that isn't true.

So many steals pock our days, they mark the horizon in drifts, like the time someone stole my hubcaps, broke into my car and took the student art I had just bought, stole my wallet (in a bank, no less), took a brand new spanking blue bicycle out from under me in the time it took for me to look away, yanked my mother's purse and left a bruise in 1963 on Easter Day, broke into my friend Patty's house and stole the Christmas gifts the night before the day, robbed the bank in which I worked of all the money in the safe. This latter act was complicated for me by the fact that the thief had been my teacher. Her name had been Gertrude before she married a Muslim man and changed it to Rashida. She was the Head Teller, a tall and slender, quiet woman partial to brownish-beige polyesters as backdrop to the thin, gold bracelet that defined the horizon of her wrist. She taught me the tricks of the tellering trade in a summer job between my semesters at college; she was all business and exacting in her job; she was unerring, and she tried to show me how to be so too, applying her supervisory signature with a flourish I quite enjoyed. One Monday, the staff returned to the bank to discover the contents from the safe, missing, and Rashida not at work. She'd stolen the money on the Friday before, and according to all accounts, fled, successfully, to Africa.

Robbery takes on a different cast when it implicates those no one suspects. Then it is lent the significance of a con, and we feel robbed of our wits as much as of our things, like the time Jean and I agreed to sublet an apartment in New York city to a person named "Lisa Arden." The building super, a Polish man who struck us as a decrepit double of an aged Samuel Beckett, warned us between drags on his non-filtered cigarettes: "Don't make mistake," but we did. We made big mistake. We believed Lisa Arden's story of a mother who lay dying of cancer in a local hospital. Of how she loved to read and would probably spend her nights reading the books in our apartment—"so many books," she cooed—after spending the day with her mother at the hospital. In fact, she ran several illegal businesses out of the apartment and paid the rent using money she had wired to herself from credit cards whose account numbers she found inside our file cabinets. She conned everyone, including the disabled people who worked for her, selling fake licenses for firearms, using phones she had set up in the apartment. She was addicted to crack, and when we finally got into the apartment—she had had the locks changed, so this was no mean feat (imagine now the rickety rail of an ever wiser Samuel Beckett having to climb in through the fire escape)—we discovered, amid the vials, the emptied closets, and blackened curtains, audio tapes of Dale Carnegie's *How to Win Friends and Influence People*. Arden was the name of the street on which we lived, and we learned from her parole officer that her real name was Lisa Rossi. She'd seen Lisa recently wearing a dress that belonged to Jean. Nothing could be done because we'd allowed her in. We allowed her in, even though her voice was raspy.

And the books, the books kept coming back to mock me, so many books belonging to such very stupid people. We were enraged by her, but we were also awed, and we were frightened: she still had the key to our mailbox, and had visited it even after we'd re-inhabited the apartment. While we fretted up above—ringing out the blackened curtains—she entered down below.

Perhaps because I was already an adult when Lisa Arden took us, and took us for a ride, I didn't experience this steal as formative. It made for a temporary hardship, but we had the stamina of people in their late twenties and were resilient. The experience didn't really mark, shape, or alter me in the way that other types of theft had, dating back to earliest childhood. You drop a pebble into a well, and these are they that sound. I can still see the sidewalk that my brother and I travelled together to get to the corner grocer on an errand for our mother. The pavement was wet with summer rain and its earthy after-smell. I was six or seven years old and was enjoying the now sweet now sour granulations of a large purple gumball as we made our way home. For these moments there was silence between us—my own mouth, at least, was intent on the distraction of a sugary concentration—until my brother asked, "Where did you get that gum? I didn't pay for that." Rather than reply, I spat the gum out of my mouth, as though I had been chewing on sin itself or the purple toe-nail of a devil's cloven hoof.

"I thought you had paid for it," I said.

"Nope," he replied. "I guess you stole it."

When we arrived home, I told my mother of the incident and she sent me back to the store with a nickel to give the proprietor. She assured me he would understand, and I could pay for it after the fact. The owner praised me for my honesty, but he sill appeared ten times his size to me. He loomed.

This incident is linked in my mind to a First Holy Communion steal—really an exchange that felt like a robbery. I'm sitting in church on the day of my First Holy Communion ceremony. I don't pay much attention to the ceremony, but instead spend a lot of time giggling and whispering with a friend of mine with whom I share a pew. When I get home, I discover, to my horror, that instead of my own little white purse with special items stowed inside it, I have the little white purse of some other girl, and it has bizarre objects in it—like a naked Baby Jesus. It was as though my things—small things, smelling of talc and delicately kept—were exchanged for the grotesquerie of an evil step-sister. I remember the feeling that things I had invested meaning in had suddenly disappeared, and at the same time, the consideration that I might appear to have taken another, sloppier girl's things. "I would never want these things!" I thought. But that's what I was now: a sloppy girl.

Such swaps are the stuff of fairytale, and always stir a sense of forces beyond our lived and visible realities. Which brings me to the third and seminal occasion in my daisy chain of incautious hits, the opposite of artful dodge. In each case, my world was altered while I was sleeping. It's kindergarten "nap time," and we are instructed to spread our blankets on the floor. The color of this memory is pinkish-brown, which was the color that softly lit my blanket as I sidled into sleep and also the hue that predominated the sheet of porous paper on which I'd just finished coloring-in the contours of a squirrel. This was our major project of the day, and we were told to stow these in our "cubby holes" during nap time. Returning home, we were supposed to give them to our mothers. I'll never forget waking to an empty cubby. No swap, just disappearance. No explanation, but a conviction that I must have awakened more slowly than my peers and that someone took my squirrel in place of their own.

These are the things we save, I guess, such memories. The things we choose not to throw away—like old letters, my father's cufflinks, or the cash register receipt from an airport kiosk from which I bought a grilled cheese sandwich the morning of the middle-of-the-night in which a friend had died. Which is different from a keepsake, or whatever we need to keep.

We save what we don't care to *throw away*.

We keep what we don't care to *give away*, though this feeling can loosen and unravel the more accepting we are of our own eventual death. Either act steadies our canoe inside a stream of past, present and beyond. Both convince us there is actually someone in the canoe.

Collecting, on the other hand, unlike keeping or saving, is more like stealing. As Bresson's *Pickpocket* demonstrates, thieves often have no interest in the things that they have pilfered. The act that makes possible their endless production is where the pleasure lies, and it's unquenchable. If saving and keeping are about securing memory, collecting and stealing are about the creation of a counter-memory. Stolen things have no history except the one the thief or collector creates. Collect or steal something and you run time's ship aground.

The thing about Bresson's pickpocket is that he doesn't wear gloves. He steals in the buff, and yet remains, for a very long time, invulnerable to capture. His skin *is* his glove, and he needs to feel, to feel all he can, directly. He needs to touch without being himself touched in turn: to touch without being felt; to touch without bearing witness to the effects of his interaction with a fellow woman or man. It's hard to know if this impoverishes him, or if his impoverishment came first, and the need to steal, second: if he's depraved on accounta he's deprived. Perhaps all theft is about access, and the pickpocket enjoys access without accountability.

At any rate, he is only engaged in petty crime which is on a continuum with petting but not to be confused with that more vulgar act, "the copping of a feel": to grope surreptitiously because you know you can. To "cop" in the older sense of "to steal" is something a man can do in the fore and after-play of theft and love, and Michel is not properly masculine; just as a woman *is* her snatch, and therefore is incapable of snatching.

Pickpocketing in Bresson's cool, filmic light is never mugging. The mugger harms you without conscience in the fulfillment of his need because he never learned the art of the pickpocket. In high school, I suffered a near-mugging that was enough to remind me of the vulnerability of being a girl walking alone in early evening time. I always stayed late at school as haven, and on this night I had more to do than usual with after school events and clubs and planning. I was just a few blocks from the school, on a street a notch down from the already working class neighborhood where I lived, when I felt someone grab me from behind, and as he did so, thrust his hands inside the pockets of my coat to either side of me, then quickly, forcefully, pat them as though exploring them in the way an animal might. In an instant, with the strength of a thousand Robert Wagners—I'd studied *To Catch A Thief* for the actor's glint and swagger—I threw the man off of me, imitating a Jujitsu move I had seen on T.V. Luckily, to my surprise, and having found nothing in my pockets but the reflex of my seventeen year old flesh, he ran. Only when he was at a far distance from me, exasperated by what he dared, and still afraid, I yelled, as if to threaten him: "Fuck you, you fucking asshole."

Marty, at the end of his autobiographical fiction, "Imagining Italy," recounts his own encounter with a pickpocket in the Metropolitana in Rome. The story is a playful study of grades of guilt and innocence, from metaphysical guilt, to involutions of innocence that are culturally determined and therefore illegible. A large man in a white shirt wedges himself between Marty's friend, Licastro, and himself, "yielding his girth to the motion of the train." Eventually, Marty feels the man's fingers with his own inside his deep, tight pocket. Marty captures him—he has felt him after all—and then releases him without accusing him. "He knew I knew he was a pickpocket, and I knew he knew I knew it," Marty writes, and decides to submit the occasion to a lesson in Jamesian hyper-consciousness. Instead of crying out, he smiles, as does the pickpocket in turn, bestowing on him, from outside the sliding door, a Roman salute.

Marty releases the man because he knows he knows *he* is also guilty, as are we all, and because he'd prefer the pleasure of this dance with him rather than exert himself a judge.

Perhaps in stealing Marty's book, I aimed to imitate him, imitation by a student of her teacher being a form of loving theft in which love over-rides violation.

II.

Reading Henry James in graduate school didn't require that I turn thief, but it did (and does) take a good deal of cunning. Reading James is like agreeing to match wits in a game of three-dimensional chess as armature for an even more intricate love-play: the triangulation of desire; the machinations of lovers whose proper object perpetually appears, disappears, and re-appears elsewhere, like the pebble inside a shell game. If to read him is to become a member of the elect, it may be why some people refuse altogether, but for me there was always a textural draw that aimed lower than "cerebration." To read James was to be seduced by a language-turned-velvet, and with the same attraction and repulsion of that fine fabric, for how easy it was, once in, to lose one's way in James's rumpled turns of phrase, to become caught in crinkled corners, or smothered by bunches of predication, to descend into his valleys, to ascend his language's creases only to get lost again in its folds.

The Aspern Papers is a novella about forms of literary predation if not outright theft. It's a book that relies on a great deal of rummaging and surrogacy, on immense hallways and foreshortened perspective, on furtive meetings in Venetian gardens and the missed chance of a Florian's water ice before St. Mark's. Because the un-named narrator cannot, himself, be a writer, he must claim the papers of another in no uncertain terms, and he will go to great, bumbling, dissimulating lengths to access them. The tale is a fable for critics, a parable of scholarly abuse populated by "wizened gnomes and a treasure trove of papers." Sexual violation plays about the edges of the tale, signaled by so many "red-tipped cigars" and "tempting buttons," as Marty had once demurred: In The Aspern Papers, we find "misogyny all wrapped up in the ideology of divine service." Living out their lives in mysterious seclusion in Venice, our two displaced Americans, the "Misses Bordereau," (the aunt, Juliana, and niece, Tina), appear to have something that the narrator-critic desperately needs. It's hard to know whether the un-named narrator is more interested in theft or in rape when, late in the story, he secretes himself before the entrance of a "tall old secretary," imagining Jeffrey Aspern's papers "languishing behind the peevish little lock." He's a plunderer of literary remains, "to be sure," and he knows that somewhere on the premises lay the buried treasure of love letters that passed between the subject of his work and the impossibly aged Juliana Bordereau (at one point her niece jokes that Juliana is 150 years old).

Like the architecture in which his characters reside, a novella by James might ask us to enter by way of its own "vast forecourt," to listen for "light footsteps on marble," and feel the atmosphere created by the "faintness of a taper"; to *dis*-embark, to become *dis*-encumbered rather than *un*-encumbered of our cameras, or of our verbs and nouns; to prepare ourselves for some unanticipated meeting inside a "long succession of empty rooms"; one moment, to observe day's light enter a chink or shutter only to be drenched by a floodlight of discovery and upheaval, later to be left to submit one's gaze to the "red immersion of another day."

It's a prose lacking the "convenient" Venetian footways James describes so lovingly, yet there are always lifts, buoys of the unsaid to keep one afloat inside the over-stated. James won't have *any* trellises enter his prose but "rickety trellises," not any old brick but "extrusions of brick that had turned pink with time," allowing us for a moment to patter, to dawdle, to introduce into our lives the "nightly practice" of a "lonely airing"; to *start* alongside the narrator for a brief moment of truth, un-sustained: that second during which he wonders why he's attached such importance to a pile of "crumpled scraps"; to laugh, ever so lightly, at Juliana's wry self-regard, "She had lived so long, she wanted to die for a change."

"Shall you study—shall you read and write—when you go up to your rooms?" Tina asks the story's strange intruder, the writer *manqué*.

In mild weather he doesn't read at night because the "lamplight brings in the animals"; in winter, he "reads a good deal," but he "doesn't often write." Nor does he *really* read, but fans the flame of idolatry for Jeffrey Aspern.

Those who taught me how to read schooled me in the necessity of tending a book much as one might a fire: it never starts on its own without your attentive effort and even-hovering skill; just when you're comfortable, it might need stoking; it could mesmerize, or catch the hem of your garment by surprise (reading was dangerous); once lit, it could warm something in yourself. To fan a flame in place of reading, on the other hand, was tantamount to torching a book.

My father, Joseph Salvatore Cappello, was not much of a reader, yet he wished to be a writer, filling his rooms in the last ten years of his life, and those to whom he posted his writing in the mail, with mounds of file folders filled with the products of his cock-eyed imagination. I tried to salvage something useful from my father's peculiar sense of humor, even to find seeds of his quirkiness in myself, a tilt-a-whirl view of things more redolent of life than the solitude of the merely oddball or the madcap. I tried to appreciate my father's efforts, if only at the level of their voluminous force of will, and not to confuse that energy with the rage or violence he'd directed throughout our childhoods at my brothers and me. My father's was an impossible personality, difficult to love, and he died, sadly, of an intractable disease, one of the most punishing disorders any body should be made to bear, Parkinson's.

My father clung so to life, outliving his doctors' predictions, that he appeared, in death, as though he had been tortured. In the working class nursing home named for Saint Francis in which he died, we weren't granted the dignity privately to attend his lifeless body; nor was consideration granted to the patient he shared a room with who had to endure the fact of my father's dead body separated from him by nothing but a curtain, and the sounds of our sobs. I couldn't bear to gaze at the angle of my father's neck, thrust ceiling-ward, or at his fully opened mouth, and wondered why no one cared enough to close it. In the place where his angry or embittered or comic voice had been remained the traces of a life force wrenched, yanked, or stolen rather than released.

Lifting a sheet in search of my father's hands, I wept to find his fingers at least, no longer tangled, curled, or trembling uncontrollably, but entirely at rest. I'd experienced a great deal of death and dying in my life, but never before had I felt this sense of bargaining with a disease, as if the only way the Parkinson's could leave was to take him with it; as though the cost of rest was a person's disappearance, and the body's remaining grace its gratitude.

Before he died, I wrote telegraphic notes to a friend:

My father entered hospice care this week. And I find myself pitching in the middle of the night. Nightmares of things swelling.

Found myself crying on the way to school this a/m—but it was a good crying. Felt flooded with memories, images, bits and pieces of my sense of my father. It was like I was trying to make some kind of coherent image of my father in my head—piecing together things, fragments, contradictory in affect, making something like a collage? ... My mother went to see my father today (in spite of their being divorced—of course she loves him in some way). Basically it seemed he just wanted to hear her talk to him. He's totally cognizant—the man has a strong mind, an unbelievably strong mind. It is very rare for someone to get to end-stage Parkinson's and not suffer from dementia. He can't eat anymore though, and this is why they are now allowing him to be released from the agony of living with Parkinson's.

Undertakers' bodies, I find, run to extremes. They are either the type whose chests are wide as the very doorways through which they will have to carry death's unspeakable weight, or wraith-like as figures out of Edward Gorey. These latter wear anachronistic bowler hats atop faces sunken from having smoked one too many cigarettes while waiting for mourners curb-side, in the rain. The wide-typed sort arrived at the nursing home to take my father's body away, while the wraith-like type appeared the day of the funeral in front of the row home where my father had lived for fifty years and where my eldest brother still lived. The narrow lane that is Concord Road had never seen doors swung open so wide, and the limousine seemed to slink in order to round its corners.

When we returned to my father's house the night of his death, my mother brought my brothers, their partners, Jean and me and my brother's children chicken soup which I suggested we serve with the sheet metal ladles my father's Sicilian father had made. Later, my brother, his wife, and Jean and I would piece together a suit for my father to wear at his viewing. I'd always thought of my father as a snappy dresser, with dashes of machismo all wrapped up in a feminine and showy South Philly flair (only so many men can get away with wearing white loafers and knee socks to match). I was surprised, then, to discover as I sought out a favorite chartreuse-colored shirt, that the collars of all of his jackets were coated with grime, and that his wardrobe really amounted to bundles and bundles of the kind of discounted garments one could take or leave in large, nondescript department stores.

My father's belongings, bank accounts, and assets were mostly liquidated by the nursing home as so many people's are in this country who have survived a great deal of living; in other words, those who have reached a certain age. Where income is concerned, it gives a different meaning to the word "disposable"; where lives are concerned, it exacts a form of pre-mature renunciation too dark to contemplate. I was, therefore, surprised when my brother announced after dinner and before we sifted through my father's remaining clothes that there was one item he had left in his bedroom if I wanted to "go through it with him."

We cleared the dining table while my brother went to retrieve the object from my father's room. It was a book. A book, with a fake leather, beveled spine and gold lettering. If you opened the front cover of the book, you would find small chambers rather than pages: it was a hollow book, a book-as-box into which a man was meant to deposit his jewelry. My brother slowly removed each item that lay inside the book for our perusal: there were pins representing each decade of the life my father had lived by working at the Philadelphia Naval Shipyard; dirty combs originally purchased at a Five and Ten Cent store; nail clippers; tie clips; campaign buttons (Muskie, Humphreys, Agnew, et al) that my brother had collected as a child and given to my father; and a pair of psychedelic cufflinks.

Now I recalled the book, and moreso the odd piece of furniture with which I paired it in my mind, a piece of furniture that marked my father's maleness, a strange combination of seat and suit hanger that, like The Aspern Papers' "secretary" could name both a person and a thing: my father's "valet." The contents of the book were pretty disappointing, even though I think my father stowed it inside the seat of his valet for safe-keeping. But the inverted glass cones with their fake gold setting and mesh soldering seemed to twirl in a way only costume jewelry can.

They were this book's hidden treasure, and they lay like tiny sphinxes found inside a pyramid. They reminded me of an era in which my father grew a moustache. I remembered my father *in* these cufflinks, and I remembered myself then too, and we are dancing. My mother had told me there had been a *day*—where that word refers to many of its kind, there had been an *age*—where that word implies a whole era, when I was four years old, that I would wait at the screen door for my father to come home from work, for when he did, he danced with me.

I asked my brother if I might have the cufflinks; if I might save them. "Sure," my brother said, I could.

In any case…
Pain
arrogates consciousness to itself
as Rabelais argues
in his great book
that the king of all men
to whom
even earthly kings bow down
is *venter,*
the body,
hunger,
a deeply materialist explanation of human events,
that life in the hospital
or in Rabelais,
though Rabelais is endlessly more exuberant,
is life in the lower body,
though Rabelais himself allows for the Abbey of Theleme
at the end of his book *Gargantua*
a realm of higher consciousness
… in any case he is fundamentally concerned as life in the hospital is
fundamentally concerned with such things as
the consistency of bowel and the quantity of urine,
the blood the bowel the body and the baby talk,
the sacred mystery of your body here revealed

the private text of your body here inscribed,
it's as if these were newspaper headlines
perhaps
you are the victim of vandals
and
graffiti.

Near the end of his life
Henry James, in medical crisis,
it's one of the most touching episodes in James's life,
"sobbed and panted and held my hand"
said his nephew, one of William James's sons,
but that of course is not the James we know,
and love,
and it is the James we can hardly imagine,
James reduced to blood, bowel, the body, and baby talk.
No
the Jamesian protagonist, as we have observed,
is out to "see, to see all she can," "to live, live all he can,"
the passionate pilgrim of a higher consciousness,
one who like John Marcher in the *Beast in the Jungle* awaits the event,
the distinguished thing,
(James called "a distinguished thing" the onset as he thought it of his
own death)
awaits the unique experience,
Mrs. Prest says in *The Aspern Papers*, "One would think you expected
to find in
those papers, the riddle of the universe,"
these papers
which elsewhere are called "sacred relics,"
with
whatever
admitted irony,
and, which are characterized as possessing esoteric knowledge
again,
with

whatever
admitted irony.
These are, in any case, high stakes
and stakes away from the lower body.
Or so they seem.

When Marty Pops gave this lecture on *The Aspern Papers*, he hadn't lineated it, though I'm certain he did *compose* it in the way a musician creates a score. He was the age I am now when he wrote this lecture-as-incantation, and I am the age he was then listening to it as though hearing it for the first time and with the fullest, most startling force of its import, of what it not only addresses or invokes but *intones*. I'm literally listening to the lecture again because I have a cassette recording of it and still own a cassette recorder. I've remembered the recording because I've re-found Marty through the not-so-circuitous route of my father's death.

It makes sense that in contemplating the impossible (my father, for example), one is put in mind of the possible; that in the doomed-to-fail attempt to tailor the self to suit "the" father, one is put in mind of fathers in the plural (may they be fruitful and multiply); that in losing kin that was never really kind, one finds oneself inspired, if one can be, by "elective affinities," the fathers that one chose over and against the One that was thrust upon us. It didn't require a great leap of consciousness to find myself thinking vividly of Marty Pops in the weeks that followed my father's death, nor was it surprising that I thought of him as I sat in my own professorial office, and with a window, too, that affords a view of the university's gold weathervane (which I never knew existed until now); the rare specimens of a college arboretum; and the winding pathways that carry students to and from their rooms.

It goes without saying that we tend to lose touch with those who most deeply touch us. Marty and I had lost touch over the years, and I found myself wondering, in between classes at the start of a new semester, *how he was*, when another old Buffalo friend informed me that if I wanted to contact Marty, I "should do so soon": as far as she knew, he was seriously, possibly terminally ill.

In the course of any one day, week, or month, there are numerous conversations that amount to nothing, that fail to make us feel, or come to matter; and then there are occasions on which so many feelings are broached in one short call, so much of a life both compressed and told, that our entire bodies might tingle afterwards with a surfeit of aliveness. I don't know how he had me laughing, but he did, and crying too, and I, him, both. Marty answered the phone as though he were expecting me, and then recounted the circuitous route to a diagnosis of *ALS* [Amyotrophic Lateral Sclerosis] starting with difficulty walking and weakness in his legs on a trip to Lucca, or perhaps, Florence, or perhaps what he called "that most sociable of cities," the Venice of *The Aspern Papers*. Italy was beloved by him, and to feel unwell in a place that we love is always un-mooring. Vague symptoms gave way to mis-diagnosis and an unnecessary back surgery from which he failed properly to recover, and which ultimately gave the true source of the condition away.

Marty was a famous *raconteur*, and he found a way to tell the story of the eventual discovery of ALS to bring out laughter in me: it had something to do with the way the doctor asked him to un-robe, and repeated, "Mr. Pops! Mr. Pops?," something about the utterly odd crunch and lilt of a new word for tell-tale lumps or fleeting twitches in his chest. Now he shifted his tone to a matter of fact that was crushingly sober as he described the place he found himself. He was at the end of the three year clock his manifestation of the disease granted, he explained, wheel-chair bound, and the course ahead of him might incur a choice: whether to be tracheotomized but to lose his voice, and live by way of a tube inserted into his side body for the delivery of nutrients, or to forego this "option" and allow himself to die. I told him how his work was ever with me, how it had mattered most in all I'd set out to do. The disease made him more quick to cry, the drugs did too, the way the disease had changed him made him more likely to cry, or maybe my words had been the thing to make him sob.

He put the question, as he had many years ago, with the same directness of a proposal to take his hand in-relationship if not in marriage: "Do you think you could come to visit me? Would you be able to come to see me?"

We settled on the week before Thanksgiving when his friend, the

poet, Carl Dennis, planned a yearly pre-holiday gathering, ritually defined by the baking of numerous pies, to be hosted this year at Marty's
house because of Marty's immobility.

In the days before I re-visited him—and wasn't this to be a kind of
pilgrimage to Buffalo?—I remembered the recording of one of his lectures and looked for it among my things. It was I who had suggested the
tape recording when Marty was otherwise to miss his class on account
of minor surgery. "I'll bring my recorder to your house," I said. "You can
record your lecture in your own time and then I'll bring it to the class
so we can listen to it. It appears you're not too ill to lecture, right? It'll
be fun."

One might wonder what references to the hospital, the lower body,
and Henry James's final days could have to do with *The Aspern Papers*,
but I knew that such references were the diamonds Marty had mined
amid the swill of his surgery for hemorrhoids and anal fissures in the
early 1980s. Though I never shared a bed with him, I still recall the
way the donut-shaped pillow interrupted the horizon of his pristine
bath tub. Only now did I really make the link between the eloquent
opening lines of Marty's lecture and his butt pain, only now that I was
a professor myself did I know how often the eternal verities I waxed
about in class were but a cover for the discomforts of my daily life. To
hear those opening lines again of course spelled out something excruciating to take, a punch in the stomach neither of prescience nor of
poignancy, but something for which I've yet to find a word: the horror
that our lessons might come to meet us where we live; the relation or
the gulf between what Marty claimed to know about death and dying
at 50—the way illness instructs us in the four B's: *the blood the bowel
the body and the baby talk*—and what he knew now on ALS' terms and
course at 75. Of all the diseases that could befall a person, ALS was the
one a trusted physician I knew told me she hoped never to get; ALS,
she explained, was the very worst of all diseases in the way it slowly,
stealthily robbed a person of each and every bodily function (even if it
kept one's "faculties" intact) until there was nothing left to take. Was
illness the thief to which all other thieves bowed down?

I re-visited Marty's lecture and continued to learn from it 25 years
after the fact, understanding just a little bit more than I had at 25 years

of age. These were the utterances not of an emergent but a fully formed voice which doesn't mean that the lecture wasn't full of gaps and tentativities. It is hard to know, listening back on it, how the unformed blob that I was heard it, or what part of it I was able to then take in. I only know that I don't lecture like this, and that no one does. My own classrooms are structured around challenging questions, and I rarely pronounce things from on high. But then Marty's lecture was not really preachy, though it was pronounced in sacral tones; it preserved the bass-y concatenations of a chant underscored by the textures of a Brooklyn Jewish accent (the sound of one kind of leather—a baseball's, hitting another kind of leather—the glove). It's a genre that may have gone out of fashion, if it ever existed at all: it is a parsing of knowledge riddled with enjambment. It's thinking as a form of breathing.

Though it sounds authoritative, it is all about submission, since it asks a student to witness a reader submit himself to a book; to listen to the sounds of an idea played upon the improvisatory instrument that is the teacher's voice.

"Arrogate" was a new word for me even at middle age. "Pain arrogates consciousness to itself"; pain claims consciousness for itself, leaving no room for anything but itself. Here was a more nuanced intra-psychic notion of theft, and it pointed to one of many forms of usurpation beyond our control, a kind of inward thieving.

I'd agreed to visit, but what could I bring to a dying man? And then I remembered the book. Of course, I would bring to Marty the book of his I'd stolen those many years before.

I didn't return to Buffalo alone but in the company of my close friend, Jim and of Jean. We'd all met in Buffalo, and Jim had worked with Marty too. None of us had ever gone in for official reunions, and had rarely returned to Buffalo since our graduate student days, but together we agreed—with Jim travelling from as far away as California—that now was a time for a coalescence of returns: Jim and I had both turned 50 the month before our journey, and we decided that Buffalo, through Marty, was calling us to converge again in a celebratory rather than strictly somber way. We were experiencing after all the chance to see

Marty again before losing him, and to remember how Buffalo shaped us.

In the course of a few short days, we went to a European style bistro that hadn't existed when we were in graduate school, and to its obverse: a favorite meat and potatoes diner featuring live music of the Barry Manilow variety. It seemed like a place where no-longer-Anonymous Alcoholics gathered, or people down on their luck in search of the kind of glow a neon light can shed inside of a warm, dark cave. I'd always said that what made Buffalo interiors so divine was the fact that they were conceived as an antidote to the huddling imperatives of the weather, and the Victorian houses off of Elmwood Avenue now loomed even larger, not smaller, than I had pictured them, just as most of the streets now exposed themselves as boulevards much vaster than the crabbed and snowy lanes I had remembered.

A "We're Talking Proud" campaign with accompanying signage to that effect had dotted Buffalo's imperiled façade in the 1980s, but on this return, I apprehended the traces of what I failed to notice as a student but what had never gone away: a grandeur, monumentality, and cobbled bustle that bespoke "Boom Town." The TRICO windshield wiper plant bore a blinking sign, so angular and red against a snow squall, that it still figured in my mind's eye as the city's metronome, splitting the days into shifts rather than cradling them like church bells. Jean and Jim and I made the rounds of haunts: the North Park Cinema whose Brill-creamed, gap-toothed ticket master had apparently never left the circular ticket booth and who welcomed us for the same affordable price to a showing of a very fine film that would never enjoy a wide release; the seedy bar called Nietzsche's whose sticky dance floor was the scene of my and Jean's first full-fledged rapturous encounter, and the bathroom where we confronted each other afterwards in a shared stall.

And we ambled. Into a new, vast art gallery named for Charles Burchfield and honoring artists of Western New York, complete with jars of pigment Burchfield had concocted. Slate green meets lime green meets underwater green to make Burchfield's conception of grass as glimpsed through a quivering snow. We exited the gallery into a rose-tinted nightfall that made rows of warehouse windows into crimson sheets, and pushed us each separately to arc our backs in awe or mildly focus our gaze from a separate corner of a parking lot.

In one part of the day and of the city, we inhabited an envelope of celebration and return; in another, we individually nursed our willingness to enter a place we might want to reject. Not the old folks home, but the place where we might fail to recognize our teachers or they, us; to Marty's home now altered: the first thing to be noticed was the installation of a massive industrial wheel chair lift at 111 Lexington, and we had trouble finding the door.

If our former teachers were now "ancient," we were, it must be admitted, "old." Our former professors were all head and no body. But perhaps this is how it had always been. One appeared as a bobble head hovering so close I could feel his helium breath inside my own; another short-bearded, dry-eyed figure was now a dot floating astride the ebb of a lake-colored couch. The young among the assembled guests formed a constellation of caretakers in Marty's home, including a girl who now lived with Marty, Marty's wife, R., and his stepsons. The young woman had bonded with him, and, though the term of her employ had ended months before, she wished to see him through to the end.

The house, Marty apologized, was no longer what it had once been, and indeed there existed a disarray one associates with people living inside a house. A boiling pot of cider left brown splotches on the stove, and stray items here and there appeared on the floor like things that had fallen out of the paintings that comprised his art collection. A cat appeared, but I couldn't tell if this were a cat of the past, present, or future. The cat was extremely old, and it spent the evening trying and failing to fetch a sweet meat from the dining room table toward which it would jump only repeatedly to fall. Had we been apart long enough for the cat to have died and another as replacement to have grown to a ripe, old age? Or was this the cat that rubbed against us and of whom it might be said: 'we had known each other in our youth'? How long had it really been since Marty and I had last seen one another?

Only Marty maintained the same brilliant buoyancy and spring, in spite of the changes wrought by ALS upon his body. He might cry more easily—*he sobbed and panted and held my hand*, but he was still "the man I knew/and loved." We talked, and laughed—so much joy had we brought, Marty's family could not stop repeating it, and as the night progressed, I became more aware of the privilege we enjoyed of those who can "drop in" with good cheer over and against those whose faces, strained by the fatigue of the daily-ness of caring for a beloved, were in for the long haul, and always had been.

Everyone's movements, the arrival of more guests, the departure of others, the passing round of pieces of pie and clanking of drinks, even a trip to the bathroom, threw the fact of Marty's forced fixedness into high relief, and made me painfully aware of how the wheel-chair bound person is always being left, or how a person frozen into place by ALS can no longer seek attention but must wait for it to come to him. At a certain high point of ig-norance by most of the other people in the room, glued to a spot on a stool next to Marty, his hand in mine, I decided to present him with his copy of *The Melville Archetype*.

"I brought you something."

"What's that sweetie? Your presence is all that matters. I'm so glad that you're here."

"No, I really wanted to bring you something."

"What gives?"

"Do you remember this book?" And I brought my wares out from inside my purse.

"I stole it from your office, and decided that tonight I should let you know."

"Imagine that! My *Melville Archetype*. That's quite wonderful. Heh heh. I'd wondered where it had gone to. I'd thought [my friend] Licastro had borrowed it and never given it back. I remember asking him about it. Well, it's about time!"

"Oh, but I'm not giving the book back to you."

"You're not? How's that?"

"And I'm not confessing anything."

"Ok."

"It's better than a confession."

"Yeeessss?"

"It's an admission. An acknowledgment, you know? Of my love. I just wanted you to know that I had it, and I took it in order to be close to you."

"Fair enough. Fair Enough. But you still need to deposit something in its place. I insist that you give me a copy of your most recent book in return for mine."

I happened to have an advance copy of my most recent book with me, but it was my first and currently my only copy. Which I agreed to give to Marty even though this wasn't the book I wished to have him read. I'd rather have given him the much better book, the something better of the not-yet-written, for who is ever satisfied with what he has wrought? I wished to give him the book that none of us can ever live long enough to write.

Instead, I agreed to slip with him inside a shift and play of substitutions: his book, my book, my book, his.

My father, Joseph Cappello, died on September 24, 2010, and my mentor, Marty Pops died almost precisely to the day a year later, on September 29, 2011. "Martin died in his sleep last night and a service will be held for him here this Sunday," began the letter that I received from Carl Dennis, and even though I knew that ALS was sure to take Marty away, I didn't believe it, because he'd written me, and I, him, as recently as a week before. In the nine months that passed between our meeting again in Buffalo and this day, we enjoyed a frank and vivid correspondence, some of which was marked by his sense of feeling more and more imprisoned, crimped, and blunted, emptied, robbed, and of my attempts to contradict this by reminding him that he remained essentially vast, bright, unchanged.

Illness encroaches and abridges, yet it seemed with Marty that he remained inviolate. This isn't true for us all. It wasn't true for my father. But, wait, that's not right either. My father, as I have noted, *remained* recalcitrant to the end as evidenced by his forcibly opened mouth. Resistance or acceptance, stasis or metamorphosis, the fact of the body or the belief in an over-soul become so highly attenuated at "the end" that we insist on one at the exclusion of the other. Whether it is more like a wriggle or more like a poof, the fact of the matter is that we do disappear.

Not only at the beginning of each semester, but also at the beginning of each class that I teach, I always feel as though my students and I return to the beginning. If a beginning is what initiates, how can you return to it? Perhaps the feeling is merely the sign of a desire for a second, third, fourth, or fifth chance—this time we really will learn some-thing!—or, better, a splendid acceptance of that Cageian dictum that we are always getting nowhere and we should learn to enjoy that while we can. I didn't really believe that my final correspondence with Marty would go on and on; what distinguished the letters that passed between us in that year was that they were last words. I knew that in returning to each other, we'd been allowed a chance that some might flee from: to confide in and salute at an end, to meet precisely at a point of no return.

Jean and my and Jim's visit to Buffalo to see Marty couldn't be com-plete without a visit to Niagara Falls, but before this, we waved to the winds that blasted and brewed inside the tunnels that ran like runnels inside the faux outdoor atriums of Clemens Hall. We stayed in the car for this, dis-believing that our bodies had once slogged with books against bursts of air impossible to buffet. The Falls were more accepting and dear even though they reared like the mane of a wild horse tempt-ing us to touch it. Simultaneously fierce and calm, they were a raging pulse in Autumn; and, wasn't the mere thought of the color of those leaves enough to invite a levee or a sluice?

"I assume that one of your caretakers is reading this letter to you," I began a paragraph to Marty, "and I hope that if you prefer to hear it in installments like a serialized nineteenth century story, you will ask for it to be read that way rather than all at once. There's something to be said for savoring sentences, and I so wish for my sentiments to fill your rooms for more than the brief while it takes to read this." Or again, "part of me wants simply to chat with you in this letter, to keep up a patter of this moment's details, as if they could together make an enve-lope of comfort or even stay the moment of what I know is the truth of the matter—this terrible suffering you describe."

That "suffering" now involved the unimaginable reckoning with the fact of Marty's wife, R., being diagnosed out of the blue with a terminal lung cancer, tragically turning tables, and jettisoning her to a place she was not supposed to be. She was at least ten years younger than he; she was supposed to outlive him and mourn him even as she missed him. She had sons to tend, and a life to keep living. And he wasn't supposed to be asked to face a mortality other than his own, the loss of the per-son he called his "lodestone."

I digitized *The Aspern Papers* lecture, having told him that I'd kept it all these years, and he replied with difficulty in typing:

> dear mary,
>
> simplified system, no caps…you might be very qualifiedly amused to know that i played the aspern tapes, flanked by r. on one side and heather [his caretaker] on the other. here comes the sad joke. they recognized my every word. not only did i not recognize any word, i didn't even recognize my voice. so heather put a different speaker behind the computer and i did r m v but only half the words. i've more or less finished my love letter to r., which turned out to be a semi-fictional portrait of her as well. amiri baraka, i seem to remember, once entitled a text, a 20 volume suicide note; my letter is only ten pages long, but it took two months to write with one cramped fibger. [i'm not going to correct that.]
>
> or no l c: LOVE TO YOU, SWEETIE,

I have asked to be scattered to the winds in two places/ I hope it doesn't sound strange for me to say I love hearing this/my cat is asking for attention and tossing paper butterflies from the table where I sit!/*the first thing I should tell you is that I am not writing this letter, I am in fact dictating it, the first time in my life I've ever dictated a letter/*there are no lawns to speak of in Italy, right? gardens should have paths but not lawns/*I am dictating because my arms and fingers have grown so heavy and curled respectively that I cannot write or use a computer/*I found it best to get her a pogo stick and for the party guests hula hoops/*I am, more than before, confined in a smaller and smaller circle, that is one of my worries/*I'm about to brave the heat this afternoon and "inspect the garden," as my grandfather used to put it/ I always heard that as a poor translation of something more subtly wondrous like "study": to study the garden and see what it has to say/*in a quieter moment of my being I felt the margins of my being expand and knew that it couldn't have happened without the ALS, and for a moment I thought it was almost a fair trade/* flowers respond but not grass (which seems to require engineering best left to the makers of what a friend of mine calls 'shrub-urbia')/but isn't it always the case that the psychologues will come in with a damper of a stupid-sounding phrase? "Post-traumatic growth" sounds like something that might happen to one's bunions but not to one's Being/*as for my health, the neurologist who recently examined me put on his thumbnail a metaphoric lemon drop and flipped it toward me as he said "See you in three months"*/ You speak of, for the first time in your life, dictating a letter, but I want to add that this puts you in the company of Henry James/*so he granted me three months/*in one of your books you had written how, according to Melville, all writing was a form of amanuensis/*a word about the book*/we had a hail storm here last night at 2 a/m, my cat let out a loud meow as though the earth were cracking open and she were in conversation with her cat ancestors and then the hail storm hit and high winds brought down some trees/*a word about the book*/I was also able to devote to some Sicilian fare—in this case, mackerel (for lack of fresh sardines) stuffed with currants, roasted lemons (a new favorite thing)/*so these are the worst days of my life*/

What turned out to be the very last line of the last letter I would ever receive from Marty demanded that I read and re-read it:

"Anyway, I offer you this foolish letter as evidence of where I am and who I am, your old—I'm beginning to weep—student/ colleague/friend—I'm still weeping—whom I love."

I will never know if it was he or his amanuensis who mixed the pronouns up, and in this way created a riddling entwinement, but I've neber seen an error seem so right.

Some things have no analogue in the computer age—like the passing of a note in a crowded room, and the tacit agreement of others not to read the note but only, one by one, deliver it to its intended recipient. The closing scene of Roman Polanski's 2010 film, *The Ghostwriter* seems nostalgic for the power of paper culture in a newly paperless age. It's an incomparable moment in recent cinematic history, though it's not without precedent. The beautifully timed and carefully choreographed passage of a slip of paper through a series of hands whose faces are not revealed serves as a witty and deliberate paean to Bresson. When the camera steadies on one hand in particular that makes of its index and middle fingers a bird's bill, or a clothespin with which to pass the note, we can sense a friendly nod from Polanski to his predecessor. It's a breathtaking scene, and the parlaying of the note is executed with the same smooth velocity as in Bresson but from the opposite direction: rather than chart the sudden progress of an object's removal and disappearance inside a thief's endlessly subtle cloak, Polanski's camera elaborates an obstacle course of dispersal and delivery, the suspense of disclosure made possible by the passage of a note into or out of the right or wrong hands.

Polanski's mediums are not a band of practiced thieves whose sleight of hand makes crime into art. Mere servants of the note's passage, and also victims of its recipient's deception, they could become her equal if they dared to open the note, but they will not. As a playful gloss on Bresson's balletics, the scene helps us to see something we might otherwise miss in Bresson: that thieves don't only pass the stolen goods from one pickpocket's hand to another, but they *make use of* the bodies of their victims—their ticks, tendencies, pauses, bends, attention, direction, even their breathing—in the passage of the item that's been picked.

See the embodied twists and turns—the strange path it takes—for a message to get from one person to another, Polanski's scene seems to say, reminding us again, of Bresson. But in Polanski, yet another kind of embodiment is pictured, since each person's way of handling the note tells us something about the kind of reader he might be: reading as a matter of hands and eyes. There's the feeble hand; the limber hand; the hand that makes its fingers into a money-fold; the hand that needs to center the note in order to read the inscription of its recipient, to bring it near or far; the hand that passes it as though holding primly onto the corner of a napkin or lifting a tiny fork by its tine; he who steadies and frames it the way a lawyer might his ledger. Note the turned back thumb, the tap, the pudge, the hand that scrutinizes it in the way an eye surveys a secret ballot, all of this culminating with the intended recipient who enjoys the pleasure, or horror, of unfolding it.

Lest we get lost in the distance across a crowded room that the letter needs to traverse, the camera pans back to its sender, our smug protagonist (the "good guy") who has decoded a devastating secret that he has found inside a cryptogram inside a book, the manuscript pages of which he holds in his hands. He's not exactly found "the riddle of the universe" in these papers, but has uncovered a chain of deceptions and murderous political machinations. The note is meant to communicate to his deceiver that he knows that she knows that he knows, and that truth will out. But not yet, not now. The passage of the note was only his secret, private errand. Once he knows that she knows that he knows, he exits the room, he thinks, triumphantly, carrying in his hands the manuscript that will reveal all.

He steps into the street, attempts, and fails to hail a cab, and then, off-screen, we hear it: the thud and thump of his being hit by a car. We don't see his body. We only see his papers, strewn, scattered, blasted, flicked by the wind down the tunnel of the street. No one tries to gather the papers, just as no one runs to see if the writer is dead. People move slowly, mildly intrigued but unalarmed, as though keeping pace with the lethargy of a whining computer in a post-paper age, letting pieces of the manuscript stick to their legs inside and against the wind. Most of the spectators are busy answering cellphones, and well, he wasn't really a writer anyway, but a writer for the new age of simulacra. A ghost writer.

Like most people nowadays, I don't have hand-written letters to hold fast to, and *The Aspern Papers* is a narrative whose center no longer holds, relying as the narrative does on the meaning attached to a bundle of letters. Where Marty is concerned, I can't access the full course of our e-mail correspondence because I switched e-mail as well as operating systems mid-way through the year, and my former e-archives are buried inside a broken computer inside *Eudora* files. Among the letters therein is one in which he responds to my latest book, referring to its being written with "characteristic brio." This is all that I recall. When he was alive, I returned to his lecture on the tape as a way of being with him again, but only now do I fully appreciate the joke embedded in his referring to "The Aspern *Tapes*," a witty hint that puts me in the position of the un-named plunderer and he into the position of the writer,

Jeffrey Aspern. Though I suppose his devotion to Henry James could make *him* into an un-named plunderer, leaving me to consider how there might exist a little of the un-named narrator in us all. James's creation of such a tyrant makes me want to indulge in the biographical fallacy that James so eschewed: it seems clear, does it not, that the story is a screen for James's fear that some sycophantic critic might pry into his papers when he died and discover his queerness, for the only love letters he ever penned were to other men.

If we pry, it's so that we might cry, so that we might remember. When a teacher whom we loved who is a writer dies, we can re-read what he's written, or choose another kind of remembered intimacy by re-reading a book that he taught us how to read. I desired nothing more upon learning of Marty's death than to steal away inside *The Aspern Papers* as return to a place where we'd been together, to the paths he'd taken me down as guide. But this was difficult. For one thing, I was living across the continent, far from my home in Providence, so I couldn't enjoy the pleasure of resuming my original copy. Immediately, I ordered it on *Kindle.* Nine dollars and ninety five cents later, I still couldn't re-enter its pages so as to read. The font was all wrong, made of round and squat letters like those found in a nursery school primer; the blank space between the letters sprang up like moats to throw off the balance of James's labyrinthine interiors; there was nothing to finger, or to hold, and before too long—novellas taking a good long time to read—the image of a blank oblong box came to replace James's words: it was the signal that my battery had drained.

I considered that I should be able to get a copy at a used bookstore, so I took a bus then walked the rest of the way to a Vancouver landmark called MacLeod's. The interior of MacLeod's induced vertigo. More books than the eye could see were packed inside bookshelves, but the sea of edifices was obscured by teetering piles of books that had nothing to hold them in place but their own girth and hopefully hard covers. The bookstore was a series of Towers of Babel in-progress whose proprietor sat at the base of a literal avalanche of splayed and jumbled papers. It was early afternoon, and he sat slumped at the bottom of this precarious mound, looking both tired and resigned as though he'd long given up pushing back against the world's tendency to topple. Hills of books are slick and steep and slippery, and not until I'd ventured into the basement of MacLeod's had I ever really considered the possibility of death-by-book.

Paper weighs. Here were so many books in so little space that I felt the fact of each book's contribution to an ontological state we might call "tonnage." I expected the walls to buckle and ceilings to heave until I lay buried beneath them.

The man at the desk who behaved like the store's owner (its "collector"?) now resembled a figure from earliest childhood: of course, Jack of the broken crown. As I wandered distractedly in what called itself the "J" section, Jill appeared to ask if I was "finding everything ok." The best way to proceed in a madhouse is to pretend to share in the collective delusion, so I smiled and said "yes," and before long, the method worked. I found a used copy of the Penguin classic version of the book that paired it with James's other famous novella, *The Turn of the Screw*.

Orange pants. A balustrade. Liquid light. The pavement not all too far from the Peggy Guggenheim collection where James's friend and fellow writer Constance Fenimore Woolson had thrown herself to her death. Jim and Jean and I had gone to Venice on a whim one Fall during a trip to Northern Italy for an international silent film festival. The food that time of year was chestnut-and-mushroom-inspired, and the little towns outside of Venice kept Prosecco on tap. A fake fireplace, fake logs and white cuckoo of a furnished room whose kitchen cupboards were filled with an unbroken line of white dishware. The only image in the room was a large caricature of a white-faced lamb. I re-read *The Aspern Papers* following Marty's death in an apartment I had sublet on Vancouver's East Side, and as I read, conjured the orange pants of Venice and Jim's red hair. Red when we'd met, of course; not now. Now it was turning grey along with Jean's.

James's critique of late nineteenth century culture—"that hour at which photography and other conveniences [had] annihilated surprise"—strangely resonated with the conditions of our present age. "In the age of newspapers and telegrams and photographs and interviews," the narrator is astounded that Miss Juliana had been able to go unnoticed, and especially that she could do so "boldly settled down in a city of exhibition." *The Aspern Papers*, this time around, reminded me of the self-cancelling protocols of appearance and disappearance that define the moments of the 21st century in which we live. New technologies had added a new substratum of psychic ambivalence around seeing and being seen, hearing and being heard. I often enough felt compelled to wave "hello" from my place in the screened-in world—peeping, I peep, not with my eyes but with my voice. The moment I submit to the self-simulating and self-stimulating game, I become horrified that peeps in the age of the internet get transmitted as screams, and that even if we don't agree to be seduced into announcing ourselves via the WEB, we live in an age in which it is impossible to hide. We are now always and ever visible and locatable, at the same time that a new anonymity anoints us.

I know: "the computer" doesn't disembody us, it creates a different body than the one we know (no, the one we never had the chance to know), and I know a technophobe is what the *technos* wants of me to make me want it more, but also because this will help to distinguish me from a presumably more savvy but stupider generation. Technology can't exist without the creation of "generations."

I can imagine the way I'd inscribed *The Aspern Papers* when I read it originally with Marty. I would have left a connect-the-dots thread of literary historical marginalia as a border. Hawthorne's "Minister's Black Veil" was a lot like Juliana's green one. How was it different? The narrator was another version of James's Marcher without a name who was another version of the false suitor in *Washington Square* (think Montgomery Clift yelling, "Cath-rine!" "Cath-rine!" while he bangs on the door that will no longer open to him). The book was a tale of cooped-up eccentrics out of Poe newly fashioned by James complete with a purloined letter. It also enjoyed a secret cabinet with release mechanism that could describe a Gothic aesthetic going back to Brockden Brown.

In my re-encounter with the story, I could use it more freely; I could enter it and wonder about points of identification, not between the novel and those that came before it, but between the critic and the writer James aimed to drive a wedge between. No one would want to identify with this narrator, but I felt I could see myself in him like never before. My white-washed white-faced rented rooms weren't as beautiful as the narrator's nook, but the time-space dimensions of toiling in oblivion, ever braced by papers, papers and more papers, the writer's endless reckoning with material and immaterial futility struck an hilarious chord. In his Venetian quarters, he "took more and more care to be in the garden whenever it was not too hot":

> I had an arbor arranged and a low table and an armchair put into it; and I carried out books and portfolios—I had always some business of writing in hand—and worked and waited and mused and hoped, while the golden hours elapsed and the plants drank in the light and the inscrutable old palace turned pale and then, as the day waned, began to recover and flush and my papers rustled in the wandering breeze of the Adriatic.

"We have entered the age of criticism," Marty echoed James in his gloss on the book, naming Criticism over and against Economics the truly "dismal science." Of course James was as much a critic as he was a writer, and his books are in so many ways commentaries on those that came before him. It wasn't critique that he opposed but a new kind of critic who would confuse the writer with the books that he writes and vice versa. A writer can be a critic and may even need to be; one can both comment upon and make art, but nowadays "comments" are a kind of pilferer's remarks that take the place of books themselves. "Victims of vandals and graffiti," most books are now preceded by comments, replaced by comments and their constant din. The commentators have tag names and no rooms to speak of but issue from an airy no-place of commentary sans books, certainly without notebooks or pens.

"Beware too much critical publication of too little caliber, its triviality, its dossier building, its industry for its own sake," Marty advises in his lecture.

Melville "was doing what he could do easily rather than chancing what he could not," he writes of *Redburn* in *The Melville Archetype*.

Each admonition and assessment was directed by Marty at us—his students and his readers—but were really meant for him. Pedagogy is nothing more than dissimulated efforts at self-instruction however unselfish it may be or seem. Such lessons could not have held much meaning for me at the age I was when I had heard or read them, but what about now? Was it too late for me to take such lessons to heart and live by them? To write by them and do right by them?

At the ceremony that brought my father's funeral to its close, I followed the need to feel his name engraved on his Ford-Falcon-blue coffin. And then to utter something loud, and clear, final and true. "Arrividerci, Papa." "E, viva la Sicilia."

Re-reading *The Aspern Papers* following Marty's death, I felt myself walking with him down a *riva* of long ago in the present. There are mettles to be tested and uneven terrain, and with each shadow cast by firelight across each turning of a page, I accept the invitation to saunter, greeting interludes like turnstiles, and the confident resumption of agile feet.

III.

Releasing the kickstand of the new blue bike with the chocolate-colored seat made the bike's bell jostle inside its casing to the tune of one satisfying "ping." The bike was a collection of pleasures consisting of glides, grooves, grease, and three gears. Riding it was like playing a trombone—it required the same heady lung-strength and bearing down, with the same resulting smack and blare once you got going. It was untried, and so new blue that its paint glistened like caramel on a recently dipped apple. I had only stopped for a moment to get a newspaper at the drugstore on Buffalo's Elmwood Avenue or maybe a pack of gum or maybe "The Swap Sheet" in search of bike accoutrements I could afford. It was to be a quick in and out, so I didn't lock the bike, figuring I could keep it in view. Perhaps I'd expected the bike would bark if someone dared approach it.

There was a long line that day and the only cash register was one that didn't afford a view of the street, so I performed a dance while waiting of stepping out of line at five second intervals and bending my head toward the door to catch a glimpse of the bike. It was as though I'd set myself up to fail the game described by Sigmund Freud of "here/gone"—which didn't make me any less stunned when my next peekaboo yielded a blank: I can still feel that instant of reckoning with the empty doorframe, the way it drew a line around the nothingness like a bad piece of Pop Art with the joke on me. It's what I'd wanted in place of the blue bike's pleasures, wasn't it? This feeling of death.

I ran up and down the thoroughfare and its side streets, astonished that there was neither bike nor thief in view, not even as a pinprick on a far, far vanishing point. Thievery can reduce us to baby talk, and I'm sure I thought nothing more than "That's that." And, "All gone."

Walking home, I'm sure I cried.

I had bought the bike in an instant at the insistence of a man whom I was presumably dating named Bobby Delmonte. Neither Bob nor Robert, he was Bobby. He wore very round glasses inside a pageboy haircut like a figure out of a Hans Christian Anderson tale, and our relationship consisted of one walk, one bike ride, and a visit to meet his parents for a spaghetti dinner. He had recently been divorced and had a child, but, I, too was just a child. I was definitely too young for him, but he seemed developmentally disabled or borderline retarded so maybe the person who set us up thought a graduate student would be just his speed. He would periodically pause in the middle of a date as if to remind himself of where we were and blurt a bulletin: "I'm Bobby Delmonte! And you're Mary Cappello!" I swear he'd followed this revelation with a squeak, a giggle, and the word "wheeeee."

Though the bike wasn't something I could afford on my graduate student wage, Bobby Delmonte insisted that it was the only way to explore Buffalo's boardwalk, which together we must do. To this day, I do not know where in Buffalo there lies a beach, though of course I understand the city was built on one of the Great Lakes; to this day, I only have two memories of ever visiting a Buffalo beach: once with Bobby Delmonte, and once with the woman who had set me up with him, which made for an interestingly paranoid structure: they must have been in cahoots to render this lesbian straight. Either that or they were part of a bicycle theft ring.

Peggy, who'd set me up with Bobby, had been a friend of Jerry McGuire who was a Buffalo grad who had taught my mother at the college near Philadelphia where at mid-life she earned her BA. When Jerry learned that I'd applied to Buffalo, he invited me over to his house and gave me my first lesson in the teachings of Derrida. He also put me in touch with Peggy who was dating Licastro who was Marty's best friend, but I didn't intuit this chain of conduits to Professor Pops except retrospectively.

All that I recall of my first visit to Buffalo and its campus was getting lost in a series of interlocking stairwells that menacingly arrived at locked metal doors. (Later I would learn that the campus' architect had also designed prisons; later still, studying Foucault in the university's cell-like rooms, I'd come to see how all schools were modeled on prisons and vice versa). The only other image that lingers from that first trip was the freak accident whereby a gust of wind funneling inside the un-buttressed walkways outside Clemens Hall literally yanked the contact lenses from my professor-host's eyes requiring him to balance them on the tips of his respective index fingers while steering his car on the drive back to the airport. It was the Shakespeare and Psychoanalysis seminar I attended that convinced me this was a great place to be, and on my second visit I stayed in Peggy's apartment while she stayed with Licastro in his.

I didn't sleep well that night. Peggy had a friendly black cat, but at the time I didn't know how to co-habit with a cat and was afraid that, sensing my trepidation, it would attack me. The office of off-campus housing was just across the street from Peggy's apartment, and the next day I holed myself up there with another inhabitant of its tiny, anxious room. Jim Morrison wasn't exactly a flaming queen, but he was wry and russet-haired, red-bearded, and jubilant. He made the plodding prospect of looking for a place to live on a grad student's salary into a form of *cavorting*, and I felt instantly I'd found a new, fast friend. He was clearly gay, but what was I? He'd pause to ask about what I was reading and who I aimed to work with; he had read all of Nabokov—I mean everything—and was looking forward to a class with Irving Massey. Reluctantly, he'd suggest we'd better turn back to the task at hand, but then he'd be prevented by a gaspy, wheezy laugh every time he read out the description of another apartment whose paltry promises knew no irony. Details like "hot plate included"; "new shag rug"; "located atop pet store"; "Chihuahuas and other small dogs ok"; and, "ten short blocks to 44 Bus Line" were not lost on us.

Peggy was petite, but she wore open-backed high heeled clog-like sandals that made her taller. She had long, dark hair and was young and muscular in a floral print dress. I was surprised to meet her boyfriend, Licastro, who, at my twenty something years, struck me as a grand-dad. He'd recently undergone surgery which may have explained why he was cranky and ashen. A striped, off-the-shoulder shirt applied a feminizing European touch to his ailing body as did his Italian cross-width slipper-like flip flops. These did nothing to off-set the disturbance of my glimpsing a drain or catheter tube that was still in place or of my sense that he was overly-thirsty and generally un-well.

Once at the beach, Licastro made an even deeper, lasting impression. There weren't many other people at the beach and even though the three of us shared a blanket, we seemed nestled into the individual cubbies of our separate books. I had brought W.S. Merwin's translations of

Antonio Porchia's aphorisms with me to read. Licastro must have asked me about my plan of study, and I replied that I was "a poet." He must have used one of those peculiarly Italian plosives to express his exasperation like "Boh!" or the in-breathing, "Oofah!" before he launched into a lecture that shames me to this day.

"Poet!" he screeched. "How do you dare to call yourself a poet?!"

He then explained how a "poet" was something that only a handful of people in the world could claim to be. How the appellation required age, experience, toil, and so much more—it was a sensibility and a lifestyle, it depended upon maturation and a higher vision along the order of Dante. It was possibly not something that could be taught, and it should certainly never be claimed for oneself.

He winced as though my using the word "poet" to describe myself were more painful than the effects of his recent surgery while he continued disbelievingly to murmur the four letter word under his breath: "She says she's a *poet*!"

"Say instead you 'write poetry.' That's all any of us can claim to do," he said.

I heard him say, "Don't claim what you cannot be."

There is always a ghosted quality to theft. Something was there, that is no more. Someone was there, but you could not see him.

Licastro was an absent presence in my relationship with Marty, and I now understood that Marty may have come to know me before the party at which I thought we first met. He could have first met me by way of Licastro, his special friend, the mate who serves as interlocutor and co-adventurer in so many of his autobiographical fictions. Licastro was my refracted double since he was the person whom Marty assumed had been the accidental confiscator or keeper of the book for all these years. My role was off to one side, if we could imagine a Nabokovian inversion: Lolita attempting to steal the equivalent of Humbert Humbert's lingerie.

I have cast Bresson's *Pickpocket* as a study in love and theft, but it's not exactly about these things. It's no more reducible to any one concept than it is a study in human psychology—something it most assuredly resists. It's a film about billfolds and newspapers and most of all *rhythms*. It's also a study in beguiling groups of three. The inter-title that opens *Pickpocket* refers to two souls who otherwise would never have met, brought together through paths of theft, but the souls in question don't necessarily belong to Michel and Jeanne; they are also the souls of Michel and other thieves. Michel and Jeanne hardly ever meet without the presence of another, a third man; an absent, third term cranks the machinery of displaced desire, just as a kind of queerness hovers and haunts Bresson's characterization of the essential pickpocket.

Asked in an interview if he'd "ever met any thieves," Bresson replied, "I think I've met many thieves but you don't know until after you've been robbed." And then he describes being in a room once with a host and a third person—"*un autre*" (an other)—and the "feeling of something mysterious that I can't put into words," the feeling that the other was a thief. (Or a gay man?) We must wonder what would happen if the figure sensed but never fully seen, if the suspected other, were allowed to be brought into the light of day. If the requisite third man were made to appear, what would happen to a definition of desire based in unquenchable longing? What would happen to a hetero/homo divide, the sequestering of queer from an ever dyadic straight?

Our pickpocket—one of what Bresson called his "models" since he rarely used real actors in his films—is lank, stoop-shouldered and remote. The hovel he lives in is so derelict that there's no need to lock the door. Oh, but of course there is, and his flagrant disregard for locking up is the surest betrayal of the stash of stolen things he keeps hidden behind a floor board and inside a mattress. Interested in nothing, hollow at a core, nihilistic, he's got nothing to hide and nothing to show for himself so that when the cops do search his apartment, this is what, resoundingly, they find: Nothing.

Pickpocket is a film about the infinite substitutability of all things, and Michel's audacity, too, keeps switching places with the things themselves as meaningful focal point. The camera bathes each thing in an individuating light—each purse, bag, satchel, clutch, wallet, valise, compartment; each folded newspaper, ticket, billfold, map, and note; each crease of paper money, each crack in a piece of wallpaper, each folded hand. But it also draws a taut line around Michel's temptation to trespass, his ability to sidle rather than to grab, the stark contrast between the boldness of his acts and the vacant space of his desire: his deadpan face, his placeless façade.

We could say *Pickpocket* is a study in ennui as cover for illicit desire. It's hard to know if the emphasis on theft is an alibi for queerness, or its medium, in which case *Pickpocket* would have to be understood as Bresson's most exquisite contribution to a camp aesthetic (the much later *L'Argent* isn't exquisite but ghoulishly gaudy). Is *Pickpocket* a film about queerness, or a queer film about rhythm? No wonder Bresson originally wished to title it "Uncertainty."

There are so many ways to recognize queerness in the film's leading questions—"Are there others like you?";

or, "Do you think I'm a thief? I won't shake your hand then";

or, "Do you know what a prison is?"

Or, in the coding of pronouncements laced with the unspoken, as in, "you know there is nothing worse." Than what? Stealing? Stealing from your mother? Or having sex with other men?

"Thieves *disgust* me," a character says to Michel's face, "they are idlers," or un-(re)productive men. Drifting and penniless, Michel cruises; he steals for days on end, and goes home only to sleep; he keeps a book on pickpocketing techniques by one "Barrington" containing an illustration of two men and the special hook-like device invented for the purposes of one man reaching inside the pocket of the other. It may as well be a different kind of penis, the kind that likes the feeling of another male mouth.

If I find *Pickpocket*'s penultimate scene to be one of the most erotically thrilling scenes in film history, what does that say about me? If "sex" is what is being enacted here, it's sex re-designed as a feeling for each other's buttons and a reaching in; it's sex as an opening of the other that isn't vulgar, and it happens from behind. More to the point, in this scene Michel makes love with his hands behind his back, feeling for the buttons of another man's jacket behind him, opening them past the lapel, hoping perhaps to be penetrated by this man but instead having his wrist grasped then violently cuffed: Michel has been lured and betrayed in the way a gay man is baited by police, and the scene is a gut-wrenching mix of beauty outstripped by horror.

This scene is prefaced by others like it of course, but in earlier encounters something is released rather than staunched as when a thumb frees a watchband prong from its buckle, or in the little "puh" sound that a purse makes as it pops only partly open, and as it does so, unleashes the sound of the pound and throb of horses inside the purse's soft leather and stiff boards, a suddenly unbounded heartbeat unearthed inside the gentle turning of a twist-lock made of brass. For Michel, a wristwatch is more beautiful—certainly it's more attractive—than the girl who wears it, but then it's neither the watch that draws him nor the girl, but the wrist of another man, his pulse, and this is one of many ways in which rhythm enters in.

Michel and his cohorts form a wave, an anonymous mass of pulsation, entirely public but invisible. There are as many thief-lovers as there are purses, watches, wallets, and cash, as there is a panoply of movements so intricate you won't or can't know who among the populace the thief-lovers are. The film is surely a form of *cinedance*—that formalist invention whereby "the camera becomes an extension of the director's body, its purpose not the photographing of choreography but the choreography of motion." Tracing the contours of modern dance in his essay, "Sleeping Beauty Spurned," Marty describes dance "as the art that requires you to put your body on the line, that reifies itself on the pulses" even if it no longer issues in blood sacrifice. "Painting and sculpture," he goes on, "sometimes do aspire to the condition of dance, although the plastic art of the closest structural affinity is film."

Enter the dancers that Bresson doesn't find or feature but *makes* out of "everyday" people. Enter the external rhythms of a metro station, a fairground or a race track; the internal rhythms of a bedroom, a church, or a bar. A nearly silent film, the mute carapace of *Pickpocket* is periodically broken by the sound of music that crashes into it in sudden swells. At such moments, the images seem to become their music (in case we missed their rhythm or because the film frame can no longer accommodate their force).

Pickpocket is a silent opera, and a dance of hands and things. It's a gorgeous film about "evil" acts, or bolds acts environed by nonchalance. If we respond to its rhythms, do we risk our dignity in the way that all dance requires us to according to Marty, or do we risk feeling the trill and thrill of the thief within?

225

In the context of cinedance, Marty cites the great Serbo-American montagist, Slavko Vorkapich, who worked behind-the-scenes-of-Holly-wood: "I shut off the sound [of my TV set...]," Vorkapich had written, "and try to feel for the movements of the screen in my body. It may be a truck passing by, or an old newspaper blown in the wind. And, if these were so organized as to produce in us implicit rhythmic reactions, then we would have filmic choreography."

I turn off my computer, and listen to Marty lecture, startled by an aesthetic both sudden and subtle, tending disobediently to lunges and pause: "So the quester of our tale is obsessed,/obsessed before, and no less obsessed,/after/his story is done." It's a reminder once again of the way that poetry is made, and with it, untold meaning, and inside of that the charging of desire, never its closure or completion, by a combina-tion of suspension and release. I hear the difference in our voices as a difference in relation to a glide or a partitioning, a rise or a fall. While I would pronounce the word "hurriedly" in the sentence, "I have hur-riedly put this lecture together," in three-syllable fashion, "hurr-ed-ly," Marty says it in four, "hurr-eeh-ed-ly." Each rhythmic repetition of a word pulls me forward along a path then returns me to a starting point both distinct and the same: a head turns, a knee pivots around the ad-verb, "hardly," barely, yes and no-ingly:

> [James's un-named narrator] tells his tale, but *hardly* as an un-burdening, *hardly* as a confession, more as a bewildered con-versation piece, *hardly* with a sense of his devastating witless-ness, *hardly* as a cautionary tale.

In Italy, if pickpocketing is an art, it can skirt moral opprobrium (which is also a horribly difficult word to say, ugly in the mouth that it prevents from whistling or cooing with its fish-like puckering against a glass). One "Inspector Bardi" in Marty's "Imagining Italy" explains to the victims of theft that Italy's pickpockets have "'fingers of velvet,'"

> ...and he lectured us on the local academies, particularly in the San Frediano district where pick-pocketing has been taught father to son for two hundred years. 'It's a skilled trade,' he

said, 'like carpentry or lacquer work. Or painting. Go to the Uffizi…Do you see how many sons and daughters follow their fathers—the Lorenzettis, the Bellinis, the Gentileschis? If you can teach a child to paint, you can teach him to pickpocket. It's a civic tradition, not a moral question.

Marty ends his charming tale by addressing the reader directly and imagining her or him sharing the middle seat opposite him and Licastro in a compartment of a train bound for Florence. The narrator-as-Marty sits by the window, Licastro sits by the door, while altogether the three-some gazes upon the Tuscan countryside whose virtues, he assumes, the third man or woman already knows by way of Henry James: "its garden-like culture and nobleness of outline, its teeming valleys and delicately fretted hills, its peculiarly human-looking touches of habitation." The seating scheme makes possible "an arrangement of bodies that facilitates a three way conversation," though the rocking of the train, one could imagine, might bind the three together into sleep.

Reading and writing, like pickpocketing or desiring, is a three-way game, though here "*un autre*" isn't to be suspected but is hoped for, conjured, and sought out. The making of a story according to this scheme emerges from a dialogue and requires a witness. Writing and reading choreograph a *pas de trois*. In the best such trialogues, neither reader nor writer need stay in their places but are invited to feel how their pulse changes when they trade places or move around.

Where the pickpocket had once been, the benign listener now appears. The threatening comrade in arms (and hands) on the Metropolitana is replaced by a companion traveler, a reader and fellow storyteller as stranger-on-a-train. But this makes for a felicitous moral-of-the-story that feels too neat: that bands of innocents are just as bad as bands of thieves; that a reader is just as likely to want to reach into the deep, tight pockets of a writer as much as any thief, and with the same ardent skill. Triads of love and conveyance seem much more complicated and not at all as interchangeable as this, just as not all arrangements of three can be lumped together under an ancient Oedipal sign.

Finding a form that could make a complete dance of our desires and our fates would seem impossible; even here there was already an accretion of threes as of Mom, Mary, Jerry; Jerry, Mary, Peggy; Peggy, Bobby, Mary; Peggy, Mary, Licastro; Marty, Mary, Licastro; Jim, Jean, Mary; Marty, Mary, Jean; Mary, Marty, and a private, hidden lover yet to be discovered, or revealed.

No book arrives in our hands scot-free, and especially not a stolen one. If you take something that isn't yours, you have to face the consequences of its bearing traces of things you hadn't bargained for. You can't expect it simply to contain between its covers the pure spirit of your pure intentions.

It was with a little shocked intake of breath that, as I turned the pages of Marty's *Melville Archetype* with the careful satisfaction of a devoted copyist, I happened upon a hand that clearly was not his. I don't remember discovering these traces of *un autre* in the super-vision I brought to the book, post-theft. The weight of the book and its satiny blue-green cover was not all that I had wanted from it then. What I relished was the fact of Marty's marginal comments. It was the chance to have access to the hand writing upon the hand that had written the book that moved me to take it; it was the intimacy entailed by listening in on a conversation he was having with himself. I suppose the marginalia gave it the feeling of a text not meant for the eyes of others, but with a different effect or motive from reading another person's diary. (Diaries bore me to death, though I admit, early in our relationship, of having once read Jean's—which I found as hurtful to myself as it was thrilling—then, in true Catholic fashion, telling her I had done so.) What I was interested in here was being made privy to the book's being-in-time: the chance to glimpse the "work" a writer was still doing on his *work*. Which was different, yet again, from reading the "teacher's guide" to a particular book, or a personalized Cliffs Notes to a greater, harder literary masterpiece. I was of course intrigued by what he wished to re-illumine in the already written text, and perhaps I thought it would make it more difficult for him to teach the book (or Melville's books) without reference to his hand-hewn annotations. But I don't think I thought much of how the necessity of my acquisition would make things hard for him. The student is always the laborer who imagines her teacher moving through the world with effortless ease. I know I placed great stock—not in the monetary sense (I was never a collector of inscribed books)—in the handwriting as the sign of his body, breath, and life. It was what made the book special. But only to him. And to me.

If I had found something sensual about the notes having been written in dark pencil, I felt embarrassed to discover the trace of a fainter, lighter hand, also in pencil. The marks, which were entirely confined to the section of the book on "Bartleby, the Scrivener," were a sign that someone else had owned the book, however temporarily; someone closer to Marty than I had been. The unnamed reader's notes appeared casually alongside Marty's as the bodies of lovers in a shared bath might. At a worst possible extreme, it was like holding in my hands another couple's crumpled, love-stained bed sheets, a prospect, I hope it goes without saying, I neither wished nor bargained for when I took *The Melville Archetype* from Marty's office.

Some people consider writing in a book—and especially if one chooses indelible ink—to be a worse offense than stealing one, but marking up books was almost always how I read them, though I would never claim affiliation with the despicable sorts who write in library books. (Sure!) Other people make distinctions between hardback and paperbacks, as though it's acceptable to write in the latter but not the former. Either we want to police the effacement of the beautiful, the pristine, the public, or we want to reserve the right to be alone inside a book. Reckoning with a wily contradiction is harder: that we are ineluctably alone; and that we never really are alone when we are reading.

So, first there were her "marks"—the private hieroglyph no psychologist has ever studied. From whence does each of us derive this abstract painting of the mind, the particular way each has of indicating inside the margins of a book different orders of meaning, of index, and response? Didn't such doodling-on-a-higher-plane bespeak a private language? Marty used vertical lines in rows of one, two, or three; brackets; and squiggles. I used asterisks, dots, arrowheads; I underlined some things with a straight or wavy line (there was a difference), drew boxes around others, and at other times cradled the start of a sentence with a half-moon. Her coded lexicon consisted of tiny loops like the cursive "e" used in proof-reading to mean "delete" though this was not what her "e" meant. A circled "c" that did not stand for copyright appeared and re-appeared, as did question marks, exclamation points, and my favorite: a backward slanting check mark that seemed either to indicate she was left-handed, adept at mirror writing, or better: that at just those points she hoped to drive a lever or a wedge between Marty's sentences and insert her own. A complex interlocution was here inscribed, a reciprocity of mind, and even the development of a thesis in the spare, austere occasion of this reader's graphite impressions of one marginal word here, another there.

In case we've forgotten the tale ("with the exception of *Moby Dick*, Melville's most successfully realized fiction"), let's turn to a lovely précis in Marty's hand: "Bartleby is a wisp of a man who subsists on ginger-nuts, who glides quietly or is motionless, who lives hermit-like, who speaks almost nothing at all, and who, eventually, does as little, preferring to stare from his window in a 'dead-wall reverie.'" Bartleby is deranged, Marty says; he's autistic, she replies. Bartleby is like Ahab, Marty remarks; Bartleby is like Job, she replies. "Does Bartleby perhaps remind us of that other fittingly silent, forlorn man trapped in the workaday world he never made, the character portrayed by Charlie Chaplin?" And she turns this sentence side-ways by inscribing a hill of momentously in-companionate names alongside his:

Christ
Buddha
Harpo

These weren't Licastro's notes—his most intimate friend who, as we learn from "Imagining Italy" underlines the parts of Marty's work he doesn't approve of in red, and draws an excising line through any portion that smacks of "self-nomination." Which wasn't to say there wasn't a form of love and eros in such critical displays as when Jean, for example, wrote between each line of a line of mine I'd shared with her. I'd chosen to give her nothing but my "best" prose, but hadn't told her that, hoping to impress her. I lied when I said I wanted "feedback." I was never so turned on as by her critical reply—her critique, not her cowardly commentary, no baby talk of "wikes" and "diswikes," but

the production of sentences that literally turned mine inside out and
bade me start again; that took flight from the margins and entered into
the text by its entrails; in Jean's hands, I felt like a bride stripped bare
by her bachelorettes. Let me show you how to thrust your tongue up
against your teeth and ar-tic-u-late, her interstitial enunciations said,
and I let her take me down like that, and un-do me, and it went on like
that in the form of lattice-work.

This unlikely trio, the brilliant collocation of

Christ
Buddha
Harpo

was the indelible remainder, I surmised, of a failed love affair, and I
don't like the feeling of having it in my possession, but there it is. If
Marty had been more Italian than Italophile, the woman whose trac-
ings these are could have become the victim of a "crime of passion,"
he hated her so. He might have called her "the behated," he loved her
so, which would have been prettier than the phrase he reserved for her
when I met him. Not merely the worst word in the language for "woman"—the word applied to a woman who behaves like a man, the word
for a woman who takes liberties—Marty supplied a special phrase for
her of greater intensity. He called his former lover, "the c--- of all the
universe" with special emphasis on the letter "t."

What kind of feminist could I possibly have been to have remained
friends with a man who spoke this way of women? I was only 25, remember; and here I might add, "etc., etc." She was a sort of senior to
myself as freshman; she was already working on her dissertation when
we (never really) met. She'd been the previous woman to have access
to Marty's office, and I'd occasionally glimpse her from behind. She
might turn her head back for just a moment, as if to say, "who the
hell are you?" before moving on, she was always moving swiftly on,
while I plodded and meandered, and when she turned, I'd be struck by
the force of her features which were beautifully androgynous inside of
thickly curly, long and golden hair. She had the air about her of "muscle"—not the muscle born of working out but of working in; I imagined

her walking down the hallway of the mind opening books, and then writing them; I imagined she created ideas of great force and beauty. Who's to say that in courting Marty, I didn't want to arrive at her?

She had betrayed him, was the story that he told, by leading him on in a many month love affair without having told him she was married. Happily so. I guess you could say that from his point of view she led him to think he was exceptional; that they were the only two-in-one. In any event, Marty had been more than spurned by her. If they'd been married, we could say he had been cuckolded, but they weren't, so we could say she thought of him as an auxiliary fuck-buddy and sharer of ideas. Who's to say she didn't love him? For all I know, she had an open marriage. For all I know, she did not. I believe that Marty felt he loved her. He must have because he lent her his book. And she must have loved him because she wrote in it before giving it back. And maybe she'd never told him she had done so, and her comments were meant as a love letter for him to later find.

In one of those moments of magisterial magnitude for which James's fiction is known, in a sentence that could serve as a compressed soliloquy to close *The Aspern Papers* with, the unassuming Tina informs the narrator: "I have done the great thing." Long pause. "I have destroyed the papers."

If the great thing, (the "distinguished thing"), we will recall from Marty's lecture, is death, it is not within the human compass to "do," just as it is equally impossible to wait and watch for the great thing in the manner of *The Beast in the Jungle*'s James Marcher. In Marty's reading of the scene, Tina achieves an ironic re-birth by this act, a form of "fortunate fall," but it's hard not to find the teeming of a metaphysical futility here. If to destroy the papers is to perform a task equal to the "thing" that awaits us all, Tina, it may be said, courts authorship in her attempt to extinguish the source of her unnamed narrator's obsession, the thing he was bound and determined to want and to have in lieu of her much less desirable self. She could be understood as determining, at best, to un-do, at least to affect, her pre-determined plot or lot. As always in James, irresolution wins the day: you can destroy all the papers you want, but another *thing* will always introduce itself between two people to supplant the possibility of immediate contact; another set of papers will come to take the place of those of Jeffrey Aspern. Papers, like objects of desire, have a tendency to proliferate, just as a thief will always stand at the ready, eager to identify yet another object worthy enough to steal.

"Papers, letters, a few photos" constitute what's left of Michel's mother's remains in *Pickpocket*, which is probably no different from what any of us living in the age of paper leaves behind. How will Michel handle his mother's papers? Where will he stash them? And will they have the same or a different status, will they serve the same or a different purpose than the papery artifacts he is daily called to steal? Papers, dormant or inert, ready for mock-up, mark-up, or make-up. Awaiting us as conduit, go-between, ombudsman, intermediary, or the more romantic-sounding "liaison." Will we feel compelled to read between their lines or read the writing on the wall? To consign them to the fire, or keep them in a fire-proof box. Leave them to their own devices, or fashion something from them, say, an essay, a poem, or a film. If in *Pickpocket* the police never check stolen merchandise for prints, this is because the film is the print we need to mind, to study, and to read.

If there still are papers left behind, some of us will feel called to shuffle them; others to smuggle the papers in or out; still others will not be able to stop themselves from writing upon the papers, and through this act of writing upon, to read them. So be it if our act enables nothing so much as a kind of mesmerized doting, a devotion to a sacred, tactile flame.

END

Autumn is "a season of strong effects." Gradually cooling temperatures meet the fire of changing leaves to mark the start of new school years. By age six, I had already developed a full-blown dog phobia that was encouraged by the swish and chink of a tiny set of chain links sewn into the back of my raincoat to hang it by. I came to confuse its sound at the back of my neck en route to school with an approaching mongrel that moved toward me the faster I moved. The walk cultivated deep listening even if a paranoid one. The coat smelled of my mother's morning coffee and a rubbery synthetic. In spite of its blue floral pattern, I associated it with early morning darkness and sunless days in which I couldn't tell my feet from the sidewalk.

If a pulley clanked against a pole, it could mean the flag before the school hadn't risen yet, but when it did rise, it never quite billowed, it never quite sailed the way it did in comic books, like ducks heading northward in a stiff wind. The sound of the pulley hitting the pole was periodic as a foghorn only maybe striking an hour but more frequently. Lank and susceptible, it kept time with the wind, creating its own horology, and qualm. I can be as old as a teenager, and still make the walk to school into a game of "kick the rock" for want of "kick the can." A roundish pebble is all that's needed first to kick the rock, then to follow it. However errantly, it must be followed, until it takes me in a zigzag path, outpacing me, to school. Arrival was an accident, or after-thought, of reverie.

We didn't live far enough for a school bus, and yet the walk seemed far. Very far. School was a very far distance from home if you considered that an entire jaw breaker could melt in your mouth in the time it took to get there. According to my first grade report card, I'd made the walk 187 times in one year. I'm sure in all the time of my school years, I made many a journey between home and school arm-in-arm with friends or, in my earliest years, accompanied by my mother, but the dream-time of walking solo most impresses me now, as though the distance wandered between two points gave rise to a bell wrapped in tissue paper or a rollicking acorn—the birth in a six year old of something we could call "thought."

I must have been sixteen or seventeen years old when a particular teacher began to offer me "a ride home from school," such offers being universally infamous in what they suggest. I can't remember the particular circumstance that first gave rise to her invitation, though it was true that as a teenager I often stayed late at school. I was the kind of kid eager to "get involved," and after-school activities provided a place to "hang out" without also getting "in trouble." If the alternative was to risk getting mugged, perhaps I thought a ride home with her was a good idea. One ride home from school with the short Italian woman with the short black hair would have been fine, but the rides home started to turn into a ritual. Rather than drop me off and wave good-bye, she would park a ways down from my house, turn off the ignition, draw one leg up onto the seat behind the steering wheel, and settle in for an evening's chat. Sometimes she would keep me for hours in her car.

I agreed to linger with her, and talk, and must have felt that I was being invited by her into the confidence of an adult friendship if only such confidence hadn't felt creepy—but how could it not? She introduced me to the word "mind-fuck"—a word she used to describe my teen-age angst, "That's called mind-fucking, Mary! But in your case, you're mind-fucking yourself!" And I know she occasionally described sex that she had had, wasn't having, or might some day have, or just sex in general. And the way her periods messed with her emotions—this was another topic we would cover in her car: when she was menstruating, she said, she could burst into tears at the drop of a tennis ball. When my mother once asked me what it was that I was talking about for so long with this teacher in her car, I'd answer, "things." If she'd asked me what I was doing with her, I probably would have said, "stuff."

As the rides home became more frequent, and the chats grew longer, I think one day I decided to invite her in for dinner. Is it possible she thought she was dating me? I believe my mother was relieved to meet this person, this teacher of English literature, face to face, and it would have been nice if what she really wanted was the chance to meet my mother, the poet. The apparent basis of our pedagogic bond was that she was the Yearbook advisor, and that year, I was its editor.

One day, she invited me to her home. She was still living with her mother at the time, and I think she just thought I might enjoy hanging out with her in the manner of an afternoon with Gidget. At some point, she took me into her bedroom and lay her head on my lap Patty-Duke-style. Though this was the late 1970s, it was the sort of gesture that might give way to a word like "dreamy," as in "he's so dreamy!," "you're so dreamy!," "isn't this dreamy?" when really it was all very trippy. I sensed there was something not quite right about my sojourn in her bedroom—I didn't especially like having her head in my lap, and I didn't know what to do with my hands just as I wouldn't have known what to do if someone suddenly presented me with a jelly fish. She, on the other hand, seemed perfectly at home with the pose she had struck, and continued to turn the pages of the book she was reading. Within a few moments of our retreat to the bedroom, her mother burst open the door to check up on us and thereafter eyed me with suspicion. It was clear to me that her daughter's behavior worried her. I wasn't sure if she was particularly concerned about me.

I might, from this distance, want to compare this teacher of yore to James's corrupting governess, or to one of Maisie's parents, or to the sort who might seduce an innocent Pearl, but the relationship wasn't as interesting as all that, and she never seemed as knowing or as conniving as a character in James. Mainly, she seemed lonely, and I suspect, in the end, she was just a run of the mill repressed lesbian out for a drive. If the student/teacher dyad turned perverse, it was because of what she *wanted* from me, and she seemed to want a great deal. Something reached a head when one day she burst into tears (irrespective of her hormonal cycles) when I explained that I couldn't give more hours of my time to the Yearbook. It was as though she expected the uncompromising devotion of a lover, and I responded in kind by marching toward my locker and punching it as hard as I could, so hard, that my hand was swollen for days and the locker bore a dent that forever reminded me of her heartbreak and my helplessness.

Because I'd never been her student, but only ever her advisee, it was easy for me to avoid her once the yearbook went to press and thereafter. She must have known that a breach of her professionalism had occurred because she didn't seem to challenge my refusal to make eye

ured as hidden connectors between one indiscriminate building and another on Buffalo's campus. I remember one in particular since the point of crossing it more frequently than my classes had required was to court a chance meeting with Jean. A coffee cart stood in a corner of this particular architectural conveyance, and occasionally one of us would be compelled to stop and sit at a table in the breezeway so as to sip something warm while we read. People rarely socialized in the breezeway. It was more about catching a glance en route to elsewhere.

I'd seen Jean once there, then twice where we'd slip each other pages of new writing as if it were the drug that bound us and we were dealers in the trade. When I'd pass Jean in the breezeway, she'd lift her face from her page as though expecting me; then, without saying anything, she'd raise one sly eyebrow in the manner of Emma Peale, and it was all she'd need to do to catch me up and make my knees wobble.

I don't know how the contact lens decision had been made, though I'm sure vanity took center-stage, and the idea that love could flow more freely if there were nothing to obstruct access to my eyes. This was the early 1980s when astigmatism called for hard lenses and a little suction device resembling a golf tee for insertion and removal. The question of how Jean might find me without my glasses—would she *find me* fair?—would she recognize me, would she thrill to the removal of so significant a part of my physiognomy as my aviator goggles, would she want to know me more, was all that I needed to propel my contact-lensed self along the breezeway.

The problem was that the lenses were sending shooting pains along their radii making me feel as though I had pieces of glass stuck in my eye—which I no doubt did (these were the type purchased at a Mall)—and that, rather than help me to see more clearly, they'd rendered the world tediously blurred and ridiculously doubled. Jean seemed both charmed and bemused by my appearance, especially as I sputtered, tilting my head to make her two lovely faces appear as one. Later that night, one of the lenses became lodged in the corner of my eye, and when neither Jim nor I could properly manipulate the golf tee to take it out (without also pulling my eye from its socket), he sped me in his make-shift ambulance back to the Mall to retrieve my glasses. I'd never felt so glad for a bodily accessory as I did for the resumption of glasses and their assembled parts—their ear mounts and nose pads, their hinges, and especially their way of literally framing reality as though the world were one vast art gallery, except in sleep, when it became one big kaleidoscopic idea.

This memory might be about the traversing of distances and movement, but something coalesces at a still point of desire inside of shoes. I never took myself to be a foot fetishist, but it seems that the past, and romance in particular, comes back to me in the shape of footwear. What's more significant a moment at the start of a love affair? The taking off of glasses or the removal of one's shoes? Undressing oneself, undressing another, or letting oneself be undressed by the other? Purposely dressing down or suddenly getting dressed up? I realize I could narrate every step of my relationship with Jean, but more, a sense of who Jean is, by the shoes she wore at particular moments, in particular settings, on particular days. Dark brown leather sandals with very thin soles and a separate loop for the big toe; blue pointed sneakers with white eyelets; most of all, an array of espadrilles suggesting she lived a separate life in a Parisian *pied-à-terre*—white, beige, red, and the ravishing sort that featured laces that tied around her ankles and calves.

Where does memory leave us? Where does life leave us? Deposited on the other side of what? What do we leave? In Marty's absence, I'm currently left with a staccato heart beat, the windshield wiper regularity under a day of dense cloud cover in British Columbia where I currently live: it's the Morse code stutter of a computer printer's re-fabrication of the work; the letters; the obituary.

A cat wants me to turn away from the work of mourning, my cat is hungry and is calling me to stop, until I realize it's Marty's cat I'm hearing through my headphones. Suddenly, she presents herself from the room inside his house in which he spoke his lecture into the machine. It's the voice of a cat that is no more, and it startles me to hear her voice track her wandering toward and away from him, as she paces and paws, and inquires not about anything in particular, in short playful "meh" sounds at first, gradually turning to bolder caverns of long "meee-aaaaahs." She vies, mid-lecture, for his attention to his own sentences, and those of Henry James. It's an ambient sound lost to any written text, a doubling of one past by another, the synchronous call of the lives as small as our own that share a room with us.

The papers once spat out of a printing machine seem paltry as a bulk by which to measure one's contribution, the final tally of a deposition into the great bank of existence, the embankment of being, the shoring up of an edifice of crumbling plaster. And if afterward the books go un-read or if reading is imperiled, a sterility persists that is too terrible to bear like the keen and absolute isolation of the thief and his wares.

Where does life leave off and memory begin?: according to a journalist's obituary for Marty Pops in *The Buffalo News*, with a *ratemyprofessor.com* graffito and the acknowledgment that you were a Pulitzer-prize winning poet's decades-long sounding board. Of course there is no *proper* way to remember our dead, and our memories are riddled with fault-lines, but it's horrifying to imagine the Internet being granted the final word, or even to imagine it as a *place* where future generations will go to find those who preceded them, to gauge meaning, and calculate "worth."

I don't try to remember Marty in broad strokes, though that could serve as a means of deducing a satisfying portrait suitable for wedding toasts delivered by the groom's best man, or epitaph-makers at a funeral. When asked how he was, Marty was known to answer neither good, nor bad, nor ok, nor not so bad (in Italian, *non c'è male*) but "as well as can be expected." Marty liked to tell a story about the time he mis-recognized himself in a shop window, how he judged in an instant the demeanor of the reflection of the face he didn't recognize as his, and how this demonstrated the limitations of self-knowledge. Among my favorite of his one-liners, I'd include, "As naturally as a spider spins a web, man extrudes a maze out of and around himself." And, "death completes us, or we suffer dread of failure to become finished personalities."

Suddenly I feel I've unfairly pictured Bobby Delmonte. I recall someone having told me he'd suffered the effects of one too many psychedelics in the 1960s that had caused him to snap, but that basically he was benign. And I've faltered, mis-remembering crucial details from my past, like the purse I left behind during my First Holy Communion ceremony that couldn't have smelled of talc as I've suggested, but had contained little things that had been carefully kept in a man-handling sort of way by the Tomboy who was me. I'm sure there was a rosary in my purse intermingled with a tiny G.I. Joe; a portable plastic crossword game made of flat moveable tiles that you could shift to make new words inside a black and white frame; and a favorite pebble, rock, or stone. It was the purse that had been mistakenly exchanged for mine that smelled of baby powder, which is the same as saying that we cope with our losses by becoming their replacements.

Having stolen from Marty, I did come to wonder if he'd kept, collected, stolen or saved a piece of me. I wondered in particular after his death whether he might have kept a photo-montage that Jean had made of him and me, or if, given his tendency toward austerity and order, he'd discarded it. If I was taken in by the crenellations of High Modernism, Jean applied herself to the more difficult demands of a fractured Post-, theorizing expression as a form of extortion in the works of Samuel Beckett. Posing went against the grain of her David Hockney-esque photo joiners, and one day she chose spontaneously to capture a lunchtime meeting between Marty and me in shards of overlapping pieces, emphasizing the corners of the table, the room, and of our smiles, picturing the bona fide vibrations of a friendship.

Photo Joiner of Mary Cappello and Martin Pops
circa 1986 by Jean Walton

The cross-hatched repetitions of the restaurant's mundane interior that Jean's photos map allow certain elements in our meeting's composition to resound: my white glass of milk to Marty's amber iced tea (I'd been on a "health kick" at the time). The red and white stripes of Marty's short-sleeved shirt and the scratchy down I'd feel on hugging him (if Marty had been gay, he'd have met the criteria of a "Bear.") The band-aid on my index finger and its anterior scene: I'd smashed my hand through the window of my apartment's tiny bedroom in a frenzied attempt to swat or release a trapped bee. The event had required a distress call to Jean even though we'd decided just about then to suspend contact for a while. These are the details I remember without the photo in view.

Following this line of narcissistic reasoning, I become aware not only of what Marty may not have kept *of* me but what he'd kept *from* me; or, to put it more truly, I become aware of how much I could not have known at 25 measured against all that I thought I *did* know. I'm astonished to realize upon re-reading "Imagining Italy" that Licastro not only wrote about Leonardo Sciascia but interviewed him. He wiled away the hours with him in intimate conversation. Twenty five years later, I knew and loved the work of Sciascia, and I knew a great deal more about my own Sicilian past, but I hadn't known Marty had such access to Sciascia way back then. When you're 25, you think the world is all your own, and you are equivalent to everything in it. You believe there's nothing you cannot know, and nothing you don't know. This state of mind I'll call "twerpitude," derived from the long lost term that deserves re-entry into our lexicon: "twerp." Only a twerp fails to appreciate a difference between what she knows and what her teacher who is twice her age knows. I have my own experiences with this condition, but from the other side of the desk now, as when a student who came into her own in one of my classes and came out as a lesbian too, shared with me, inside an office smoldering with youthful libido, some reading suggestions drawn from the world of contemporary gay and lesbian fiction. When she offers to lend me books that she must know but at the same time cannot know that I have either studied, taught, written of, or myself written ("I read it in a book and I wrote the book I read it in"), she accedes to the condition of a darling twerpette. No matter how old I get, I maintain a fascination for spinning tops, and watching her is beautiful, and watching her is mesmerizing, so I don't slow her down, and I certainly don't correct her. I honestly keep pace with her, and know that I can learn from her if I'm patient enough to wait to see at what point of interest, at what angle of entry into thought she will land.

Digging the front teeth of a snow-shoe into rising drifts inside of cypress groves at night; tripping on clown feet into snow mounds face-forward; cracking gum before and after violin recitals; waiting to see how long it takes for my cat, stoned on catnip, to stop sticking her tongue out; admitting a fear of heights; refusing to skip the way she did when she was five, or to dance; humbly submitting fluency in French and giggling at my lousy pronunciation; pretending to watch the Brothers Quay with me but checking her Facebook page on her I-phone not even on the sly. I think about the spaces I inhabit with my fifteen going on sixteen year old niece in the midst of the long stretches I live inside this writing. What will it mean to her to know many years hence that this writing was where I resided at the same time of the real time of what she knew or thought she knew we knew together? You could be making pudding or making sentences, but those acts required entirely different latitudes to make them rise, and a piece of prose might not be ready, might not ever be ready to read or to hear.

As for the book…the price is an astonishing one hundred and ninety-nine dollars and ninety-five cents. Assume it weighs two hundred pounds, then we can sell the book, a dollar a pound, as if it were ground steak. Libraries and other institutions, we hope, will buy the whole steak, but I see no reason why individuals wouldn't like a tasty slab for say five dollars. Isn't it worth the price?

There is a point in our lives when we stop lending and start to give away books. A point in our lives when we know we don't have all the time in the world in the way we did at 25 to read, read all we can, to write, to write every book we have inside us. A point in our lives when we accept the fact that some of our books are better off in better hands, or should be read by better hearts, or as a contribution to their preparation for greater things. In just this way, I gave my Albert

Pinkham Ryder books to an aspiring young visionary in my charge; as I explained it in a letter to Marty, "I say I lent the books, but I probably won't ask for them back. She's a visionary artist in the making, and I believe she should have the books." Of course this idea of arriving at a point of facing your own mortality, as in, being able once and for all to part with your books, is hogwash. I'm determined to let her have the books, I confessed to Marty, "because I know a better, grander, finer Ryder book will replace these mere *catalogues raisonnés*. I await your book with the greatest enthusiasm and pleasure. Let me know where it is at this point."

Though when I first met Marty, he filled the academic position of a specialist in nineteenth century American literature, having already written the book about Melville's entire *oeuvre*, he was just completing a book on the entirely different subject of Vermeer, and he would go on in those years to write essays about dance, and popular culture, labyrinths and quick fixes, perpetual motion machines, and the "metamorphosis of shit" in literary and visual art. In the early 1980s, he was also beginning to devote his attention to an anomalous nineteenth century American painter named Albert Pinkham Ryder who fashioned his paintings to self-destruct. Ryder's output was "small" by certain standards, but singular; his methods were eccentric, or so it seemed, since he purposely applied his paint in layers before allowing it to dry and thus created a cracking effect that scarred his canvases. He sometimes took a hot poker to a canvas mid-painting singeing the image at an edge or at a core; he mixed oil paint with candle wax to make his figures waver, and all in all, to create a repertoire of images as organic as their source in earthen pigment and as likely to disintegrate. If you look for a Ryder in an art museum, you're more likely to find a sign along the order of "men working," or "under construction," or "under repair." Ryder's work thus leaves us with the vexing question of whether it is "right" to "restore" a Ryder painting or better to let it "go" the way he intended for it to, for who are we to say that these images borne of a private eschatology should not be allowed to return to their original alchemical source, a source that Ryder was trying to reach to the very ends of in his art? These are some of the lessons in paraphrase that I recall learning twenty five years ago about Ryder's strange paintings from Marty Pops, but it was only in the last year of his life that I learned he had drawn to completion his 600 page book on the painter—in musical terms, it must be Marty's *magnum opus*—and that he was hopeful to see it placed before a reading public before he died.

Art books are costly, long books are prohibitive in a tweety-bopper age. Art is long, life is short; this, my essay on my kindly teacher's work is long-short, short-long, and Marty's last letters to me show him to be unconvinced that *The Life and Art of Albert Pinkham Ryder (1847-1917)* would ever metamorphose beyond the status of "in press," or date of publication, "TBD." I am confident to acquire, fetch, or steal a copy of this book—in spite of its heft (where there's a will there's a way), for the very reason that we buy so many things beyond our means (and when we cannot buy them, we beg, borrow, or steal), because I know, as I can only in my heart of hearts know: that this book is something *I cannot live without.* "Paragraphs from the Studio of a Recluse"; "From *Passing Song* to *Pegasus Departing*"; "Centric and Eccentric"; "Life in the Unreal City," are the names on the marquees I await an escort for, impatient for Marty as usher in his private cinematheque. "An Excursus on Some Clouds in Ryder," I've convinced myself, is the key without which I won't be able to open the work I'm currently involved in on mood and sound, on atmosphere and clouds. "Moonlight Marine" might inter-animate my own contribution to a chapter in American arts and letters, "my secret private errand."

But I mis-speak. Either Marty got the phrase wrong in his lecture—I refuse to double-check—or I had erred in pronouncing it so, for the strange words James feeds his narrator to describe his obsessive quest for Jeffrey Aspern's papers was "my *eccentric*, private errand" not "my secret, private" one. Though I'd prefer not to joust with Henry James, I can't help but notice that, linguistically (but what other way is there?), a secret, private errand is more interesting than an eccentric one. All that the word "eccentric" does to "private errand" is to make the narrator's compulsion peculiar; if the word distinguishes his private errand from yours or mine, it only does so in a way that makes his errand disreputably queer. Bring secret together with private, on the other hand, and either one word redounds in the other, or they cancel each other out; on second hearing, one presses upon the other for emphasis and urgency; on third feeling, so nearly, hardly, maybe, merely closely to one another are they that they rub against each other creating that libidinous smoldering I earlier ascribed to the longed for and longing student. On fourth glance, they only appear to enjoy the perfect fit of a raccoon's mask or a thief's: they only seem the same but are quite qualifiedly different.

Secrecy is more permeable than privacy, though what they have in common is their ignition of an uncanny space between the things we can't bear to share and the things that we cling to. Secrecy involves rites, whereas privacy involves rights. A secret society is not the same as a private club: one is underground but open, while the other is exclusionary and closed. Secrecy has to do with *logos*; privacy has to do with property. Secrecy does time with the sacred, privacy, the profane. In James, a secret, dissimulating self is a requirement of modernity, and the private, impenetrable self, its curse. Both secrecy and privacy make neurotics of us all.

The mundane necessities that organize a day or a grand pilgrimage dictated from on high, errands free us by keeping us moving however furtive their preparations or demands. I'd like to know the path by which the errand as grand scheme, spiritual pilgrimage or mythic quest got confused with the tic-tac-toe of filling the daily larder. It must have to do with the death of God and the birth of suburbia. I'd like to understand why an errand is something one "runs," or to try to explain that locution to a non-native speaker. If there is currently an Errand I must make or am called to carry out, I do not know it, and I wonder if it's the same for you—if, like me, you're wondering if your (1 c) errands are your distractions from a greater, truer purpose. Had my private secret errand been the theft of Marty's book, or its return? Has my secret private errand ever been fulfilled?

There are so many orders of theft, as there are of experience, that I hesitate to treat the *grand mal* type the same as the *petit*. In the course of this writing, Jean became convinced that her wallet had been stolen. We were leading a small group of friends toward the swelling seascape of a Vancouver beach, when she felt a sudden pang of vacancy in her pocket where the wallet had once been. There's nothing more striking than the conviction that everyone else's day has remained the same when your own has been altered by theft. Following an afternoon's re-tracings, and collisions, of crawling beneath parked cars on busy thoroughfares and reaching into trashcans, we gave up our search. Several days later, a kind person called to say she'd found it: the wallet had fallen from Jean's pocket in the seaside parking lot, and, being orange, was indistinguishable from autumn leaves. It had been wet that day, extremely rainy, and all 150 dollars of Canadian currency was still inside, though sopping. When we gave the stranger who found it a basket of oranges, and chocolate, and cheese to show our thanks, she practically refused to take it, she was so surprised.

There are worse things than theft that follow the form of dissimulation: like purposely giving someone wrong directions, or the sundry forms of Internet "phishing" our fellow men subject us to, and the anguish when we take the bait, and the sense of ourselves as ir-real. There's the disappointment we have got to feel when a university's undergraduate student body cannot succeed in a free bike-lending plan: one by one the very grantees of the loan steal the bikes instead.

"Bait cars are everywhere. Steal one. Go to jail." I don't know why the Vancouver billboard pretends to be addressing me. I have no intention to carry out a car heist before I die, but nor do I think that there is such a thing as a "class" of people who are likely to steal a car, even though it is evident that there are some people whose sole purpose in life is to watch and wait for the vulnerability of others, and then, when those others least expect it, to break and enter, to violate, and *to rifle through*.

What calls me are the "give-us-this-day" of our daily rends. The diurnal breaks in our surface routines through which we hope to slip, un-noticed. Untouched by anything but the solitary peach in our pocket. A high-powered Canadian radio producer who is a friend of Jean's asked if I'd come to her kitchen on American Thanksgiving and "cook up a Sicilian storm." She banished Jean and her own partner to the living room while allowing me entry to the privacy of her culinary sanctum. Of course, I didn't steal anything—that's not my point—but we talked con-spiritedly, consorted-ly, in confidence the way people do when they cook together or are caught inside a rainstorm in a stranger's car. We were talking about her recent divorce from a several decades-long marriage and the amicable but strained dividing of "things," when I slipped in the question of whether she'd ever stolen anything. She told me that from time to time at the grocery store, when approaching the counter, she'd separate a piece of fruit, a peach, say, from her basket and put it in her pocket before checking out. She didn't know why she did it, she said, but just that, from time to time, she did. I was stirring onions and capers and currants; I was filleting sardines; I was slipping basil inside of layers of red and green and yellow peppers, but I couldn't get my mind off the peach. Strange to say, the peach made her more interesting than anything she had told me about her life which it seemed quite aside from, and more real. I considered that she might want access to what she can never have again, to what it is impossible to have: I know, just as you know, that there's not been something equal to a flavorful peach on the North American scene in at least 30 years. I wondered if she reserved a special place for the peach when she got home, or if she tossed it triumphantly into the bowl with the other peaches? Maybe she bit into it the minute she left the store, not bothering to wash it first. There are so many colors on the surface of a peach, each shade turning from an already unexpected salmon toward yellowish pink, and then it also had the fact of its fuzz going for it like icing on the cake of a sensuality scale. Perhaps in a disused corner of her mind, she fancies herself a starving artist who needs the extra peach for a still life. Perhaps in stealing it, she hopes to un-make, make, and re-make the peach as a painter would instead of eating it.

Now is a time for final definitions, so here's one: "Dance is the art of obedience: to tend to move as though drawn." Marty's re-casting of dance in this mind-torque, this sentence, makes dance seem akin to erranding. Errands make dancers of us all; death, on the other hand, requires that we stoop.

See me kneeling, not beside my father's coffin, but beside the bed on which he is beginning to die. He's trying to say something, but I can't hear him well enough to know what he might be asking for, or to learn what he might need for me to do. His bed was low and his voice had grown smaller, and before I knew it, I was, in a single bound, kneeling, not on two legs like a supplicant, but on one leg like a knight. I knelt easily beside my father as though this could be an habitual stance. I felt filled with the strength of a thousand men and as nimble-limbed as a child. I lingered there, my ear to his mouth; I only awaited the word if he would utter it, ready to do his bidding like an eager, patient swain.

JAMES MORRISON is the author of *Broken Fever*, *The Lost Girl*, *Everyday Ghosts*, and several nonfiction books on film. His collection of stories, *Said and Done*, was a finalist for a Lambda Literary Award in 2010. He teaches film and literature at Claremont McKenna College and lives in Los Angeles.

JEAN WALTON is the author of *Fair Sex, Savage Dreams: Race, Psychoanalysis, Sexual Difference* as well as essays on film, modernism, and culture in *Critical Inquiry*, *differences*, *Discourse*, and *Hotel Amerika*. *Mudflat Dreaming: Waterfront Battles and the Squatters who Fought them in 1970s Vancouver* appeared with New Star Books in 2018.

MARY CAPPELLO is the author of *Night Bloom*; *Awkward: A Detour* (a *Los Angeles Times* Bestseller); *Called Back*; *Swallow*, based on the Chevalier Jackson Foreign Body Collection in Philadelphia's Mütter Museum; and, *Life Breaks In: A Mood Almanack*. She is the recipient of a Guggenheim Fellowship in Nonfiction and a 2015 Berlin Prize.

CPSIA information can be obtained
at www.ICGtesting.com
Printed in the USA
FSHW011956261018
53346FS